PSYCHOMYTHICS

Sources of Artifacts and Misconceptions in Scientific Psychology

BOOKS BY WILLIAM R. UTTAL

- Real Time Computers: Techniques and Applications in the Psychological Sciences
- Generative Computer Assisted Instruction (with Miriam Rogers, Ramelle Hieronymus, and Timothy Pasich)
- Sensory Coding: Selected Readings (Editor)
- The Psychobiology of Sensory Coding
- Cellular Neurophysiology and Integration: An Interpretive Introduction
- An Autocorrelation Theory of Form Detection
- The Psychobiology of Mind
- A Taxonomy of Visual Processes
- Visual Form Detection in 3-Dimensional Space
- Foundations of Psychobiology (with Daniel N. Robinson)
- The Detection of Nonplanar Surfaces in Visual Space
- The Perception of Dotted Forms
- On Seeing Forms
- The Swimmer: An Integrated Computational Model of a Perceptual-Motor System (with Gary Bradshaw, Sriram Dayanand, Robb Lovell, Thomas Shepherd, Ramakrishna Kakarala, Kurt Skifsted, and Greg Tupper)
- Toward a New Behaviorism: The Case Against Perceptual Reductionism
- Computational Modeling of Vision: The Role of Combination (with Ramakrishna Kakarala, Sriram Dayanand, Thomas Shepherd, Jaggi Kalki, Charles Lunskis Jr., and Ning Liu)
- The War Between Mentalism and Behaviorism: On the Accessibility of Mental Processes
- The New Phrenology: On the Localization of Cognitive Processes in the Brain
- A Behaviorist Looks at Form Recognition
- Psychomythics: Sources of Artifacts and Misconceptions in Scientific Psychology

PSYCHOMYTHICS

Sources of Artifacts and Misconceptions in Scientific Psychology

William R. Uttal
Arizona State University

LEA LAWRENCE ERLBAUM ASSOCIATES, PUBLISHERS
2003 Mahwah, New Jersey   London

BF
38.5
.U88
2003

Copyright © 2003 by Lawrence Erlbaum Associates, Inc.

Lawrence Erlbaum Associates, Inc., Publishers
10 Industrial Avenue
Mahwah, New Jersey 07430

Cover design by Kathryn Houghtaling Lacey

Library of Congress Cataloging-in-Publication Data

Uttal, William R.
  Psychomythics : sources of artifacts and misconceptualizations in scientific psychology /
William R. Uttal
    p. cm.
  Includes bibliographical references and indexes.
  ISBN 0-8058-4584-4 (cloth : alk. paper)
  1.   Psychology—Methodology. 2. Psychology—Philosophy. I. Title.

  BF38.5.U88 2003
  150'.1—dc21

                                                        2003040828

Printed in the United States of America
10   9   8   7   6   5   4   3   2   1

For Mit-Chan

Contents

Preface

This has been a very difficult book for me to write. In it, I embark on a critique of a science of which I have been a part for almost half a century. It is a science of the utmost importance, perhaps more so than any other, as it asks the question: What is the nature of human mentation?

However, important as it is and as far reaching as are the discoveries of scientific psychology, this science is characterized by some of the most recalcitrant and refractory problems ever encountered. Sheer complexity is the least of the challenges faced by scientific psychology; perhaps even more significant are the interactions that any study of mental activity or behavior (take your choice) has with so many other views of our place in nature and in society. So much of what we try to do and so many of the discoveries we make conflict with the goals and aspirations of other approaches to understanding the mysteries of human existence.

We are making some progress, of this there is no doubt. But, what is becoming increasingly clear to me as the years go by is that there is much, much more that we do not know and perhaps even more seriously, much that we cannot know. The result of this mix of importance, relevance, our desire to know, complexity, and intrinsic difficulty is that there is a tremendous opportunity for mistaken or incorrect ideas, concepts, and theories to develop and then become entrenched in psychological thinking. I call these erroneous beliefs about the nature of mind *psychomyths*. By a myth I refer to that part of the dictionary definition that uses this term to denote "a fiction or a half truth, particularly one that is associated with an ideology."

By a *psychomyth,* I specifically refer to those mistaken ideas about the nature of mind and the relationship it has to the neural substrate that produces it. Psychomyths arise out of a multitude of misinterpreted experiments, leaps of logic, fallacious assumptions, ignored caveats from other sciences, and misunderstanding of the limited power of the tools that are used by psychologists to study their chosen topics. They also arise out of extrascientific approaches to the study of behavior or mind that impact on and distort scientific findings.

Others, most notably Dawes (1994), have spoken to the psychological area most susceptible to psychomyths—psychotherapy. Unfortunately, his message has not yet been effective in making any major changes in the status quo of that huge industry. Frankly, I do not expect any better result of this current book. Nevertheless, no one can be true to oneself or to one's science without taking a deep look at the problems faced by it as well as the veracity of the "progress" that has been made.

The purpose of this book is to examine the sources of psychomyths and, by exposing them, to reduce their influence on our ideas about human thought. In my previous books in this series (Uttal, 1998, 2000, 2001, 2002), I concentrated on some of the psychomyths themselves. Here I examine the sources, but identify the psychomyths only by way of example and emphasis. I suspect this will make many of my colleagues uncomfortable and some others angry—many of our erroneous ideas are deeply held, almost to the point of axiomatic immutability. I am convinced, however, that constructive criticism can only enhance and improve the contributions that have already been made and will continue to be made in scientific psychology. If the critique I present here makes some small contribution to changing psychology into a more accurate description of ourselves, I will be content.

ACKNOWLEDGMENTS

No study of this kind goes on in isolation. I have been the recipient of a considerable amount of wisdom from a number of my colleagues here at Arizona State University. In particular, I am deeply grateful for the advice given to me by Professors Jeff Cochran, Kevin Dooley, John Reich, Cindy Greenwood, Norma Hubele, and Peter Killeen. I am especially grateful to Professor Cyril Latimer of the University of Sydney for his many helpful comments on an early draft of the manuscript. I was also privileged to have had a particularly distinguished senior citizen of experimental psychology, Professor William Verplanck, read and make suggestions on a portion of the manuscript. This is not to say that any of then agree with all of the arguments presented here. I am also continually grateful to the chair of the Industrial Engineering Department, Gary Hogg, and to the Dean of College of Engineering, Peter Crouch, for their continued support of my work following my 1999 retirement.

Finally, as ever, Mit-Chan, it is you who continue to make all this possible.

—William R. Uttal

Introduction

1.1 PURPOSE AND GOALS

Psychology, like any other natural science, is dedicated to the goal of analyzing, describing, and understanding the nature of a particular subject matter. Although it can legitimately be debated whether the subject matter of this science is externally observable behavior or inferred internal cognitive processes, we usually are able to identify a psychologist by what is being done in the lab or what is being written. That is, psychologists by experimenting, hypothesizing, theorizing, professing in oral or written form, and to be completely candid, often wildly speculating, seek to define, and to the extent possible, "explain" cognition.[1] There are many ways to explain something. One is to describe it thoroughly. Another is to hypothesize, infer, or speculate about what kind of internal, unobserved mechanism could account for an observed behavior. Another is to determine what are its primary causes. That is, to identify the properties of the environmental stimulus or of the organism that *cause, trigger,* or *lead to* a particular behavioral response. Over the years, many "phenomena" have been attributed to func-

---

[1]Although it is impossible to define it exactly, I use the word *cognition* here to denote all of those mental processes that are associated with observable behavior. Those that do not are for all practical purposes invisible and cannot be the subject of scientific inquiry. This is done with compete understanding that the very definition of this word is fraught with ambiguities and loaded with connotations from its use in the mentalistic field of cognitive psychology. I may well have used the words psychological or mental, but they are much too general and even less precise.

tional properties of the mind–brain that represent and transform incoming stimulus information.

However, in many instances and for many phenomena, it turns out that what we believe to be cognitive in origin is not and what we believe to be an adequate theory is totally incorrect, not just in its details, but also in terms of its most fundamental axioms and assumptions. The purpose of this book is to demonstrate that the variety of misinterpretations and misconceptions of the causes of psychological phenomena is substantial. That is, a large number of observations and findings are incorrectly attributed to information transformations and processes within the nervous system in place of the true antecedent causal conditions. Logical and conceptual errors of many different kinds provide the basis for the invention of psychomythical interpretations, theories, and sometimes deeply held convictions about cognitive activity. Expanding upon the definition presented in the preface, by psychomyths I am referring to the generally accepted, but erroneous, gamut of reductive and descriptive theories, metaphors, and conclusions that do not hold up under close scrutiny. This book examines this aspect of the conceptual foundations of psychological explanation to winnow out the valid from the fanciful.

1.2   A PROPOSED TAXONOMY

Given that much of the discussion in this book deals with an interacting set of topics and issues, it is imperative that I make an explicit effort to categorize and organize the subject matter that is considered. This section develops a personal taxonomy of the sources of what I believe are some of the main driving forces behind psychomyths. At the outset, it is clear that such a classification system, of necessity, will be quite arbitrary and there are likely to be many overlapping and redundant categories. Nevertheless, I propose the following outline of the various categories of sources of psychomyths:

1. Confusion of the exogenous with the exogenous
2. Inevitable natural laws
3. Superpowerful mathematics
4. Self-organizing systems
5. Misconceptions about measurement
6. Miraculous graphs
7. Misleading statistics
8. Erroneous assumptions and conceptual errors
9. Nonillusions
10. Persistent mysteries

In the remainder of this section, the nature and significance of each of these categories is discussed.

The Endogenous–Exogenous Confusion. Chapter 2 begins the discussion of the origins of psychomyths by examining the role that the external environment plays in defining the information content of our perceptual experiences. I argue here that, like the rainbow, many other illusions are actually defined by transformations or events occurring long before the physical stimulus is coded into neural activity. Therefore, what has often been identified as a distortion or illusion produced by a neural or cognitive transformation of the information carried by a stimulus by the nervous system is, in fact, a veridical response to the stimulus.[2] I also emphasize that this is not a new debate but one with an immensely long history in which the controversy became incorrectly framed in the antagonistic terms of a conflict between rationalism and empiricism. As I argue, this false dichotomy has to be eventually resolved in favor of an eclectic compromise.

The point here is that some processes that produce particular perceptual phenomena are due to simple geometrical effects such as diminishment of retinal size with distance. Others, furthermore, are attributable to the inevitable outcome of much more complex natural processes. I argue that many "illusions" previously attributed to endogenous psychoneural transformations are actually caused by exogenous events occurring in the external environment.

Inevitable Natural Laws. Throughout the history of science there have been some relationships that are "facts of nature" that seem immutable and constant. The most obvious ones are to be found in the physical sciences where a relative organizational simplicity obtains. Newton's laws of motion (e.g., force = mass × acceleration) have been replicated again and again and are generally accepted as universal laws of physical action at macroscopic scales of measurement. The precision with which we launched and controlled our spacecraft during the last four decades is clear evidence of their applicability and generality.

In contrast, there are relatively few such persistent and universal laws of psychological activity that hold across all individuals and situations; observations of human behavior are notoriously variable and especially sensitive to what may often seem to be random influences. In the large, however, some relationships that reflect an average description of the behavior of individu-

---

[2]Later, I make clear the obvious—namely, that the nervous system must transduce, encode, and interpret the information in the stimulus for it to be perceived. The emphasis here is on where the critical information transformation occurs. Obviously there is much more to the generation of a complete perceptual experience than just the key point of information transformation.

als have been observed sufficiently often to justify generalization to groups. Even within this limited range of psychological laws, there is considerable variability and, thus, limits on the generality of their application. Some, for example, the Law of Effect (i.e., reinforcement increases or produces learning) are not intended to be exact in the same sense that the quantitatively precise laws of physics are. Although this famous psychophysical principle (Thorndike, 1913) and a close modern corollary—Hebb's (1949) principle of synaptic usage—express general tendencies, different situations, and different individuals could and presumably do apply the general law in different specific ways. Thus, the roles of effect or usage were and are probably intended to be qualitative generalizations that had to be fleshed out by specific experiments. Although these and related principles appear in quite different forms in a variety of contexts, no one expects them to be precise predictors of individual behavior.

In other, even subtler, cases, similar processes, subject to mathematical or statistical laws and solutions, occur regardless of the specific properties of the system being observed. For example, linguists are familiar with a relation called Zipf's law (Zipf, 1935/1965), which asserts that the relation between the frequency (F) with which a word occurs and its rank order (r) in terms of the number of times it appears in a piece of English prose is closely approximated by an inverse power law. It was originally assumed that Zipf's law reflected a psychobiological property of human linguistic activity. That is, that it was a putative law describing a property, attribute, or transformational characteristics of human linguistic skills and, therefore, of the mind–brain. Indeed, Zipf's initial tome was actually entitled *The Psycho-Biology of Languages* (Zipf, 1935/1965).

However, there is an enormous complication to the simple suggestion that Zipf's law is a valid psychological law or description of an attribute of human linguistic information process. Zipf's law works as well for many other rank order-frequency relations as well as it does for language! There is, therefore, an emerging implication that however good the fit between the law and the behavior of some natural system, there is something more general implicit in it that transcends the particular aspects of human linguistic behavior. Topics of this kind are discussed in chapter 3 along with an examination of how superpowerful mathematics often lead to the error of attributing properties of the mathematics to the mind–brain.

Superpowerful Mathematics. Cutting (1986) summed it up exceedingly well when he said: "Mathematics is too powerful to provide constraints on information: it models truth and drivel with equal felicity" (p. xi). The problem is that, in point of fundamental fact, mathematics is neutral with regard to underlying processes. It is the tool par excellence of description but contrary to the view of many mathematical psychologists it cannot, for reasons of deepest principle, delve deeply into underlying structure. For example, some kinds of mathematics (e.g., Fourier analysis) are capable of providing analyses of complex processes in terms of simple fictional or hypothetical components. The output of a totally nonsinusoidal machine can be analyzed into sinusoidal components that have no underlying physical reality. The point is that mathematical methods have properties of their own and on occasion these properties have been inadvertently attributed to the system being described. In short, as Cutting highlighted, mathematics is too powerful to be uncritically applied. Chapter 3 also details how some kinds of mathematical models can give rise to psychomyths.

Self-Organizing Systems. Biology is replete with examples of self-organizing systems. For example, chemical affinities and repulsions between the lipid molecules that make up the membrane of a cell cause them to organize themselves into regular linear structures. Biological clocks of one kind or another are omnipresent in organic tissue. Other physical and chemical forces control the development of patterns of growth in embryological development. Even the growth of the coloring patterns of fish or of the pattern of sulci on the surface of the cerebral cortex are now known to be at least partially dependent on self-organizing properties once the basic genetic code has been expressed. Resonant effects in which a low level stimulus energy produces a high level of response as a result of a special sensitivity or specialized tuning to some aspect of the stimulus is another example of how a system's self-organizing properties can lead inevitably to responses that are too easily misinterpreted as active cognitive transformations.

However, there is also a caveat to this theoretical approach. Such an argument parallels discussions of the emergence of macroproperties from the microproperties of a system. It is often asked: Can the whole be more than the sum of the parts? The only really plausible answer to this question is, No, if you include the rules of interaction between them in the property list of the components! No mysterious or supernatural emergence need be postulated. Individual parts of a complex system have definable properties that are only exhibited when they interact with their fellows. These properties are the ones that govern the rules of interaction and when included among the properties of the parts, in principle all is predictable.

There is an enormously important caveat embedded in this last assertion: What can be done *in principle* cannot always be done *in practice.* Simple numerousness precludes knowing the effect of all individual interactions, particularly in nonlinear systems in which there are a huge variety of feedbacks, feedforwards, and other kinds of contingent interactions. From this practical epistemological limitation arises totally unjustified ideas of mystical "emergence" that are supposedly outside the normal rules of science. Such subtle, complex, and inexplicable self-organizing interactions can sometimes be invoked without adding anything to our knowledge of how the mind–brain system is performing. This topic is also considered in chapter 3.

Misconceptions About Measurement. There is perhaps no greater source of psychomyths than those arising from misunderstanding about the role of measurement in psychology. Some new ideas challenge some of the most widely held assumptions of the role measurement including what can and cannot be measured. The problem of whether or not psychological processes can be measured in the same sense as physical dimensions is not yet resolved. In the event, that the answer to this question is negative, many putative explanations of cognitive processes may also turn out to be psychomyths. Chapter 4 delves deeply into the role of measurement in scientific psychology.

Miraculous Graphs. The necessity for displaying data in an easily digestible form often provides a fertile seedbed for the kind of erroneous conclusions I have designated as psychomyths. If a set of data extends over very wide ranges, it is often necessary to nonlinearly compress it in order to see the details, particularly at the lower values of the range. For example the dynamic range of brightness and loudness perception are usually compressed so that details of the relationship between stimuli and responses are not obscured. Such a compression (e.g., when a logarithmic coordinate system is used) can, in some cases, produce an illusion of order when disorder is actually a better description of what is happening. In some cases, highly processed data of this kind can produce graphical relationships that may appear to reflect something about the psychology of the observer but actually hide important microdetails of the functional relationship. Graphs and inevitable laws can strongly interact to mislead the unwary and create psychomyths. Chapter 4 also considers the roles of graphics in the study of cognition.

Misleading Statistics. No other branch of mathematics has been of such persistent or profound utility to psychology as statistics. The reasons for its particular value in this kind of research are obvious. Psychology deals with responses and individuals and situations in which there is an enormous opportunity for variance. The multidimensional determination of psychophysical responses generates enormous variability from person to person and from day to day, indeed very often from trial to trial. No single instance or sample typically tells us anything useful about the transforms carried on a stimulus by an entire population. This is why anecdotes (very often those from neuropsychological clinics) are so mischievously deceiving—they obscure the actual variability between individuals. For these and related reasons, psychologists have been led to the use of statistical estimates of the central tendency or variability of a set of responses. Indeed, given the variable nature of human behavior, they have no other choice.

On the other hand, no other branch of mathematics or analysis of any kind offers greater opportunities for erroneous conclusions and interpretive mischief than does statistical analysis. Naïve applications of "cookbook" statistical methods may provide what appear to be highly precise measures of human performance while at the same time leading the researcher wildly astray to draw erroneous conclusions. Even as straightforward a process as a "simple" test of significance can mislead an unwary or unlucky scholar. Nor does one have to use intricate statistical analysis to expose oneself to misleading inferences. Even a process as simple as averaging is likely to hide the details of individual performance in ways that may lead to incorrect conclusions. Furthermore, most statistical analysis techniques are based on hidden assumptions about the distribution of data that often do not hold (or cannot be shown to hold) in real situations. It is surprising, as we see later, how far back this chain of logic goes and how often the limitations of the logic are ignored in psychological research. The roles of measurement, graphs, and statistics in generating psychomyths are also discussed in chapter 4.

Erroneous Assumptions and Conceptual Errors.   Perhaps the most egregious source of mistaken theoretical conclusions—psychomyths—is a fuzzy or careless interpretation of the foundation assumptions on which a theory or research project is built. It is a truism that in the everyday efforts to "produce" new knowledge by carrying out experiments, that an initial "barefoot empiricism" can often lead to errors of conclusion. Yet few investigators seek to make their critical assumptions explicit. The variety of ways in which the assumptions underlying one's work can be overlooked are innumerable. From a ubiquitous underestimate of the complexity of the mind–brain system to false a priori estimates of the ways that results are likely to be distributed to assumptions of the existence of rigid mental modules, there is a plethora of ways in which invalid assumptions can produce treacherous foundations on which to base a theory or even a descriptive "law." I consider this category in chapter 5. Chapter 6, in which I sum up my conclusions, follows.

Nonillusions and Some Persistent Mysteries.   Finally, I briefly mention here two other topics that are relevant to the emergence of mythical theories and explanations. The first topic concerns phenomena that have been traditionally designated as illusory when in fact they are not discrepant, but are processed by the observer in an entirely appropriate manner. For example, the irrepressible impossible object (Penrose & Penrose, 1958) has become a mainstay of popular perceptual psychology. This weird appearing

FIG. 1.1. The Penrose Impossible Object. Drawing from an anonymous source after Penrose and Penrose (1958).

object (shown in Fig. 1.1) is presented as a psychological "illusion" in virtually every text on perception. Yet, if one thinks about it a bit, the perceptual response (a difficulty in organizing the figure into a coherent form) to this kind of stimulus is actually a perfectly appropriate reaction to a highly ambiguous and internally inconsistent stimulus. An endogenously generated illusion? No! A near veridical response? Probably yes! An interesting and curious perceptual response to an ambiguous stimulus? Indisputatively yes!

The second topic only briefly mentioned here includes several phenomena that simply cannot be understood in terms of their primary causes at the present time. One of the most curious is the close relationship between certain mathematical series (e.g., the Fibonacci numbers in which each successive term is the sum of the two preceding numbers; i.e., $a_n = a_{n-1} + a_{n-2}$) and the extremely vaguely defined cognitive experience we call visual pleasure or beauty. If each Fibonacci number is then divided by the one previous to it, this new series converges on what has become a magical number— 1.61538. . . , otherwise known as the *golden ratio*. The golden ratio appears ubiquitously in a wide variety of biological systems including the arrangement of seeds on a flower, the structure of fruits and vegetables, and the shape of the spiral shells of a Chambered Nautilus. Most interesting in the present context, however, is the fact that if an observer is asked to identify the width and height of the "most beautiful" rectangle, the usual answer is close to the golden ratio. This phenomenon appears through the history of art with the pyramids, Greek temples, renaissance art, and contemporary views of female beauty all showing evidence of the golden ratio. It is also observable in musical compositions. More details about the Fibonacci numbers and the golden ratio can be uncovered in Dunlap (1998).

Thus, there appears to be a close relationship between a subjective aesthetic judgment and a fundamental number appearing in a mathematical expression. The problem is that this is a purely empirical observation; there is no theory of why these two domains should be linked in this manner. This mysterious relationship suggests, however, that mathematics and human aesthetics are intimately tied together for totally obscure reasons. Perhaps it is due to evolutionary forces of which we are only beginning to understand, but even this is only the loosest kind of speculation. Nevertheless, there are some well-established links that are considered.

Methodological Flaws. As subtle and esoteric as the problem of the mathematical basis of cognition may be, I must also point out that there are other much more pragmatic issues that confuse and misdirect our understanding of the sources and origins of cognitive phenomena. One, of course, is the perennial problem faced by psychology: There are so many different topics of interest that key experiments are not replicated sufficiently often or well to provide a robust basis for some of the drawn conclusions. Closely associated with inadequate replication, indeed, perhaps the major methodological failings of psychological research are the inadequate control of, improper designations of the range of, and the underappreciation of the complexity of the salient stimulus dimensions. The end result of such methodological errors is that much of the database of what are collectively designated as "high level" cognitive processes is fragile. By "fragile" I mean that findings are all-too-often repudiated in subsequent studies undertaken in a different context or cannot be replicated when only slightly different experimental conditions are used. Indeed, at one point I choose to point out that what seemed to be the prime law of cognitive research—*Slight changes in an experiment protocol can result in huge differences in outcome!* The more complex the judgments involved, the more susceptible are experiments to such drastic changes in obtained results.

There are numerous other methodological flaws deeply embedded in the culture of empirical psychological research. Some are extremely subtle. It is not always easy to detect the influence of experimenter bias in the selection of data or subjects. Perhaps the most difficult constraint on validity to overcome is the psychological analog to what physicists refer to as the uncertainty principle. Just as the moment and position of a microcosmic particle can not be simultaneously established because of the impact of the measurement itself, so too in psychology is there likely to be a ubiquitous effect of any effort to measure on the state of a cognitive system. This type of difficulty ranges from the interfering effects of light adaptation caused by the test probe in an experiment designed to measure visual sensitivity to much higher level influences on the behavior of respondents in opinion polls as a result of the formulation of the questionnaire itself.

In other words, the conventional view of an experiment as a rigorous means of defining a specific relationship between independent and dependent variables may have to be replaced by a unconventional view of the experiment as a adaptive control system in which many "uncontrolled" variables are likely to influence the experimental outcome. Although the topic of methodological contribution to the developments of psychomyths is not considered in detail in this book, it should not be overlooked as a major source of conceptual contamination in scientific psychology.

These are but a few of the most obvious sources of what I believe are causal misattributions scattered throughout the literature of scientific psychology—a class of explanations that I designate with the term *Psychomyths*. That is, explanations of cognitive functions that are based on incorrect data, models, theories, methods, and analyses. Psychomyths represent nonexistent entities in psychological theory in much the same sense that unicorns, centaurs, griffins, basilisks, mermaids, and dragons filled the tales of older mythologies. Although based on some semblance of fact (e.g., narwhales, dugongs, and large lizards and their tongues) exaggeration far outpaced reality. So, too, it may be for some of the dragons of cognitive psychology. Identification of various contributing causes discussed in this section provides a beginning for us to cleanse our bestiaries in the same way biological science has cleansed its mythologies.

1.3 SOME DEFINITIONS

It is clear, that many psychological controversies are based on differing understandings of the meaning of certain key words. Because of the iconoclastic and critical tone of this book, it is of special importance that I define as precisely as possible some of the terms used. There is probably no better place to start than to consider the specialized use I make of the terms *endogenous* and *exogenous*. As ever, the place to begin is to examine the standard definitions of these words as revealed in a dictionary. My American Heritage dictionary suggests the following definitions for

en•dog•e•nous *adj.* 1. Produced or growing from within. 2. *Biology* Originating or produced within an organism, a tissue, or a cell: *endogenous secretions*.

And

ex•og•e•nous *adj.* 1. *Biology* Derived or developed from outside the body; originating externally. 2. *Botany* Characterized by the addition of layers of woody tissue. 3. *Medicine* Having a cause external to the body.

The primary criterion of difference between these two words—external versus internal—has to be elaborated a bit to make clear how the terms are going to be used in the following discussion. There is no bark or membrane between the internal and external worlds to which I allude. There is, however, another kind of boundary—a functional one separating the world of physical energy from the world of neural energy. This boundary is very specifically defined as the site of the final action of a stimulus before it is transduced, for example, from light or acoustic energy to the common energy of ionic transport utilized by the nervous system. According to this criterion, there are some exogenous (i.e., external) forces at work well within the anatomical boundaries of our bodies. Optical processes occur within the eye, mechanical ones within the ear, and chemical reactions within the tongue, skin, and nose that are, in my lexicon, all "external." The criteria of "external to the body" or "within an organism" are replaced by one based on the boundaries identified by the functional transductive processes that convert physical stimuli to neural responses. Such conversions often occur well within the boundaries of what demarcates our "body" from the outside world. Specifically, this includes the point of absorption of photons by the photochemicals in the retinal receptors or the point at which mechanical acoustic energy alters the membrane permeability of the cilia base plate on a hair cell in the cochlea.

A more meaningful attribute of these terms, however, is their adjectival denotation. The key concept underlying my use of this critical pair of words is that they refer to the locale at which the critical causal forces leading to a perceptual experience are exerted. That is, do the processes that produce the causal forces occur within the actions of the nervous system or as a result of processes and transformations that occur prior to the neural interaction processes? In other words, should the primary cause of a given experience be considered to be an action occurring within the nervous system and thus, to whatever extent it is possible, be explanatory for both biology and psychology? Or, to the contrary, as I have already illustrated, is it a veridical outcome on the part of the nervous system of some physical action occurring external to the nervous system?

It is important to appreciate that even though we are not able to understand all of the explanatory links between nervous function and psychological processes, it is possible to at least determine on which side of the transduction process, the key information transformation (i.e., the primary cause of an experience) takes place. The bottom line is that there are some processes that are patently and unarguably neuropsychological in origin and some that are not dependent on the action of the mind–brain system. To determine which is which we must examine on which side of the transduction process the key causal process occurs. This is an initial criterion for distinguishing between the endogenous and the exogenous. It is, however, extremely difficult to apply.

Another key word used throughout this book is *inevitable*. The dictionary definition of this term refers to something that is "impossible to avoid or prevent." My connotation is slightly different. I refer to something as inevitable if it is the logical or natural outcome of a process. Some endogenous processes are highly malleable, tractable, or adaptable. Indeed, one of the most serious problems facing any student of human cognition or mentation is the ubiquitous *cognitive penetration* exerted by high-level cognitive activity on what may seem to be simple decisions or perceptual experiences. The classic exemplar in this case is the fluctuating criterion level that must be measured or controlled in psychological experiments to avoid highly misleading sensory psychophysical observations. On the other hand, some endogenous processes, for example, some of the classic visual illusions, are extremely difficult to counteract or alter regardless of criterion levels.

Exogenous processes are also very difficult to overcome. It would be virtually impossible not to see a rainbow (short of simply closing one's eyes) or to initially see a well-camouflaged or fractured (Leeper, 1935) object. The perceptual experiences driven by linear perspective, produced by the natural geometry of the world, are also difficult, if not impossible, to override in one's perceptual experience.

The terms *veridicality* and its antonym *nonveridical* also deserve some elaboration. The dictionary says

ve•rid•i•cal *adj.* 1. Truthful; veracious. 2. Coinciding with fact or reality; genuine or real.

My use of the word is close to this meaning, but it is particularized to the present context in the following way. An experience is veridical if its properties agree with the properties of the stimulus. Thus, the experience of identical relative length of two lines is veridical if the two lines have the same length when measured by some independent (external) means. An experience is nonveridical if there is a discrepancy between the properties of the experience and independent measurements of the object's properties. In short, veridical is to truth as nonveridical is to illusion.

Another word that appears often in this book is *law*. I do not refer here to the legal, social, grammatical, or theological use of the word but to its scientific and mathematical one. A law is either a proven relationship (in mathematics) or a well-established or consistent correlation between two measures (in natural science). Not all laws of natural science are perpetual or immutable. Some well-accepted "laws" have ultimately turned out to be invalid; others have been shown to vary as new measurement procedures become available; and others have been shown to be corollaries or derivatives of even more fundamental relationships. Nevertheless, the idea of sustainable relationships between various measures is one of the cardinal characteristics of any science. Should nature's laws vary from instance to instance, a science would be hard pressed to organize itself in any coherent manner. Unfortunately, many of the laws of psychology are impermanent, gross approximations, or so selective and specialized to particular experiments, that they do not withstand the tests of replication or generalization.

There is another problem that confronts psychological science beyond the fragility and short lifetime of many of its laws: Does an observed lawful relationship exist because of the properties of the observer or is it a mandatory outcome of the applied methodology? For example, if a law is the inevitable outcome of the properties of the mathematics or statistics used in developing that relationship rather than of the relationship itself, then we are not characterizing the nature of the lawful relationship between a physical stimulus and a cognitive behavioral parameter. Quite to the contrary, we are observing something about the nature of the mathematical process itself. In other words, the measuring "instrument" is imposing its own properties on the measurement when, ideally, it should be neutral. Therein, also, lies a source of psychomyths.

Finally, it would be useful to be more specific about my use of the terms *causal*, as well as *essential, primary,* or *key causes.* I have earlier argued (Uttal, 1998, 2000, 2001, 2002) that a coherent scientific psychology is only capable of *describing* the transformations that occur between stimuli and responses and not *reductively explaining* them. This is the foundation assumption of a behaviorism; an approach to psychology that I have come to believe is the only sustainable one.

Stimuli interacting with the active and adaptive properties of the mind–brain often produce a response that is more or less veridical with the stimulus. To the extent that it is veridical, the causal explanation can be claimed to be exogenous. To the extent it is not veridical, the causal explanation can be considered to be endogenous. However, in each case (with the possible exceptions of hallucinations) there is a causal link between some aspect of the stimulus or the organism and the response. There is a definable attribute of the stimulus, either absolute or relative, or a property of cognitive processing that is the primary trigger of whatever cognitive response may occur. This is meaning of the phrase *primary cause*—the attribute of the stimulus that is the essential or key force in eliciting the response—whether it be an endogenous or an exogenous one.

As a simple example, the wavelength of light of an isolated spot of light is, to a first approximation, the key or central stimulus that causes the resulting chromatic experience. Wavelength, in this case, can be asserted to be the exogenous critical cause of the perceptual experience. In more complicated cases, however, there is not always a direct relation between wavelength and the chromatic experience. The relation of several adjacent patches of light may alter the chromatic experience of each of them (Land, 1977). In this latter case, the key or primary cause of perceptual experience is the observer's[3] interpretation of the spatial relationship of the patches. The stimulus and the perceptual experience are not veridical and the primary causal factor in this case must be considered to be an endogenous one.

The concept of key, primary, or essential causes is, without question, closely related to the choice each experimenter makes of an *independent variable* as an experimental protocol is constructed. But, there is a more general sense of these terms; there is always some aspect (or aspects) of the situation to which the perceptual experience is best attributed. Inspired speculation or experimental finding notwithstanding, a major axiom of the argument presented in this book is that some of these key causes may be exogenous and some may be endogenous and which is which, in large part, can be determined. Thus, a second criterion for distinguishing between the endogenous and the exogenous is the degree of veridicality between stimulus and perceptual response. We must add this to the criterion previously mentioned—on which side of the transduction process the critical transformation occurs. This second criterion has the advantage of being much easier to apply!

It should also not go unmentioned, that philosophers for millennia have dealt with the word "cause" and its implications. This is not a simple word whose usage can be fully appreciated by any kind of a simple dictionary definition. Therefore, it is all too easy to trivialize the meaning of this word. My colleague Peter Killeen (2001) reminded me that Aristotle listed four kinds of *causes*, each with a slightly different meaning:

- The efficient cause by means of which something is made to happen.
- The material cause or that which is changed.
- The final cause or purpose for which something happened.
- The formal cause or final result.

Only the first of these four definitions comes close to the meaning of the word *cause* as I use it here. Indeed, it is the one with which this book is concerned. The other three *causes* may well be legitimate topics of inquiry for others to pursue. However, the target of this book is understanding what Killeen and Aristotle called "efficient causes."

---

[3]By my use of the word *observer*, I am simply personalizing the abstract idea of the mind–brain. I am not suggesting that any effortful or attentive "interpretation" (*cum homunculus*) is being consciously carried out by the observer. As we see later, perfectly automatic endogenous mechanisms are well known.

The philosophical difficulties that have led so many since Aristotle to give such special attention to the word *cause* are manifold. The problems for psychology in the search for efficient causes are particularly complex because the subject matter is itself so terribly complex. It must be remembered, for example, that correlation is not always causation even within the meaning of the first of Aristotle's four definitions.[4] Two events can be concomitant without one causing the other.

Another problem is that the constancy of a presumed causation in the study of cognitive processes is especially problematic. Do the putative laws of psychology remain constant? Are they universal or local to cultures, languages, religions, individuals, and so forth? Are we, on the other hand, such a dynamic system that we change from moment to moment and experience to experience? Is causation unidirectional from the cause to the effect or bidirectional between cause and effect? (Considering this latter question, we are impelled to ask: Is there a kind of uncertainty at work in the psychological domain?) Are all causes multiple or are there singular, isolatable, and unique causes? Many of these issues transcend the intended goals of this work as they do even the limited sense of the Aristotelian meaning of "efficient" causation.

In concluding this brief lexicon, I acknowledge that I am deliberately avoiding the linguistic trap of trying to specifically define such mentalist terms as mind, cognition, perception, phenomenon, and other closely related mentalistic terms. I use these words in the general sense that all psychologists and, for that matter, all human conversants do. Unfortunately, I must leave to my readers the imposition of the denotative and connotative meanings with which they are most comfortable. To do otherwise is to encourage a kind of empty and endless debate filled with circular definitions and unsatisfactory efforts to define such vague and unsubstantial terms as *consciousness* or *free will.*

This then concludes the preparatory discussion. In this chapter I have identified my goals, organized the topics with which I deal, and made preliminary definitions of some of the key terminology. With this introduction, I now turn to the substance of my consideration of the source of many of the psychomyths that permeate modern scientific psychology.

---

[4]See page 124 for a further discussion of the correlation versus causation issue.

Chapter 2

Endogenous and Exogenous Causal Forces in Perception

2.1 ON MISINTERPRETATIONS OF PERCEPTUAL TRANSFORMATIONS

It is the thesis of this chapter that some (but certainly not all) perceptual phenomena often attributed to internal (i.e., endogenous) brain processes are actually veridical reflections of external (i.e., exogenous) or natural processes. I argue that many so-called perceptual phenomena actually reveal nothing about the characteristics of the mind–brain system beyond the bare fact that it is sensitive to the parameters and properties of the causal agent. These external processes may be preneural transformations or the inevitable results of certain other external causal events that determine what is perceived. The point is that all such exogenously determined events occur independent of any *informationally essential* cognitive or information processing within the nervous system.

This is a subtle distinction, but one that is important in designating which observations can serve to define the properties of the mind–brain (i.e., which are patently cognitive) and those that should more properly be attributed to the properties or dynamics of the external world. This does not mean that the effects of these external causes are not perceived or even further transformed within the nervous system, but rather that the primary causal explanation of what is "seen" is to be found outside the nervous system either in the physical nature of the world or in the ways that information is processed by preneural activity. The information coming through the senses, although some external force or process may have transformed it, is then processed by the brain in a more or less informationally passive, but from all points of view, veridical way. That is, the percept agrees with the stimulus as defined by independent external measurements, events, and transformations—all subsequent mechanisms carrying out their usual communication and decoding functions without further altering the meaning or cognitive significance of the stimulus.

The generic empirical question faced here is: To what particular causal factor is the form of the perceptual experience best attributed? Is what is seen determined by the content, processes, and arrangements of the attributes of the external world or is it a cognitive distortion[1] caused by an internal interpretation or transformation? In other words, we must distinguish between internally generated *illusions* that are demonstrably nonveridical with the incoming stimulus information and the kind of perceptual experiences that are "caused" by transformations occurring prior to those occurring within the mind–brain. Clearly, both types of causal forces are not only possible but also probable.

Perhaps my distinction between *endogenous* and *exogenous* causal factors can be made clear by comparing simple and uncontroversial examples. First, consider the beautiful rainbows frequently occurring after a rainstorm in the Hawaiian Islands. An observer perceptually experiences these phenomena, however, they are obviously attributable to an *exogenous* transformation. The light entering a drop of water is internally reflected and refracted in a manner that physically disperses the mixed wavelengths of white light into a spectrum of constituent wavelengths, each component of which is transmitted to the eye at a slightly different angle (see Fig. 2.1). The visual system responds to the dispersed spectrum of different wavelengths by means of its usual photosensitive mechanisms to produce an experience that is veridical with the physical aspects of the stimulus.

The important point is that the critical cause of the experience—wavelength dispersion—itself is not accomplished within the nervous system. Rather, the visual system is faithfully responding to the stimulus as defined by the optical properties of a myriad of water droplets. The colors we see are in accord with the usual primary transformations between wavelengths and chromatic experiences. Clearly, it would be incorrect to assert that the "cause" of the perceptual experience of the rainbow should be attributed to some property of the nervous system; this particular visual phenomenon is totally accounted for in terms of external transformations—reflective and refractive dispersion. Of course, there are many uncertainties concerning how we transduce, encode, and transmit this physical instantiated information to the brain, not to mention the totally intractable problem of how this encoded information is then transmuted from the activity of a pool of neu-

---

[1]The term *distortion* is not used here in a pejorative sense. Information may be added to an ambiguous or incomplete stimulus in a way that adds to the quality of a cognitive experience.

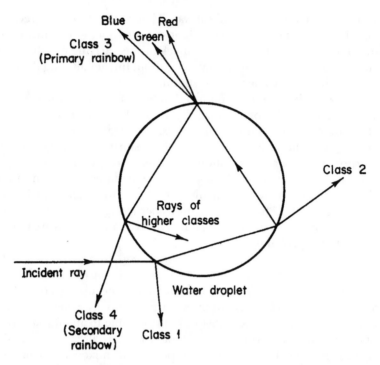

FIG. 2.1.   The refractive and reflective light paths in a droplet of water producing the visual experience of a rainbow.

rons to the awareness of conscious experience. Nevertheless, the primary,
salient, key, essential, critical (take your choice) causal factor in the case of
our perception of a rainbow is clearly an exogenous one.

On the contrary, there are many perceptual phenomena that are dependent on causal factors that do reflect the transformational properties of
the nervous system. The familiar visual illusion known as the Müller–Lyer illusion shown in Fig. 2.2 is nonveridical in the sense that what is perceived
(the two horizontal line segments are not perceived to be of the same
length) is not congruent with the stimulus (the two horizontal lines are
physically the same length) as measured by some other independent device
such as a ruler. Although there is still no compelling explanation of this illusory response, the lack of stimulus–perceptual response agreement (i.e.,
the essential nonveridicality of the perception) must be attributed to a
transformation occurring within the mind–brain system. In this case, the salient causal factor is clearly an endogenous one.

The argument presented in this chapter is that there are a number of
other so called visual "phenomena" that should have been attributed to
similar exogenous factors, rather than endogenous ones. Furthermore, it is
argued that many such processes have been systematically misrepresented

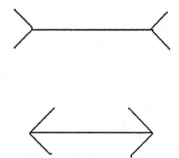

FIG. 2.2.   The Müller-Lyer Illusion. Although identical in length, the two horizontal lines appear quite different.

in the psychological literature as endogenous transformations when in fact they are exogenous. The problem is exacerbated when we consider several other classes of even more subtly misrepresented sources of psychological theory. For example, there are some external processes that have an inevitable outcome, regardless of the mechanism that happens to be instantiating them. For example, geometrical perspective and its companion—the vanishing point—is a result of the nature of geometry at the scale of space at which we operate. The visual angle (the angle subtended by an object at a given distance) is determined by spatial geometry in a way that produces a compelling optical effect (things further away produce a smaller retinal image than closer objects of the same physical size). However, the first order visual experience of perspective—the diminishment of size with distance—is totally independent of any cognitive or precognitive processing; it is an inevitable outcome of spatial geometry and is fully defined and caused, in the sense proposed here, within the information that specifies the physical stimulus.[2]

My goal in this chapter is to explore further examples illustrating the point that not all perceptual phenomena are properly attributed to endogenous processes carried out within the mind–brain system. The next section presents a brief history of thinking about exogenous and endogenous perceptual processes.

2.2   A BRIEF HISTORY

The problem that is the concern of this chapter can summed up as the task of determining whether a particular perceptual experience is caused or de-

---

[2]As usual, even exogenous factors can be modified. Perturbations of the basic phenomenon are well known. Endogenous illusions of apparent size can sometimes wildly distort the effect of visual angle.

termined by information that is inherent in the stimulus or by representations and processes that are executed within the nervous system. The criterion proposed to resolve such uncertainty is the degree of veridicality between the stimulus and the percept. If the percept and the stimulus dimensions are in agreement, the primary cause may be mainly attributed to exogenous factors; if, on the other hand, there is an informational or meaning discrepancy between the two domains, the primary cause is more likely to be attributable to some kind of endogenous or mediated information processing. The essential and eclectic core of this point of view is that both endogenous and exogenous forces are at work and examples of both can be identified throughout the study of human cognition.

Such an evenhanded or eclectic view has not characterized the history of this problem. Rather, the history has virtually always been in the form of a vigorous debate between proponents of radical and extreme positions. Argumentative controversies between radical proponents of direct (i.e., exogenous) and mediated (i.e., endogenous) perceptual processing typify even some of the most current theoretical positions. This debate has taken many forms. On the one side have been those who championed *unconscious inferences* or *rationalist* philosophies in their many varieties. On the other side were those *empiricists* who argued that the stimulus (S) determined the response (R) in what was a much more direct and automatic way. The rationalists argued that the stimuli were only clues that had to be interpreted by the visual system—our percepts had to be actively constructed from these clues. The empiricists argued that the environmental stimuli exerted a direct influence on our perception and this influence accumulated as a result of the experiences of the observer.

Perhaps the most important point to be made prior to a consideration of detailed history of the exogenous–endogenous issue with which I am concerned here is that both classic positions (originally incorporated within the twin rubrics of empiricism and rationalism) are certainly correct to a certain extent. There is no question that both external environmental and internal neurocognitive processes are at work determining our perceptual experiences. The main point made now is that the extreme dichotomy drawn between the two alternative positions is certainly a false one. Phrasing the issue as an either–or controversy has led to meaningless and irresolvable disagreements that have diffused down through the history of our science. Empirical support for either side is available in copious quantities, but this is not because of the truth of one extreme contending theory or the other, but rather because both types of causal influences are at work in producing the enormous varieties of possible perceptual experiences.

It must be also appreciated that even a successful search for answers to questions concerning the locus of crucial causes (either external or internal) does not imply that the entire system consisting of the physical, neural, and psychological worlds is not involved in any perceptual process. All stages of the process are obviously involved. The physics of the rainbow would not produce the beautiful experience if the other parts of the visual system were not fully engaged. This fundamental truth must not be ignored in our search for the critical causes of any perceptual phenomenon; both the stimulus and the organism must play a role in any perceptual experience.

The argument here, on the other hand, is that a strict adherence to either extreme theoretical position—empiricism or rationalism—is potentially misleading and disruptive to psychological science. In perhaps no other historical controversy in psychology is eclecticism more desirable and yet more dishonored.

It is also important to note that the use of the word "empiricism" in this context is not directly related to the nature–nurture controversy. The connotation of that alternative use of the word is more concerned with whether cognitive skills have to be learned or are innate. In that context, empiricism is intimately entwined with the enormously complex study of development and learning. The issue here is a much more tractable problem—simply determining if the primary cause of some phenomenon occurs prior to or following the transduction process—whether, the critical transformation is "direct" or "mediated" for an observer who has achieved a stable and mature level of cognitive development.

Nor is my search for the determinants of perceptual experience congruent with the debate between those who feel that our behavior is determined exclusively by our environment (or by some supernatural force) as opposed to those who champion another of the great red herrings of psychology—free will. Such a controversy is most likely unresolvable. The argument presented here is based on the assumption that both automata and sentient beings could exhibit identical behavior. As much as it may disappoint aficionados of Artificial Intelligence (AI), it seems to me there can never be an effective "Turing Test." As I have discussed earlier (Uttal, 1998, 2000), both behavior and mathematics are neutral with regard to internal structure and neither can provide any compelling evidence about the detailed nature of the underlying mechanisms. Thus, no behavioral test, including Turing's, can possibly discriminate between an automaton and a human.

The goal of this chapter is much simpler and vastly less ambitious than these other persistent controversial issues in scientific psychology; it is to examine the question of the locus of the critical or essential determinants of some experience. To recapitulate, to the extent that the perceptual response is nonveridical with the inducing stimulus, a perceptual response should be attributed to endogenous transformations. To the extent that independent measures of the stimulus and the perceptual response are veridical, then the critical transformations should be attributed to exogenous transformations.

2.2.1 The Classic Arguments—Whence Come the Universals

The endogenous–exogenous dichotomy presented in the previous section closely maps the more familiar direct-mediated debate. Indeed, the history of the direct versus mediated origins of perceptual experience is one of the oldest in psychological history. Stripped of its close relation to the related, separable, matter of nature versus nurture (or as it is otherwise known—innate vs. learned) the issue has traditionally concerned whether the stimulus or an internal cognitive process was primary in determining our perceptual experiences. Both controversies are closely related to various epistemological debates that have emerged through the centuries. How we know (or, better, what we can know) is a superargument that contains these perceptual issues within it.

That the direct-mediated controversy is ancient if not classic can hardly be overstated given that it posed one of the main conceptual differences between the two greatest of the Greek philosophers—Plato and Aristotle—two and a half millennia ago. Plato (c. 428 BCE—c. 348 BCE) may be considered to have been among the first, if the not *the* first, rationalist. A student of Socrates (470 BCE—399 BCE), Plato followed his teacher in championing the power of reason and logic. Plato generalized the "Socratic method" into the idea that acquiring knowledge required thinking (i.e., we can know only by virtue of our mental activity). Within this historical precedent, as far as we know, lay the earliest origins of the entire rationalist position, one that places the responsibility for knowledge acquisition (including, presumably, perceptual knowledge) on internal processes. Here, also, can be discerned the roots of the endogenous theories of the origins of perceptual experience that dominate so much of contemporary psychology.

Aristotle (384 BCE—322 BCE), Plato's student and Socrates' "grandstudent," however, took a major new intellectual direction that eventually led to the exogenous cum empiricist position—the antithesis of the Socratic–Platonic philosophy. In his earlier years Aristotle had supported the Platonic point of view and its emphasis on the mind and the soul as well as the internal determinants of our experiences. The later Aristotelian position, to the contrary, was one that not only championed empirical science, the epistemology that asserted we can learn about nature better by observing it than by speculating about it, but also, more subtly, by stressing that the outside world also has enormous influence on how we gain knowledge and what we see and think. Aristotle stressed that the mind or soul had to respond both to internal forces and external ones. Here lay the germ of a determinist and empiricist view of the origins of perceptual experience.

It should also be noted, however, that some scholars who have studied Aristotelian philosophy felt that his acknowledgment of the effectiveness of both internal and external forces supported both kinds of mental activity—active (i.e., rationalist) and passive (i.e., empiricist). A link is thus made between rationalism and what is commonly meant by the term *endogenous*, on the one hand, and between empiricism and the term *exogenous*, on the other.

A more extreme empiricism was proposed by Epicurus (341 BCE—270 BCE). According to him all knowledge came from sensory experience, an idea that was to resonate down through the years and culminate in the empiricist, structuralist, and associationist psychologies of the 19th and 20th centuries. Epicurus' position was, therefore, dominated by the role played by external causal factors. We can now say that his point of view was "hyperempiricist" and overwhelmingly emphasized exogenous causal forces. Indeed, not only were perceptual experiences driven exclusively by external causes according to him, but also these same external causes could interact directly with the "soul."[3]

The debate about the sources and causes of knowledge (including cognitive and its special case—perception) continued into the next millennium. One group of philosophers shifted their positions away from Aristotelian and Epicurean empiricism in the centuries that followed and regressed to Platonic rationalism. To Aurelius Augustinus (Saint Augustine, 354–430), the dualistic nature of mind–soul and brain was taken as a given. He went beyond that point, however, arguing that the mind's powers were dominant over those of the body, a precursor position to the idealist emphasis (e.g., as professed by Bishop Berkeley, 1685–1753) that was to follow centuries later. Augustine placed great emphasis on "inference," that is, the interpretation of sensory data by the mind, thus also perpetuating the rationalist emphasis that was to reach its epitome in the 17th century.

Before that happened, however, another medieval philosopher, Peter Abelard (1079–1142) also argued that any universal ideas that we form are solely the products of the mind; and, although the mind might draw general ideas from specific empirical examples, it was the mind that was the dominant epistemological engine. Abelard's ideas were quintessentially mediated and endogenous and represented another one of the important roots of philosophical rationalisms and modern mentalisms.

---

[3]The dualism that pervaded all traditional philosophy until relatively recent times led to the invocation of an existence for mental activity that was independent of the body. However, it is clear that once one gets beyond this kind of ontological dualism, the archaic word "soul" refers to mental life in much the same way that psychologists use the word "mind" today. To theology and rationalist science, mind and soul are the indistinguishable seats of cognitive activity. It is extremely difficult to separate the two ideas in the ancient literature except in terms of their respective positions on the possibility of the independent existence of the soul–mind.

However, others reverted, once again, to what is clearly a more Aristotelian or empiricist point of view. Thomas Aquinas (1225–1274), for example, championed the priority of sensory experience when he argued that knowledge could only come through the senses. Here we see another source of the empiricism that flourished in the 16th and 17th centuries and which continues today to influence modern theoretical thought in the form of exogenous, direct theories of perception.

2.2.2 The Foundations of the Modern Controversy[4]

Around the beginning of the 17th century, a new perspective on the direct versus mediated, the empiricist versus the rationalist, the exogenous versus the endogenous, debate began to emerge. Although theology still played an important role in the discussion (throughout the first millennium and a half, theology was irretrievably intertwined with ontology and epistemology) there was an emerging tendency to minimize those aspects of the problem that had to do specifically with the influence of the supernatural. Indeed, one could say that the emphasis of the discussion began to shift from concern with the word *soul* and all that it implied to that of the *mind* and all that it implied. The major rationalist or mediated philosopher of the 17th century was Rene Descartes (1596–1650). Descartes was still undeniably concerned with theological issues, but one can begin to see the shift in the primary emphasis from a speculative theology to what was to become an experimental psychological science.

The enormous contribution that Descartes, and to a controversial degree the Bacons (Roger, 1220–1292 and Francis, 1561–1626), brought to the table was the world-shaking transformation of philosophical speculation into scientific exploration and experimentation. Descartes' contributions to mathematics (analytic geometry) and scientific method began to outshine his efforts to provide arguments for the existence of God. His dualist explanation of the relationship of the soul and the body (which were assumed to be of two different kind of realities in the traditional interpretations) were formalized in the philosophy of interactionism. However, his much more important philosophical contribution was to the idea of rationalism, which as we have seen is the predecessor of the idea of mediation, itself a harbinger of endogenous information transformation.

At their most fundamental foundations, the modern forms of rationalism argue that knowledge and experience can best be achieved by an active,

---

[4]A more complete discussion of the Rationalism–Empiricism controversy is available in my earlier work (Uttal, 1981). Here I only briefly outline the high points. The treatment there is much more complete, but is partially included as well as updated here to make this current work self-contained.

deductive, and logical interpretation of what otherwise would be meaningless sensory information. This is in sharp contrast to the antithetical empiricist position that knowledge is obtained by an inductive accumulation of sensory data in an almost passive manner.

It is problematic whether the rationalist or empiricists believed that their strategy was the only acceptable strategy—the differences for some were more of emphasis than absolutes—but the idea of a contentious controversy, if not an intellectual "war" between dichotomous positions pervades the entire historical discussion. However, it is clear that the idea of mediation, of active metal information processing, was strongly influenced by this rationalist background with its emphasis on the endogenous determinants of perceptual experience. The rationalist position was further particularized by adherence to a principle of *innateness*. The brain, almost of necessity, according to Descartes and others had to have some a priori cognitive capabilities to "bootstrap" subsequent logical processes. However, as I noted earlier, this is really a separate issue.

Following Descartes, Benedict de Spinoza (1632–1677), Gottfried von Leibnitz (1646–1716) and Immanuel Kant (1724–1804) became the champions of the rationalist position. They were followed by a number of modern proponents of neorationalist psychological systems, all of which had the quality of ascribing the primary influence on perception to endogenous cognitive processes in particular. This was so much the case that the influence of the external world was relegated to an incidental role. Examples of this mediated perspective on how we gain knowledge and perceive are found in the works of Helmholtz' (1856) "Unconscious Inference," Bruner and Postman's (1947, 1948) "New Look in Perception," Helson's (1948, 1964) "Adaptation Level Theory," and Rock's "Perceptual Intelligence" (1997).

A major problem with all of the rationalisms is that they depend on interpretations of mental processes that are for all practical purposes inaccessible to scientific examination and analysis. Thus, although effectively making the case that there are endogenous processes that affect our perceptual experience, they must fall back on hypothetical mechanisms to explain these internal transformations. In my earlier works (Uttal, 1998, 2000) I detailed some of the logical and conceptual problems that such a point of view engenders. Although it may be unsatisfying to mentalist psychologists, it may be an unavoidable fact that any cognitive, mentalist, rationalist approach is limited to identifying the transformations that take place and describing the course of those endogenous transformations without ever being able to explain the exact mechanisms and processes that account for them.

All of the rationalisms, including the most modern descendents, are characterized by active mental processing to produce knowledge or perceptual experience. There is no question that such endogenous processes influence many of the phenomena of psychology. The antithetical view—direct empiricism, however, stresses the influence of the parameters of the stimulus—the exogenous forces that dictate perceptual experience.

The alternative theoretical point of view—empiricism—has its equally deeply convinced adherents; adherents who often rejected endogenous causation outright and attributed everything to the flow and content of externally defined stimulus information. The history of the empiricist viewpoint complements that of rationalism. The 17th-century roots of modern empiricism can be found in the writing of Thomas Hobbes (1588–1679) and John Locke (1632–1704). Locke, in particular, argued that all knowledge was based on sensory experience, so much so that he considered the newborn babe to have a blank slate, a "tabula rasa" on which sensory information would accumulate and form the basis of our intellectual life. This was clearly antagonistic to the rationalist philosophy of the time. Locke's work gave rise to one of the best known schools of epistemological philosophy—*British Empiricism*. The personalities in this school are well known and include such luminaries as Bishop George Berkeley (1685–1753) (whose empiricism was mixed with a strong dose of idealism), David Hume (1711–1776), and John Stuart Mill (1806–1873). Their work presaged modern approaches to the problem, modern approaches that are more or less extreme in their support of empiricist positions.

Strong empiricist (direct) theories emerged from these essentially philosophical discussions in the early days of modern experimental psychology. Strongly elementalist and empiricist tenets were fundamental to the structuralist ideas of Wilhelm Wundt (1832–1890) expressed in his seminal books (Wundt, 1874, 1894) and in his student E. B. Titchener's (1867–1927) book (Titchener, 1896). Although both these "structuralists" felt that the study of human mental activity was the prime goal of scientific psychology, they argued strongly that what we perceived was determined by the aggregation of sensory components by direct experience of the external world. Other schools of thought, including functionalism and, of course, modern cognitive psychology—the current instantiation of rationalism—emphasized the mental (internal) processing of information. Indeed, mentalisms of many different kinds pervade current psychological thinking.

To sum up, there is no question that some percepts are defined by exogenous causes of the kind championed by those theoretical approaches included within the empiricism rubric. Equally certain is the fact that many of our perceptual experiences are defined by complex interpretations and informational transformations that fall under the umbrella of rationalism. The controversy between the two sides, therefore, is much less a controversy than what it is typically considered to be. The most fitting form of any modern theory must incorporate both kinds of influences in a way that permits them to complement and supplement each other. Viewed in this light, a major remaining task is the empirical one of determining the critical stages of the salient informational transformations and of evaluating how each contributes to the resulting percept. In the next two sections we examine some of the current theoretical positions of both modern direct (the modern version of empiricism) and mediated (the modern version of rationalism) psychologists.

2.2.3 Modern Direct Empiricisms

Gestalt Holistic Direct Realism. Despite its heavy emphasis on the global and holistic aspects of perception and its strong rejection of the elementalism of Wundt and Titchener, Gestalt psychologists can be considered to be direct or empiricist, as opposed to mediated or rationalist, perceptual theorists. Although the direct–mediated issue was rarely made explicit in their writing (both Koffka and Kohler certainly argued for the role of past experience in influencing what is perceived), an examination of the fundamental assumptions underlying their work suggests that a version of direct realism also guided much of their thinking. For example, one has only to examine the classic Gestalt laws of grouping to see how heavy the emphasis is on the properties of the stimulus as the essential determinants of perceptual experiences. For example, of the 11 laws of grouping enunciated by Wertheimer (1923), 10 (e.g., proximity and common fate) are driven by properties of the stimulus and only one deals with the internal state of the observer. That singular latter exception—Einstellung—states that what we see is essentially what we expect to see—a residual rationalist concept. Thus, although this association between Gestalt theory and empiricism might be (and has been) questioned by some,[5] it does seems that the Gestalt school of psychology was based, in major part, on a kind of direct perception in which the stimulus was strongly influential in determining the perceptual response.

Kantor and Naïve Realism. Another root of contemporary theories of exogenous or direct determinants of our perceptual experience can be found in the history of philosophical realisms. Realisms have been traditionally been the antagonists of idealisms as well as, to a considerable de-

---

[5]In my earlier work (Uttal, 1981), I pointed out that the traditional view of Gestalt psychology made their position on the rationalism-empiricism axis equivocal. There is no question that those pioneers rejected introspection and emphasized the relationship between the stimulus and perception. Admittedly, however, a definitive characterization of their position on this axis is largely dependent on the reader's proclivities.

gree, dualistic notions of mind and brain. Naïve realism, in particular, generally asserted that our perception of an object was the direct result of the properties of object itself and not of any mental reconstruction. Thus, it seems to be more closely allied to a direct rather than a mediated interpretation of the sources of perceptual phenomena.

Among the most vocal proponents of a naïve realism and the direct realism that follows from it was J. R. Kantor. In several important books (Kantor, 1924, 1926, 1947, 1958), Kantor developed a point of view, which although not a quantitative theory in any sense of the word, was based on an interaction between the stimulus world and the response world.

A collection of Kantor's papers was published in 1971. The key to Kantor's ideas found there is his concept of *interbehaviorism.* For him, interbehavior was the "essential datum of psychology" and he defined it as follows:

> The specific events which psychology investigates consist of the interactions of organisms with objects, events or other organisms and their specific qualities, properties, and relations. These interbehaviors, whether movements toward or away from things, manipulations of all sorts, speaking of them, or reflecting on them are all concrete actions based on observable events and in no sense manifestations of any occult forces or forces.[6] (p. 69)

Kantor vigorously criticized modern psychology as being cryptically dualistic and overly dependent on the mental reconstruction of objects from coded sensory signals. He suggested that, in general, all too many psychologists believe it is not the object that is experienced but a mental map or model of it. One of the prevailing assumptions leading to this perspective on perception is the implicit axiom that psychological processes can be analyzed into parts and components. This incorrect assumption, he believed, led to a de-emphasis of the global aspects of perception. It is obviously not too great a leap from Kantor's ideas to the models proposed by Skinner and, to an even greater degree, by Gibson.[7]

Kantor was also a vigorous opponent of physiologizing psychology. In a collection of his papers (Kantor, 1971) he made several critical statements

---

[6]As I noted in my earlier book (Uttal, 2000) there continues to be a substantial correlation between mentalist psychologies and theological thought over the year. J. R. Kantor was among the most explicit proponents of the idea that much of mentalist psychology was and is driven by religious principles and assumptions, however implicitly. Indeed, Tolman, Skinner and Watson all also alluded to this problem and to the anti-science that religious thinking stimulated.

[7]I must add parenthetically that I did not appreciate until recently how similar Kantor's concerns and my own were. His behaviorism, his concern with the localization problem, and his general attitude toward mentalist psychologies resonate with my own opinions. Today, Kantor's philosophy is not generally taught to our students. Mine probably is not likely to be either. But, it is very satisfying to know that there are at least a few others who generally agree with some of the criticisms made by each of us in our own times.

concerning the role of neurophysiology in psychological thinking and none of them is particularly supportive. For example:

> Although the nervous system is made to do heavy duty in psychology, as is manifest from even the slightest examination of psychological literature, it is only in the case of reflexes and similar actions that it serves in any sense as a descriptive factor. In practically all other cases the nervous system is used in psychology merely as an explanatory [i.e., theoretical] agent. (p. 289)

Elsewhere he stated:

> Never can we understand the neural mechanisms by making them into surrogates for, or aspects of, "psychic" or "mental" occurrences or events. (p. 303)

And finally:

> Probably because of the persistence of spiritistic [*sic*] postulation, under the name of psychology many workers occupy themselves with events that belong to the older naturalistic disciplines. They may concern themselves with neurological, statistical, and general biological tasks, or even problems of physics. It is hardly an advantage for psychology to substitute the data of physiology, pharmacology, or physics for psychological events. When such substitution is made we can, at best hope only for some remote advantage to psychology. (p. 546)

These quotations certainly reflect the fact that Kantor was extremely critical of the role of neurophysiology in studying behavior.

Skinner's External Determinants.   The roots of B. F. Skinner's behaviorism are clearly in the realistic tradition championed by many philosophers, his predecessor John B. Watson, and by his contemporary, J. R. Kantor. Skinner also emphasized the environment as a major determinant of our behavior. Skinner, like Kantor and Gibson, believed in direct perception, although he offered another name—*external determinants*—and specific rules by which these determinants could be made to exert their influences. The term external determinants might be better rephrased as *environmental determinants* because Skinner included the internal environmental aspects of the body (including its genetic heritage) within this class of causal events.

One of the most germane of the rules of behavior proposed by Skinner was *contingency of reinforcement.* By this term he referred to all of the factors that are involved in determining whether and how strongly an organism responds in a particular situation. These factors include the setting, the history of the reinforcement protocol, and the nature of the response itself. There are two important aspects of this definition. First, all of the factors are observable and measurable; that is, they are part of the interpersonal world and not of the intrapersonally private mental world. Second, as Skinner (1974) asserted, his operant version of behaviorism

> . . . moved the purpose which seemed to be displayed by human action from antecedent intention or plan to subsequent selection by contingencies of reinforcement. (p. 224)

Skinner did not reject internal representations or mental processes as many have suggested. Rather he simply assumed them to be inaccessible and not the proper object of study for a scientific psychology. Nevertheless, it is easy to see how this view of human mentation with its implicit rejection of "free will" could not have but caused consternation among many in our society. But, that is another story and here we are mainly concerned only with his views of the causes, sources, and origins of the aberrant behavior of psychology—the science.

Clearly, there were only minor differences between Skinner and others who were more specifically interested in perception per se. One residual difference, however, is notable. Although little interested in the phenomenology of perception, he dealt with the problem peripherally. For example, Skinner (1953) suggested that "seeing" is just another behavior when he argued that:

> If we say that a rainbow (either as an objective event in the environment or as a corresponding pattern in the organism) is not "what is seen" but simply the commonest variable which controls the behavior of seeing, we are much less likely to be surprised when the behavior occurs as a function of other variables. (p. 281)

Others like J. J. Gibson, the key figure in the next section, were mainly interested in "seeing" and its causes.

Gibson's Direct Realism.[8]   The most explicit and much more dominant empiricist modern macrotheory of visual perception was suggested by Gibson (1950, 1966, 1979). Known today as *ecological optics* or *direct realism,* his work has become a mainstay of modern perceptual science. Ecological optics is a radical empiricism; it emphasizes the direct causal effect of the stimulus in generating the percept almost to the exclusion of the transformations occurring within the observer. The observer, in Gibson's terms, responds directly without further mediation to the information in the "optic array" but does not create the meaning or significance that is attendant to

---

[8]Some of the following discussion of direct realism as proposed by Gibson and Shaw and Turvey is updated and expanded from Uttal (1981) and Uttal (1988).

the percepts; the environmental stimulus scene itself largely predetermines that meaning or significance. Meaning is thus inherent in the role played by the stimulus in the external environment (i.e., its ecological function).

Rather than the eclectic view taken in this present book, Gibson rejected or at least ignored the role of transformations occurring within the observer almost totally. Given the many examples of nonveridicalities between stimuli and perceptual response, it is, however, hard to rationalize his extreme position on this issue with modern developments in visual studies, neuroscience, or sensory coding theory.

Gibson's theory is sufficiently well structured to allow its major premises to be abstracted and tabulated. The following summary of the major points of his theoretical position is abstracted from a particularly lucid discussion of his approach by Gibson (1950) himself:

1. The world is real and is a source of information-filled stimuli, which are the direct antecedents of perception.

2. The purpose of perception is to communicate ecologically valid information about the external environment.

3. Sensation and perception are separate and distinguishable processes of systems. An example of a sensation is "blueness" and an example of a percept is "texture."

4. Perceptions are not based on the concatenations of simpler sensations nor on any organizing on the part of the perceiver but rather on the direct extraction of information from the optic array—the pattern of light at the retina, which is a linear transform of the external environment.

5. There can be "sensationless" perception.

6. When perception occurs, there is a more or less direct detection on the part of the perceptual system of invariants of the stimuli, but no construction from sensory elements occurs. Perception, furthermore, is not a triggering of recall of previously learned patterns of knowledge but a new and direct response to the attributes of the stimulus scene.

7. Perception is improved by experience; there is such a thing as perceptual learning even though learning is not essential for the perceptual experience itself. In other words, we learn to perceive, but we do not need prior experience to perceive some new stimulus. (Abstracted and paraphrased from Gibson, 1950)

Gibson's theory can be seen in terms of these basic premises to be a reaction against both an associationism suggesting that perceptions were created by the aggregation and concatenation of simpler sensations and against a rationalism suggesting some organizational, rational, mediated, or logical processes within the observer were required to construct perceptions from incomplete or ambiguous stimulus information.

Although many contemporary psychologists feel that he went much too far in direct realism, Gibson did raise important points. A particularly important contribution of Gibson's theory was his calling attention to the invariants in the stimulus scene that could determine the perceptual response. In this vein, Gibson expended much of his attention on such stimulus factors as texture, perspective, and outline. These and other aspects of the stimulus form were especially important to him because they were thought to collectively convey information about the whole stimulus scene. For example, stimuli were considered to signal the invariant aspects of the stimulus scene even though a particular attribute (e.g., texture) may be continuously varying in terms of the projected retinal image.

It is in this context that Gibson became most vague. He coined a word—affordances—that has taken on an almost poetic and mystical quality in psychological discussions. "Affordances" seems to mean something very different to each person who reads Gibson's work. The following list describes some of the ways that it has been interpreted. All of these terms are consistent, at least, in describing properties of the external environment or stimulus object.

- A potential for action
- Action possibilities
- The property that enables the observer
- Actionable properties between the environment and the observer
- Relevant properties
- Natural relationships
- Relationships between the world and the intentions of the observer
- The information needed for perception
- Dynamic meanings of the environment
- The result of environmental invariances

Indeed, Gibson himself offered several definitions:

The affordances of the environment are what it offers the animal, what it provides or furnishes, either for good or ill. (Gibson, 1979, p. 127)

And

. . . the affordance of anything is a specific combination of properties of its substance and surfaces taken with reference to an animal. (Gibson, 1977, p. 67)

And

> . . . it is a combination of the physical properties of the environment that is uniquely suited to a given animal—to his [*sic*] nutritive system or his action system or his locomotor system. (Gibson, 1977, p. 79)

Although there is a common theme through all of these definitions, there is a vagueness about them that makes Gibson's words almost useless in the scientific study of human perception. The meaning of "affordance" could be summed up as the sum of the attributes of the stimulus. Even in this case, however, there is ample opportunity for ambiguity simply because scholars would have to agree which attributes are salient and which are not. Many potentially critical attributes might well be measurable by normal metrics. However, some—specifically the global properties of the stimulus—are much more recalcitrant to quantification and require measures and measuring techniques that have not yet been developed. On the other hand, this is a difficulty faced by perceptual psychology in general. In any case, the situation is not ameliorated by the introduction of the inscrutable term *affordance* with its almost poetic connotations. It may be that Gibson actually was suggesting that what the affordances are in a specific situation depend on the animal as well as the stimulus—a situation in which uncertainty about which independent variables were critical would rise to an extraordinarily high level. In this interaction between the organism and the environment some reflections of Kantor's interbehaviorism can be seen.

Another significant aspect of Gibson's theory was his rejection of a role for stimuli as mere triggers to elicit previously stored memories or internal mental processes. For Gibson, the stimuli, which are themselves produced by the environment, were *always* the direct and immediate producers, if not the equivalents, of the experience and, thus, merely reflected the primary role of the external environment in what was for him a very direct causal chain from stimulus to perception. Ecological optics was thus radically nonrationalist arguing that processing by the mind–brain never (or, in the words of the Captain of HMS Pinafore, "almost never") occurs. Gibson also clearly eschewed any physiological reductionism. In fact, his direct realism was so "direct" that he never concerned himself with the well known anatomical and physiological aspects of the afferent communication pathways.

Gibson's antiassociationist, antimentalist point of view led him to draw what I believe is the erroneous dichotomy between sensation and perception. Gibson considered the two terms to be unrelated in a way that leads to such difficult-to-interpret concepts as "sensationless perception" (Gibson, 1966, p. 2). This concept was made even more obscure by the fact that Gibson did not define either sensation or perception in a sufficiently precise way to clarify the denotation of the words as he used them.

In his extreme rejection of the constructionist or rationalist ideology, Gibson's ecological optics was, however, very much in the empiricist tradition stressing that our mental experiences are determined by primary causes in the external world. The external world provides complex and, to Gibson, informationally complete stimuli to which there is a more or less direct psychobiological response we call perception. There is no interpretation, rationalizing, constructing, or hypothesizing; to Gibson, Helmholtz was not only dead but was dead wrong. Perceptions are the direct resultants of the stimuli and are not mediated either by sensory primitives or by any form of epistemic inferences. Characteristics of the stimuli such as texture and contour became the direct antecedent conditions (i.e., the primary causes) of perception in Gibson's (1950) highly empiricist system.

Gibson plays a curious role in modern perception theory. Although highly regarded by many and discussed by even more in a very large number of both supportive and critical articles, his research has, if fact, had surprisingly little impact on current experimental and theoretical work.[9] Some of the concepts he introduced (e.g., optical flow) however real, are difficult to manipulate and only a relatively few perceptual psychologists had the temerity to study them until the advent of the digital laboratory computer. Even fewer have been willing to abandon the essentially reductionist and rationalist cognitive tradition that dominates current theory in favor of a direct realism.

The main thrust of the criticism to Gibson's ecological optics, therefore, has usually come from cognitive psychologists who are interested mainly in the internal transformations and processes that Gibson ignores. For example, in the early 1970s, a critique of Gibsonian direct realism was presented by Gyr (1972). Gyr was very much among the proponents of the rationalist or mediated school regarding matters of visual perception. Arguing that perception and voluntary motor responses were very similar, Gyr suggested that the organism does not passively respond to the stimuli in the way Gibson proposed but that the essential aspects of perception are more akin to self-organizing processes carried out by the central nervous system of the perceiver on the afferent stimuli. Gyr noted that the enormous amount of attentive selection on the part of the perceiver is required for much of perception and that this selection is heavily dependent on the perceiver's current cognitive state. He argued such stimulus selection is tantamount to a prima facie rejection of Gibson's strong premise of an external-stimulus-

---

[9]I am sure many of my colleagues would disagree with this sober assessment, but, in fact, the mainstream of psychological science these days is concerned with measurable independent variables and the discriminative effect they have on our cognitive processes, on our nervous system, or on our behavior. Agree with its main theme or not, cognitive neuroscience—the most modern version of experimental psychology—is mainly concerned with internal processing mechanisms. This is the exact antithesis of Gibson's direct realism, a theory mainly concerned with external stimuli and their nature.

dominated perceptual response and his radical empiricism. Gibson's (1973) reply to Gyr was of interest mainly because of his early consideration of proprioception and self-awareness—the former leading ultimately to current work on dynamical systems discussed in chapter 3.

Other cognitive criticisms of Gibson's extreme position include articles by Hayes-Roth (1977) and Ullman (1980). Ullman spoke to the fact that then current theory was based on the transformations of internal representations. His point was that because most of the important aspects of perception were conceived of as internal computations, there could be little support for a theory of direct perception such as Gibson's that ignored these essential aspects of the process.

The criticism also overflowed into social theories of perception. Schmitt (1987) argued that direct influences on social perception were not supported by empirical evidence and also asserted that the introduction of the ambiguous term "affordance" simply ignored the question of how our social environment affects what we perceive. Of course, even in this context there was controversy. Costall (1989) argued to the converse that, from a historical point of view, Gibson was, indeed, conscious of the role that direct perception played in social perception.

Of course, Gibson has also had a loyal following. Authors such as Mace (1986) and Schulz (1989) provided support for the Gibsonian position, particularly in their efforts to show that it was not at all inconsistent with earlier Gestalt principles. Guerin (1990), among others made an effort to extend the ideas of direct perception to memory and cognition. Gibson's Festschrift (MacLeod & Pick, 1974) contains many other expressions of support for his ecological optics and the direct realism point of view.

Despite efforts to generalize and extend Gibson's point of view, it is clear he was an extremist on the direct-mediated dimension. His apparent unwillingness to even consider the role played by active processes in the brain on our perceptual experiences ignored a huge amount of scholarship. By doing so, he "mystified" psychological science by ignoring processes that were especially amenable to empirical examination. How much better it would have been to operationalize the debate in terms of whether the significant stimulus information is to be found in the stimulus (i.e., whether it is exogenous) or in some central transformation or interpretation of it (i.e., whether it is endogenous).

It is my conviction that any deep analysis of the debate between direct and mediated theories of perception must ultimately be resolved in the form of an eclectic theory not supportive of the extreme views of either camp. It seems absolutely necessary to accept the fact that perception is an interaction between processes occurring in the stimulus world and inside the organism. The key task is to determine how much of the variance in our responses can be attributed to each.

Neisser's Ecological Psychology.   Gibson's theory of perception—ecological optics, though not generally accepted by today's mentalist and reductionist oriented cognitive psychology, did have a nonnegligible impact on some theoretical thinking. Two important schools developed around two of his followers: Ulrich Neisser and Michael Turvey.

Neisser (1967, 1976), to begin this discussion, attempted to incorporate many of Gibson's ideas into his version of a theoretical framework of contemporary cognitive psychology. Although Neisser eventually moved on to more practical issues such as the study of intelligence and memory in real-life settings, he was one of the most important proponents of an ecological approach to learning and memory (as opposed to Gibson's main concern with perception.) In spite of his early defense of cognitive psychology, Neisser underwent a major theoretical metamorphosis under the influence of Gibson with whom he worked at Cornell University. Indeed, it is felt by many that his early book (Neisser, 1967) actually created the modern version of experimental psychology now called cognitive neuroscience. Nevertheless, just a decade later he published another book (Neisser, 1976) that criticized the very field he had so significantly influenced. In that later volume, he attacked the mainstream research paradigm of tightly controlled stimuli and precisely measured responses carried out in a constrained laboratory situation. In its place, he proposed that real-life situations provide a much richer source of information and sight into the nature of our cognitive mechanisms. In short, he was championing the same kind of direct effects on cognitive functions that had characterized the work of Gibson. As Neisser (1976) said:

> Gibson's view has certain striking advantages over the traditional one. The organism is not thought of as buffeted about by stimuli, but rather as attuned to properties of its environment that are objectively present, accurately specified, and veridically perceived. (p. 19)

Neisser, however, did not reject or ignore cognitive processing altogether in the extreme manner that Gibson did. Rather his ultimate goal was to find a middle ground in which the two views could be reconciled—a middle ground in which the direct and active transformations could be merged to form a more complete interpretation of how our perceptions evolved. As he asserted later:

> Despite these strengths, [my new] theory remains unsatisfying in certain aspects. Most obviously it says nothing about what is in the perceiver's head. (Neisser, 1976, p. 19)

Thus, as he admitted the inadequacy of his theory, he also acknowledged the importance of mediated cognitive processing. By not rejecting that aspect of our psychological life, Neisser was marking out a middle ground between the cognitive mentalism he had so strongly supported only a few years before and Gibson's direct perceptual realism. What does emerge from these discussions is, however, quite germane to the topic of this book. Neisser's discussion zeros in on the nature of the information (as well as its source) that subsequently becomes the basis of the representation of the perceptual experience. Phrased in these terms, it becomes conceptually similar to the question that is the target of this chapter—Where does the critical transformation take place that accounts for the perception? Is it exogenous or endogenous? Is the critical information generated externally or internally?

The important contribution of Neisser's work is that no matter how direct the perception, it is obvious there is a considerable amount of information processing inside the nervous system. As Bridgeman (1998) pointed out, Gibson "simply wasn't interested in it." Neisser, at least, brought ecological psychology back a little from the precipice of Gibson's narrow and radical perspective.

Turvey's Direct Realism. Another energetic step forward from Gibson's original direct position can be found in the work of Turvey and Shaw. Turvey and Shaw and their later collaborators developed a radical direct realism in a series of articles (Shaw & Turvey, 1981; Turvey, 1977; Turvey & Shaw, 1979). Like Gibson, they argued that perception is not the result of a distant, indirect relationship between the external physical environment and the perceiving observer as mediated by encoded signals, but rather that it is a much more intimate transactional relationship between the perceiver and the environment. In Shaw and Turvey's (1981) words: "The objects of perceptual knowing are functionally ascribed directly to objects in the knower's environment." This kind of direct realism asserts that the experience is not the brain state triggered by the stimulus, but a property of the "functionally specified environment" itself. Shaw and Turvey's theory postulated that this interaction is in the form of a "coalition" between the observer and the environment. Their approach, therefore, tied together the observer and the observed into a unified entity; perception is not understandable, according to them, without consideration of both observer and observed and the interactions between them.

Turvey (1977) provided us with a concise statement of what the issues were in the direct–indirect controversy:

> Presumably, the goal of visual-processing theory is to isolate and characterize that which is most eminently and directly responsible for our perceptual knowledge. In the view of indirect realism, the candidates for this honor are patently the postulated links in the internal chain of epistemic mediators from the retinal image to perceptual experience. But the view of direct realism promotes a very different roster of candidates. They are, most obviously,

the complex, nested relationships in the dynamically structured medium surrounding the observer that are specific to the properties of the environment
in which he or she acts. (p. 86)

In this article, Turvey allied himself with the ecological school that placed
such enormous stress on the structure of the environment. By his use of the
word "structure," in this case, he was almost certainly referring to the informational structure of the environment. Here, Turvey drew the important
operational distinction between indirect and direct perception by asserting
that although indirect realists suggested that an external stimulus under-
determined the perceptual response, the direct realists felt that the external stimulus was capable of fully determining the response.

In recent years Turvey and Shaw (e.g., Turvey, 1992; Turvey & Shaw,
1995, 1999; Shaw & Turvey, 1999) have extended their version of direct realism to a more complete formulation in which both perception and action
are intimately tied together. They suggested that continued development
of this line of psychological theory will ultimately replace the cognitive
movement by emphasizing the differences between the two approaches to
psychological science. Whereas cognitive psychology is deeply concerned
with representations and "knowledge is said to come primarily through reasoning, not sensing" (Turvey & Shaw, 1999, p. 106), they propose that the
more appropriate view is "a rethinking of the conceptual versus perceptual
distinction in terms of invariance detection" (p. 107). It will be interesting
to see if their approach is able to achieve the objective they have set for it.

2.3   SOME MODERN RATIONALISMS

In the previous sections, I discussed a few modern direct perception theories. There are, of course, a multitude of mediated, mentalist, or rationalist,
or indirect psychological theories presented as alternatives to the direct realism of Gibson and the others. However, only a few explicitly invoke
Helmholtzian or similar kinds of unconscious reasoning as the main way in
which we perceive. One main exception to this generalization is the work of
Irvin Rock who represented one of the most vigorous proponents of a contemporary rationalism.

Rock's Perceptual Intelligence.   To Rock, there was nothing direct about
seeing. In his writing (e.g., Rock, 1983) he argued for an indirect, interpretive, or rationalist theory of perception based on a substantial amount of his
own research or that of others. Rock described large numbers of perceptual
experiments and demonstrations he believed demonstrated that what we
see depends primarily on mind–brain interpretations of the stimulus. In

other words, from his perspective, stimuli provided the clues to a puzzle that had to be actively interpreted by the observer. He argued that these phenomena clearly counterindicated the direct realism position championed by Gibson and the others. Many of the findings he cited are associated with interactions between the various attributes of the stimulus. For example, Rock highlighted an experiment showing the perceived orientation of an object determined its perceived shape. Other experimental results were used to illustrate perceptual changes that depended on the current set or experience of the observer. In short, his argument was that endogenous forces determine virtually all of perception.

Rock (1983) designated his version of this new indirect perception or neorationalism as *perceptual intelligence* and described it as being analogous to reasoning (p. 3) much in the same manner proposed by Helmholtz (1856). He went on to cite many other contemporary psychologists who have supported the same inferential kind of perception over the years including Hochberg (1970), Gregory (1970), and Epstein (1973). The central theme that pervaded these works, as well as Rock's work itself, was that "perception is thought like" (p. 315). That is, what we see is filtered through many layers of cognitive processing in which the initial stimulus is only a set of incomplete cues, hints, and initial conditions on which unconscious logical or thought processes operate to interpret, analyze, and conclude and then to construct a perceptual experience.

There is another attribute of Rock's theory of intelligent perception that must be acknowledged—the fact that processes leading to perceptual experience are autonomous and not subject to conscious control. No matter how much we know of the incorrectness of an illusion, we are not able to suppress the compelling perceptual experience that results. Past experience may affect the perception but conscious control is ineffectual. Helmholtz' use of the adjective "unconscious" is clearly mirrored here.

Recently, a collection of papers (Rock, 1997) was published; it was edited, and introduced by Steven Palmer. This volume brought together a number of important papers by Rock and his colleagues, some recent and some several decades old. Palmer presented an excellent history of the recent controversy between the indirect and direct theoretical positions in the foreword. The contents of this book were, however, mainly empirical; a collection of experiments describing many of the results that proponents of this school of thoughtful perception believed supported the idea that perception is largely indirect, inferential, and constructive, in other words, endogenous.

There is little reason to deny the data and findings of the many experiments that Rock or his colleagues described even if the conclusions drawn were as one sided as those antithetical ones from the Gibson camp. Certainly, there are ubiquitous interpretations, illusions, and nonveridicalities

demonstrable in the psychological literature that suggest extensive processing by an "intelligent" if not "autonomous" cognitive system underlies many
aspects of visual perception. That is, however, not the point! The same criticism of the radical direct perceptionists earlier in this chapter can also be
made of those who champion unconscious processing. That is, their respective views were too dogmatic, too narrow, too rigid, too strict, and too extreme. It is probably possible to match on a one-for-one basis experiments
that were cited to support the direct and indirect views, respectively. The
problem is that neither side accepts the fact that all these findings and demonstrations are indeterminate; none is able to peer inside the behaving or
perceiving organism to determine what kind of cognitive mechanisms are
actually present. Most likely, the true situation is that each theoretical position is probably correct—at least in part. The neorationalists are correct in
specifying there are some instances in which internal processes dominate
perception; the neorealists are equally correct in specifying there are some
instances in which the nervous system almost passively responds to the external stimulus.

This chapter proposes an alternative to such dichotomous and extremist
thinking in the form of an operational analysis of the causal conditions that
lead to various kinds of perceptions. The foundation axiom of this view is
an eclectic one; both endogenous and exogenous processes are at work in
the definition of our perceptual experiences. Our job is to determine
where the critical transformations occur—prior to or following the transductive line of demarcation between the internal and the external.

Although Rock is one of the most prominent proponents of an indirect
or rationalist theory of perception, there are many, many others whose
ideas are implicitly based on the same or similar fundamental principles
and assumptions. All cognitive psychologists who seek to unravel the "modules of mind" or "components of cognition" fall into the same camp as do
any of the classic or modern faculty psychologies. It is also the case that
much of the neuroscientific effort to locate functional modules in the brain
are expressing, ever so cryptically, the conceptually identical idea of central
processing mechanisms that are supposed to selectively modulate, transform, and interpret incoming stimulus information.

A number of other perceptual psychologists also can be characterized as
being in the rationalist, mediated, endogenous camp. In large part the empirical evidence on which they depend are also the classical visual or "geo-
metric" illusions stressed by Rock. Such workers as the Australian Ross Day
and the Englishman Richard L. Gregory are among the most notable. The
American psychologists Theodore E. Parks and John M. Kennedy are also
among those who explicitly express their theoretical belief in mediated perception. Although they quibble a bit over the terminology (Day, 2001, e.g.,
sees no need for these processes to be considered as successful problem

solvers or "intelligent" in that sense), this group does generally agree on the idea of mediation and disagree on any form of directness. In general, however, interest in a radical rationalism of the kind to which this group of scholars adheres seems to be declining. A popular summary of the rationalist or intelligent theories of visual perception held by some of these proponents can be found in Parks' (2001) very readable book.

2.4 SUMMARY AND AN INTERIM CONCLUSION

The point of this chapter is that a considerable portion of what we call psychology, particularly in the field of perceptual experience, is not, in fact, defined by internal mind–brain transformations. That is, many of the critical causal relationships that define the information representing a perceptual experience are actually determined by the external environment or by inevitable natural laws, by invalid analyses, or by misinterpretation of what are from an operational point of view incontestably valid data. This issue arises in many different contexts including the direct and indirect controversy and its more modern version in which the holistic aspects of direct perception are contrasted with the isolatable components of an elementalist cognitive system.

Again, the eclectic tone of the argument I make here must be emphasized. There is no question that information transformations and forces that exist without "active," "mediated," "intelligent," or "inferential" intervention of the nervous system, largely determine some phenomena of perception. It is essential to appreciate, on the other hand, that there are also many other cognitive phenomena that are "caused" by these information transformational activities of the nervous system. Thus, it is important to keep in mind that the debate between the positions suggested by the most extreme proponents of the direct or mediated schools of thought, respectively, is probably a false one. This dichotomous debate is, in other words, a red herring that has blocked efforts to develop operational procedures for discriminating between those percepts that are, in fact, due to active mind–brain transformations and those that are simply passive responses to the information provided by external stimulus properties and conditions.

This false controversy is to a considerable degree fueled by the fact that, all-too-often, psychologists "talk past" each other rather than "talk to" each other. Scholars on one side of the debate or the other quote quite separate bodies of empirical findings to support their respective positions. Indeed, to a surprising degree, one conclusion drawn by a reasonably neutral observer is that the two antagonistic fields are not even interested in the same phenomena or experimental findings! Although superficially joined by the words perception or cognition, the universes of observed phenomena with which each is concerned frequently do not overlap. Such an emphasis on mutually exclusive databases is one of the main forces leading to the extreme positions we have encountered in this discussion. Or perhaps, it is the reverse problem—the hyperemphasis on one theoretical position leads to a narrow selection of what are assumed to be relevant experiments and results. In either case the effect is the same—a parochial and dogmatic theoretical orientation that does not acknowledge the important aspects of its antagonist's principles or empirical findings.[10]

Unfortunately, such parochial constraints on what is to be studied inhibit any resolution in terms of a compromise appreciation that both sides of the controversy were and are at least partially correct as well as partially incorrect. The entire discussion is far better structured as an eclectic search for an inclusive, if not universal, identification of the causes of all relevant phenomena. Furthermore, it is exactly in the domain of perceptual experiences that we are in the best possible position to ascertain exactly what part of the salient information is conveyed by the stimulus and what is constructed from ambiguous or incomplete information. Central cognitive processes do not enjoy such unidirectional simplicity or concrete anchoring to the external physical world.

Hopefully, the discussion presented so far highlights the necessity for eclectic resolution of the false debate between direct and indirect theories of perception. These radical and extreme positions can then be replaced with a practical and empirical question: What nonveridicalities exist between the stimulus and the perceptual response that must be accounted for by inferential, mediated, or constructive processes in the nervous system? The corollary, of course, is: What veridicalities exist between the stimulus and the perceptual response that suggest passive information processing of stimulus information? A unified version of this pair of questions is: Where do the critical information transformations that account for a particular perceptual process occur?

Obviously, these are not questions that can be answered for all perceptual phenomena. There are uncertainties and incompletenesses even in this attempt to sharpen the issue. There currently remain many unanswered or even unanswerable questions. Nevertheless, such an approach has the enormous advantage of attacking the problem from a maximally unbiased and unprejudiced point of view and thereby eliminating, if not re-

---

[10]The other possibility mentioned previously should not be overlooked. It may be that the reported perceptual phenomena are incapable of distinguishing between the alternative views. The possibility that mental processes and mechanisms are inaccessible has been considered previously (Uttal, 2000) and may be closer to the truth than either of the extreme positions. I believe that the veridicality test proposed in this book overcomes some of the problems raised by the inaccessibility criticism even if it does not completely mitigate it.

solving, at least some of the false controversies that have long plagued perceptual psychology.

It is also important to anticipate that the criterion that I have proposed—veridicality of stimulus and response—is not always going to be suitable or usable. Undeniably, a perceptual experience is always the result of an interaction between the observed and the observer. In seeking to determine how much of the variance can be attributed to each, we must remain aware that the nature of the interaction may produce a complex situation in which the two factors may be irretrievably intertwined. In such cases the very act of examining them may alter any measurements we make of the relative contribution of the endogenous and exogenous factors respectively.

A further complication lies in the fact that very similar phenomena may have very different properties. Some phenomena, for example the perception of fractured figures, are strongly influenced by supplementary cognitive information. Others, such as the Poggendorf illusion, cannot be perceptually overridden no matter how much supplementary information is provided to the observer. The point being that superficially similar phenomena may exhibit very different properties and, arguably, be based on very different origins.

Another caveat related to the problem I discuss here is that even the most *direct* response to a certain attribute of the stimulus, which may appear to be occurring automatically, is, without question, being processed by the nervous system in the manner argued by the mediation theorists. Any allusion made to *passive* processing must reflect mechanisms that have evolved over the millennia to handle quickly and efficiently some of the environmental puzzles that are presented to the observer. Shepard (1987) presented an extremely cogent argument that our nervous system has evolved under the pressure of such forces as circadian rhythms, "the three degrees of freedom of terrestrial illumination," and "the geometry of three-dimensional space" (pp. 255–256) to build internal mechanisms that operate with great automaticity and great speed. Such internalized, automatic processes, as discussed by Shepherd, are not identical, in principle, with the passive ones I invoke earlier in this chapter in the discussion of exogenous processes. However fast and automatic they may be, they still represent internal processes carried out by the mind–brain and are, therefore, intrinsically endogenous. They change the information content or interpret or transform the form or content of the stimulus; thus they do not pass the exogenous test proposed here. On the other hand, it must not be forgotten that all exogenous stimulus attributes must have some mechanism for their internalization, for their instantiation as perceptual experiences. The receptors must transduce, the nerves conduct, and the brain must respond. No matter how direct the perceptual experience, nothing would happen if the nervous system did not carry out its necessary functions. To reiterate this essential point—this is not the issue; what we are concerned with here is *where* the *critical* stimulus transformation underlying some perceptual response occurs.

It is unlikely that the boundary between endogenous and exogenous processes is going to be a sharp one. Nevertheless, by restraining our quest to the practical one of seeking the location of the critical causal information transformation, we should be able to distinguish between these two causal sources of our perceptual experience. Drawing such distinction in this operational manner will help enormously to reduce the conceptual errors (i.e., the psychomyths) that clog and mislead scientific psychology.

Inevitable Natural Laws and Superpowerful Mathematics

3.1 INTRODUCTION

Psychology, beset with all of its conceptual difficulties, complexities, and logical challenges, has always harbored some of the most aggressive and ingenious adaptors of scientific developments from other fields. I know from first-hand experience that the idea of using computers to control experiments occurred in the psychological laboratory earlier than in most other fields of science. Why this is so is patently obvious—the needs of the science are so great that the tendency to adopt anything that may help to design and execute experiments or that may provide a conceptual or metaphorical bridge to a satisfactory theory is overwhelming.

The history of psychology and all of its predecessor natural sciences and philosophies is littered with acquired metaphors and analogies—some groundbreaking and others of only temporary utility. Boring (1950), among others, suggested that psychology almost slavishly followed the current scientific Zeitgeist. Cognitive processes have been modeled by hydraulic, pneumatic, electrical, cybernetic, computational, informational, statistical, control system, and, nowadays, even by the annealing of glass or the distribution of molecules in a gas, or, most recently, by mathematics that had originally been used for the description of the dynamics of complex gravitational systems.

Most of these metaphors disappear as the other sciences move on, but some persist, if only in the vocabulary of psychology. Some, newly arrived on the scene, have not yet been tested to see if they are likely to contribute more than a few vestigial vocabulary items as did their long forgotten predecessors. Perhaps the clearest example of an attractive idea that was quickly transferred to psychology that did persist in our language was the almost immediate adoption of ideas about information processing (Shannon, 1948) by psychologists (e.g., Garner & Hake, 1951). Others, such as the telephonic and, arguably, the computer metaphor have had less persistence, only to be replaced by new metaphors as psychology progresses.

However useful a given metaphor may have been in its brief time, it should be appreciated that even the most abstract ones typically do not embody the same kind of mechanism instantiated in the biological neural network. The more concrete ones (such as modeling attention by a funnel or a searchlight) are often nothing more than graphic aides for tutoring novices. The more abstract ones, on the other hand, sometimes leave a residue of mathematical tools, but in doing so they are usually stripped of their adjunct notions of what kind of mechanism actually accounts for the system's behavior. Indeed, even what is probably the currently most popular model—the neural net—is now appreciated by at least a few iconoclasts as something other than a direct model of the function of the nervous system. On the contrary, neural networks and other connectionist models are now beginning to be considered as means of interpreting mathematical descriptions in a more concrete way rather than as literal models of psychoneural equivalence.

There is, without question, no more fertile source of metaphors for the mind than mathematics—the near universal means of describing system behaviors of all kinds. Psychologists and their counterparts in other psychobiological sciences who are also interested in human and other organic kinds of complex system behavior have, once again, been among the leaders in applying new developments in mathematics to their chosen fields of study. Psychologists repeatedly encounter new mathematical approaches to thinking about behavior that promise to illuminate some hitherto obscure aspect of the human mind. Some initially seem to have great promise, but then, like many of the more physical models of the past, slip quietly from the scientific scene.

We see in this chapter how ideas from the new mathematics of fractals, 1/f noise, and other closely related modern mathematical developments have led to exciting reconceptualizations of how cognitive processes might be implemented. Unfortunately, this translation from the physical to the psychological sciences is sometimes done without a full appreciation of the actual limits of these astonishingly powerful mathematical tools. I argue here that inappropriately deep explanatory meaning is sometimes attributed to what are purely descriptive methods. In other instances, empirical research shows that humans are not sensitive to certain parameters to which a particular mathematical model may be exquisitely sensitive.

Throughout its history, psychology, as have most other serious sciences, has turned to mathematics for help in analyzing its data and formulating its theories. Many of the mathematical methods that have been so absorbed had nonpsychological origins. In some cases there was a need to solve a particular problem (e.g., Fourier analysis arose out of the need to develop a way to describe heat flow). In others, a curious function was found to empirically describe a particular phenomenon (e.g., Pareto's law was intended to summarize economic systems behavior). Statistical methods arose primarily to meet the needs of agriculture. In many of these cases, the very power, indeed, the broad applicability of these methods to topics far afield from their origins suggested they might have equivalent utility as theoretical engines for cognition and behavior in particular. Indeed, the power of these "universal" methods was so great that it made their application to psychological phenomena virtually inevitable.

Thus, there has always been some concern that the role mathematics played in quite distant fields of study might not be properly played in psychology. One of the problems was that mathematics might introduce spurious and superfluous meaning into psychological phenomena. Perhaps, it was argued, the properties of very general mathematics might be misinterpreted as properties of the psychological system being analyzed.[1] In other words, mathematics expressed general properties of complicated systems that transcended the particulars of any given system such as the mind–brain. Thus, for example, rather than describing a characteristic of human language or thought processes per se, a relationship such as Zipf's law probably represents a general property of the organization of stochastic systems. Or, to put it another way, it had as much (or as little) to do with the properties of linguistic behavior as with any other data set that involved rank ordering. In another familiar example of a superpowerful mathematical tool leading to overinterpretation, Fourier analyses and polynomial series expansions are capable of parsing or analyzing nearly any function into sets of primitive components. The key point, however, is that the components, however well they represent the system under study, do not necessarily correspond to the actual mechanisms of that system; the analysis would produce the components regardless of their physical presence or absence.

Before I begin to review particular examples of what may be best called *inevitable natural laws* and their theoretical explanations, it is important to point out that the potential explanations of these laws and their wide applicability have implications for several different levels of discussion. At one level, they make the important point that mathematics is neutral with re-

---

[1]Of course, this is a criticism that can be levied against any mathematical model in any science, not just psychology. There are two approaches that can be taken in the application of mathematics. The first is to apply an existing mathematics developed for one science that seems to offer promise to solve an analogous problem in another science. The second is to state a problem and then seek an appropriate mathematics to solve it. Psychologists all too often follow the first rather than the preferred second approach.

gard to the topic to which it is applied; mathematics is not specific to psychology (or any other scientific domain) but, to the contrary, it reflects the general properties and laws of a system of analysis that can be applied to psychological and biological mechanisms as well as to electronic or other physical systems.

At another level, the interpretations of the mathematical laws and procedures proposed to explain psychological phenomena do make one thing clear. That is, few if any of the mind–brain mechanisms under study are simple. Rather, allusions to complexity, nonlinearity, multidimensionality, and superimposed component functions are ubiquitous throughout all discussions in this chapter. That the psychobiological system is complex is a truism: We did not need the descriptors that were forthcoming in the form of, for example, $1/f^n$ expressions[2] to know that this was the case. Complexity, interaction, and nonlinearity must be accepted as fundamental properties of neuronal systems and the behavior that they generate. The inherent contradiction between the simplicity of the typical univariate experiment in experimental psychology and our increasing awareness of just how complex the mind–brain system really is should be a warning to all concerned.

In the following sections of this chapter, I consider some of the most egregious misinterpretations of what on closer inspection turn out to be inevitable natural laws.

3.2 ZIPF'S LAW

There is probably no better place to start this discussion than with the classic and empirically accurate, but deeply misunderstood, law promulgated by Zipf (1935/1965). In his 1935 book, Zipf reported his extensive statistical studies of the structure of language. In particular, his technique was to study the relationship of the rank order (r) of words and the frequency (F) with which they were used. Zipf "discovered" that such a relationship was well fit by the power law expression

$$F \propto \frac{1}{r^k} \qquad (3.1)$$

where k is an exponent that is very close to 1 and $\propto$ means "is closely approximated by."[3] If Zipf's law is plotted on log–log coordinates, its locus is

---

[2]The superscript ^{n} in this case need not be an integer. As we see later in this chapter, ^{n} can take on fractional powers.

[3]The usual meaning of the mathematical symbol $\propto$ is "is proportional to" but this suggests a precision that is not usually obtained with Zipf-type functions. The somewhat softer tone of "is closely approximated by" comes closer to the proper meaning as it is used throughout this chapter.

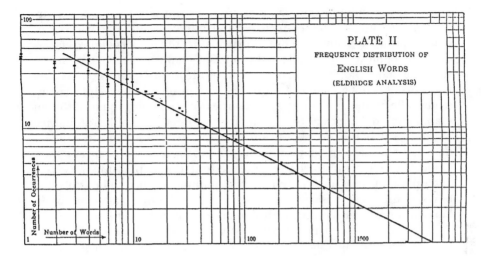

FIG. 3.1.   Zipf's log–log plot of the relationship between the rank order of
usage for English words and their frequency of occurrence. From Zipf
(1935).

remarkably close to a straight line for the language database he studied.
Figure 3.1 is an example of a Zipf law plot from his 1935 book for language.
The form of this graph is very common; as we shall see, the same relation-
ship appears in many other, sometimes quite, different contexts.

Zipf was very specific in concluding that this expression was a direct outcome of the underlying biology and psychology of language production.
For him, these curves were a means of examining the behavioral organization of the human mind. For example, in his 1935 book he stated:

> The term Psycho-Biology [*sic*] is employed in the title because it seems to des-
> ignate more concisely and accurately than any other term the present treat-
> ment of linguistic behavior in reference to: (1) man's experience, and (2) the
> rest of man's bodily functions. (p. xv)

There is no question that it was within the context of the specific attributes
of human language, cognitive processing, and behavior that Zipf sought
the explanation for this observed regular relationship.

Over the years, this expression for the relationship between rank order
and frequency of use has been repeatedly confirmed for language. As an
empirical expression, its accuracy is probably as good any other so-called
"psycho-biological" law. However, as Miller (1965) suggested in the introduction to the 1965 edition of Zipf's 1935 book, Zipf's theoretical interpretation of this incontestably valid empirical description was totally invalid!
Miller pointed out that Zipf assumed his law modeled the linguistic behav-

ior of human cognition and was, therefore, assaying a deep property of human mentation. As Miller emphasized and, as recent work has made clear, this is not the case; any reductive or explanatory theory of cognitive activity built on cognitive entities inferred from Zipf's law is indisputatively incorrect—no matter how well the data are fit by the formal expression; we now know that it is not a matter of cognitive mechanisms. Rather, Zipf's law actually reflects the fundamental properties of something quite different than the mind. Miller was one of the first to appreciate that it is an inevitable end result of the probabilistic or stochastic mechanisms involved in producing the behavior of many different kinds of systems—organic and inorganic. In other words, however excellent the expression was as a description of the data that Zipf studied, it ultimately had to be explained by rules other than those of human mentation or, for that matter, any other biological function. Even though human mentation was and is subject to these rules, their fundamental origins had to be found more broadly.

Before beginning a more detailed discussion of Zipf's law, it should be pointed out that this is a perfect example of both the neutrality of mathematics with regard to underlying mechanisms and the need to keep clear the mathematical and the mechanistic and/or physiological assumptions of any theory. As I argued in Uttal (1998), no matter how good the fit provided by a formal model, the underlying mechanisms are actually invisible to the mathematical model and inaccessible to behavioral research methods. That is, mathematical and computational models of all kinds can perfectly describe or predict the behavior of the system they model without having anything useful or authoritative to say about which particular mechanisms account for them. Nowhere is this distinction between description and reductive explanation clearer than in the history of the potential explanations of Zipf's law. Not only could this particular model not distinguish between two alternative theories from the same domain, but it was also incapable of even identifying the potential domain from which the currently most popular explanation was eventually to come. Zipf was, thus, totally wrong in his basic theoretical assumption—the belief that he was studying something about the "Psycho-Biology of Language."

Zipf's law, therefore, had nothing fundamental to say about psychology or biology or even language beyond that it shares a property found abundantly throughout the natural world; it is purely an inevitable statistical outcome of the nature of a large class of probabilistic information sources. As we see later, it has been applied to a huge variety of analogous information sources and it works as well for each of them.

Nevertheless, by 1949,[4] Zipf was still interested in the search for "fundamental principles that seem to govern important aspects of our behavior"

---

[4]In 1941, Zipf published what was most appropriately his least well-known and best-forgotten work. In it, he discussed the application of his law to the political and social structure

(Zipf, 1949, p. v). By then, however, he had expanded his goal to include not only individual behavior but also that of social groups. After having discovered the reasonably accurate empirical law that now bears his name, like any serious scientist, he was very much committed to finding a general explanation for it. It was here, in terms of the interpretation of the empirical law, that Zipf went so badly wrong. Indeed, his enthusiasm waxed as he became increasingly aware that it seemed to have more general applicability than simply to language behavior.

Unfortunately, Zipf did not take the next logical step and realize that his purported psychological law must be of even broader significance than he was beginning to appreciate, extending not only far beyond language but beyond organic behavior of all kinds. To the end, he did not appreciate that his law was actually a special case of a much more universal property of information sequences. His personal interpretation was still contained totally within the realm of human behavior, albeit greatly expanded from linguistics to include mental illness, child development, the geographic distribution of populations, and even international war.

The explanatory vehicle proposed by Zipf (1949) to explain his psychobiological law was based on what he called the "Principle of Least Effort." He suggested several properties that he believed characterized this putative general principle.

First, the least effort principle was regarded by Zipf as:

> contingent upon the *mentation* of the individual, which in turn includes the operations of "*comprehending*" the "relevant" elements of a problem, of "*assessing their probabilities*," and of "solving the problem in terms of least effort." (p. 7; italics and punctuation in the original)

Second, Zipf proposed that the least effort principle was based on estimates not only of the current rate of mental work, but even more importantly, on estimates of the "probable average rate of work." His theory, therefore, required predictive estimates on the part of the subject.

Third, the entire behavior of every individual was, according to Zipf, based on minimization of the effort required to behave in any particular situation. This "universal" underlying principle gave rise, he asserted, to the ever-increasing variety of human behavior that the classic Zipf function could fit.

---

of national entities. It does not require too much reading of Zipf's last chapter to appreciate both his explicit anti-Semitism and his pro-Nazi outlook. Particularly dangerous was his justification of Germany's aggression in terms of his empirical law. It is also interesting to note that *in 1941*, Zipf repeatedly asserted, "we have no knowledge of Mr. Hitler's intentions" (p. 383 and elsewhere). The absurdity of this statement is highlighted by both the history of the 1930s and Hitler's own statements in his own horrible book.

Unfortunately, even though the hints were there, Zipf continued to misunderstand the much wider generality of the expression that had seemed to him originally to be a metric of human language performance. There is no better way to illustrate this unappreciated generality—a generality so broad that the function ultimately had to be attributed, not to human mentation, but rather to universal properties of stochastic systems—than to review the precursors and successors of Zipf's Law. This task is carried out in the next sections.

3.2.1 Precursors of Zipf's Law

Prior to the publication of Zipf's 1935 book, a number of similar if not analogous relationships had been observed in many other fields of endeavor than linguistics. The earliest well-documented anticipation was reported in the 19th century by Vilfredo F. D. Pareto (1848–1923), a pioneering economist who proposed a mathematical law of wealth. Pareto observed that income was distributed the same regardless of the tax or political situation of a country. His law should be familiar because it was very close in form to Zipf's formulation:

$$N(X > x) \propto \frac{1}{x^{p}} \qquad (3.2)$$

where $N(X > x)$ is the number of people who have an income X greater than some lower value of income x and p is the exponent to which x is raised. This expression predicts that there will be fewer rich people than poor people, an obvious fact, but one that Pareto felt was measured by this expression for the actual distribution of incomes. As noted, the law seemed to be completely independent of the particular society in which it was measured. Adamic (2001) has shown that the Zipf, Pareto, and many of the other power laws to be discussed in this section are all actually nearly equivalent to each other.

Also in the late 19th century, Simon Newcomb (1835–1909), an American astronomer, naval officer, and professor, suggested a special case of what also turned out to be a close relative of Zipf's law. His formulation (Newcomb, 1881) was based on a peculiarity of a set of logarithmic tables that he was using. Newcomb noticed that the pages representing numbers starting with the smallest numerals (i.e., 1, 2, and 3) were more soiled than those beginning with the largest numerals (i.e., 7, 8, and 9). This suggested to him that the tables of logarithms were not randomly distributed with regard to their first digits. Indeed, when Newcomb carried out an analysis of the logarithms he discovered that the leading numeral had a probability of

.301 of being a "1", not .1, as might naively have been expected! He was able to summarize his observations by the expression:

$$P(n) \propto \log_{10}\left(1 + \frac{1}{n}\right) \tag{3.3}$$

where $P(n)$ is the probability of the leading numeral being n. In recent years, Newcomb's law was rediscovered by Benford (1938) on the basis of a much more extensive collection of data from economics, geography, and a variety of other fields. This expression also appears to be a law of extreme universality and, therefore, hardly needs to be constrained solely to logarithmic tables any more than Zipf's law had to be constrained to language.

Other scholars who observed very much the same sort of relationship in other specialized situations also anticipated Zipf. One of the most prescient was Estoup (1916). He was seeking ways to improve the newly invented stenotype system—a mechanical shorthand machine that allowed specially trained typists using a multiple key-press device to record speech at virtually the same speed at which it was spoken. Estoup observed what was essentially the same relationship that Zipf discovered some years later, namely, that the product of the frequency of a word and its rank order was a constant, another way of expressing the same essential relationship.

In the early years of the 20th century, librarians, surrounded by their huge reservoirs of human knowledge, became interested in seeking out general laws of publication, acquisition, and classification. For example, Lotka (1926) proposed a rule that approximated the publication rate of individual authors, namely:

$$N \propto \frac{1}{n^2} K \tag{3.4}$$

where N is the proportion of authors who publish n papers or books given K, the constant proportion of 61% who publish only once. Thus, for example, authors who have published 20 books represent only 0.15% of the publishing population compared to the single book author's occurrence of 61%.

A similar law of library science (not quite a predecessor as it came somewhat later than the publication of Zipf's law) was Bradford's empirical law of scatter. Bradford (1948) proposed that there were three levels of scientific publication—primary journals, secondary journals, tertiary journals—and that a third (.33) of all publications relevant to a particular topic came from each level. However, the number of journals in each level followed the expression—$n:n^2:n^3$. This indicated that the number of journals in the first level was n, that the second level contained the square of the number of primary journals (n^2), and the third level contained the cube of the number

(n^3) of primary journals. This distribution resulted in a progressive reduction in the proportion of relevant articles in each journal class. Thus, there were diminishing returns for a library to order any second or third level journal—the probability of a relevant article appearing in them would be less or very much less than in the primary journals, respectively, according to the following sequence:

$$\frac{.33}{n}; \frac{.33}{n^2}; \frac{.33}{n^3} \tag{3.5}$$

3.2.2 Successors to Zipf's Law[5]

Relationships such as Zipf's law were a natural application of what was clearly one of the most important innovations of the second half of the 20th century—the development of the digital information-processing machines called computers. It should be pointed out that it diminishes these machines to use the highly overspecific term—*computers*; these extraordinary devices can and do far more than compute arithmetic functions. They can also perform logical functions, perform geometrical transformations, and sort alphabetic sequences as well as make counts of occurrences. Indeed, based on the concatenation of simple operations, they have been able to carry out far more complex functions. The full range of their capabilities has yet to be determined, to say the very least.

The lexicographic applications of such a powerful information-processing device were as immediately obvious to lexicographers as they have been to psychologists. A host of explorative studies of the structure of language and many other topics that seemed at first to have only a minimum relevance to language proliferated in the next several decades. These near universal information-processing machines clearly opened up a wide range of data of all kinds to detailed examination.

Zipf's law, some derivation of it, or some close relative of it, have been observed in an enormous variety of different topics in recent years as the computer made it relatively easy to manipulate huge databases. (Indeed, one can only wonder at the perseverance of some of the early workers who had nothing but pencil, paper, and persistence to carry out their exhaustive and exhausting counts of word frequencies or other statistical data.) With modern equipment, however, some tasks became much easier and others became possible in a practical sense.

Despite the fact that most linguists now reject the psycho-biological inference drawn by Zipf and tend to appreciate the generality that these rules

---

[5] I am indebted to Li (1999) for the extensive online bibliography on Zipf's law that led me to some of the more obscure references cited here.

are determined by the stochastic properties of sequential databases, many researchers have continued to carry out Zipf-type analyses on language. Beier, Starkweather, and Miller (1967) expanded on Zipf's research on the more mature language of adults as expressed in books to consider spoken word frequencies in children. Wright (1979) applied Zipf's law to the study of the spoken duration of rare and familiar words equated for length. Interestingly, they concluded that the Zipf effects observed were not generally associated with memory, thus contradicting, at least in part, the original Zipf premise that the observations that were fit by his law reflected the basic cognitive processes presumed to underlay language.

New fields of science and technology have also become grist for the Zipf mill. The World Wide Web (WWW)—the Internet—is a natural for such studies; because "surfing" is not only a highly structured tree-type graphic behavior with abundant frequency distributions, it also leaves footprints in computer memories—footprints that can become the data necessary for further study. Huberman, Pirolli, Pitkow, and Lukose (1998) studied WWW surfing behavior and discovered "Zipf-like" functions for the number of pages that a reader typically examined at a single Web site. They also reported that a Zipf function also described the distribution of hits of various sites. That is, the frequency of hits is related by this function to the rank order of the site's hit rate. Breslau, Cao, Fan, Phillips, and Shenker (1998) related the hit ratio of Web site addresses to the log of the cache size and asserted that these phenomena also followed Zipf's law.

Zipf's law and derivations of it have been used to describe other relationships that seem initially to be far distant from the original topic with which he was concerned. Mandelbrot (1960) followed up on Pareto to describe the relation between income rank and income change and replicated that antique law. Vandewalle and Ausloos (1999) found only weak predictions from Zipf for simple stock market prices, but reported that a negative trend did exist, thus suggesting some prediction of the stock market might be possible. Axtell (2001) reported that the size of firms in the United States (as measured either by receipts or by the number of employees) was closely approximated by a Zipf-type function.

In a completely different domain, Sornette, Knopoff, Kagan, and Vanneste (1996) observed a Zipf-type law that described volcanic behavior—big eruptions occur less frequently than small ones in the same regular manner that word rank and frequency were related. Biology also was "Zipf-ed." Hill (1970) applied this versatile law to population dynamics. Raup and Sepkoski (1984) and Matsumoto and Aizawa (1999) considered the problem of the structure of the branching tree describing the rise and extinction of phyla and again observed that Zipf's formula fit this kind of data. Furthermore, they specifically concerned themselves with the evolved size of various phyla and concluded that this biological process was also adequately modeled with a Zipf-type law. May (1988) reported that a Zipf-type function related the numbers of species to the *average length* of the animal—rank order of size being Zipf-ed into the frequency of occurrence of the species—describing the empirical fact that there are only two kinds of elephants but many kinds of monkeys, if not explaining why. (The question of why there are so many species of cetaceans arises but is not answered by this observation.)

Zipf-type laws eventually were applied to the most modern fields of science. Even DNA structure appears to be grist for the mill of this nearly universal law. Mantegna et al. (1994) observed that noncoding sequences of DNA also followed this remarkable law.

This incomplete tabulation of the ubiquity of Zipf-type laws is sufficient to make the point: Many, many different systems are well described by simple inverse power function laws similar to Zipf's. The major conclusion drawn from this sample is that there is nothing specific in any of these domains of study that explains what mechanisms are at work to produce this family of similar and identical functional relationships. This unavoidable deficiency argues, once again, very strongly for the neutrality[6] of mathematical models of all kinds; given the form of an equation or its solution, there is no way one can infer what actually is the underlying mechanism producing the observed relationship.

The important summarizing point in this tabulation is that many of these other laws are identical to or easily derivable from Zipf's equation. Thus, all are reflecting a common property of probability that is not simply restricted to linguistics. Furthermore, as already pointed out, Adamic (2001) has shown that many other superficially dissimilar power laws also "refer to the same thing." This enormous breadth of application raises serious questions about any explanation that is restricted to one specific domain—as Zipf did. The next section examines this situation to determine what can be gleaned from the theoretical confusion into which this "ubiquitous" law has propelled us.

3.2.3 Toward an Explanation of Zipf's Law

It is likely that the catalog of Zipf-type law applications presented in the preceding section are all correct—as empirical observations of the topic domains to which they have been applied. However, the very versatility of the expression in describing so many different natural phenomena is a damning indictment of any suggestion that valid inferences can be made about the nature of the processes underlying linguistic behavior or any other Zipf-

---

[6]I must emphasize that "neutrality" should not be equated to "uselessness." There are many advantages to be gained from the application of the formal rules of mathematics. Indeed, in some cases it may reduce the full range of uncertainties by restricting possibilities to a limited class, albeit one with its own infinite number of possibilities.

type distribution. From words to stock markets to DNA, the expression does its job too broadly for it to be uniquely associated with any one of the linguistic, social, biological, geological, economic, or other situations in which it has been observed. Nor, for that matter, can it provide a means of penetrating beneath the behavior to access underlying mechanisms. Any theory proposed to explain the particular empirical successes of this law, therefore, must come from properties they jointly share rather than from those of any particular domain.

There are several possible explanations of Zipf's law that may explain its wide applicability. One possibility is that Zipf's law is driven by a general property of all ordered sequences. That is, the function is characteristic of any of a number of sometimes quite different and related activities. In this case the law may be generally true, regardless of the domain in which it appears. This means it would be a mistake to use it as a metric or descriptor of psychobiological reality. Nevertheless, it may be useful as a measure of data by placing it in an appropriate context.

A second possibility is that Zipf's law, like several others of a similar nature, is so approximate and general, that it can fit almost anything. In other words, such formulations may be so inexact that their supposed "fit" to various databases, especially when plotted on log-log coordinates (see pp. 142–143) is itself but an illusion. In other words the details of relatively small differences may be hidden in the compression of logarithmic representation. For example, Rosenbaum (1998) showed that a logarithmic law fits very well such diverse functions as the relations between body height and age, brightness and luminance, performance speed and practice, and speed and accuracy.

Clearly any explanation of the ubiquitous application of Zipf-type laws has to be framed in terms of probability and statistics, if for no other reason that event frequencies are involved and they push us toward stochastic models. The recent history of analysis of such laws has been to relate them to the general properties of probabilistic systems including the cluster of "new" types of mathematics that include chaos, fractals, and noisy systems. Readers are directed to Schroeder (1991) for a good introduction to the close relationships among these topics.

One of the most important recent generalizations of Zipf-type laws was presented by Mandelbrot (1961). Mandelbrot provided the mathematical basis for the comment by Miller in the foreword of the 1965 reprinting of Zipf's 1935 book by showing that Zipf's law would work as well even *if a gang of monkeys randomly hitting keys on typewriters produced the language being studied.* Indeed, his work supported the first of the two possibilities just mentioned—supergenerality of the law. Mandelbrot proved that the same law could describe a wide variety of stochastically driven sequences of events, sometimes in surprising and unexpected ways. It was this generalization that should have finally lain to rest Zipf's Psycho-Biological explanation of the phenomenon as well as any other explanatory theory of system behavior that was intended to peer into the inner workings of any other such system. Unfortunately, as the law keeps being rediscovered, novices entering the field of mathematical models rejoice in having encountered another fundamental "law" of the particular aspect of nature they are studying.

Mandelbrot's generalization of the Zipf law also improved on its general ability to fit data sets. Typically, the log–log plot of a Zipf law data set is somewhat irregular at its ends where high- and low-frequency words are represented, respectively. Mandelbrot (1961) corrected these irregularities by introducing other parameters that introduced corrections for the size of the vocabulary being analyzed. Thus, at the same time, he enhanced the generality of the law and reduced its ability to "explain" specific mechanisms.

Why are Zipf-type laws ubiquitous? The answer may lie in the fact that they are all power laws of the form:

$$Y = KX^p \tag{3.6}$$

where p is an exponent that may be either positive or negative and K is a scaling constant. This provides the theorist with a powerful and general law to represent many kinds of monotonic functions.

For example, during the time I was functioning as a sensory psychobiologist (Uttal, 1973) I used the power law as the basis for developing a unified approach to the problem of the neural coding of sensory magnitudes. I now see that some of my hesitation there to exploit this relationship further than I did was well taken. The enormous versatility of the power law made it possible to describe a host of monotonic functions with positive and negative as well as fractional exponents. The interpretation of this finding was that sensory magnitudes were governed by power laws. At that time many of us sought to explain why this should be the case. I chose, as a possible mechanism explaining Equation 3.6, the compression that occurred at the transduction mechanism for many of the sense modalities. I now believe this to be incorrect. Rather, the general utility of the power function to encode many different monotonic functions is a better explanation in the same way that its close relative—a Zipf-type law—exercises such great generality. In fact, they, too, may also be different versions of what on closer analysis is the same thing. Of course, this still leaves open the questions of why Zipf studies of word distributions repeatedly generated exponents close to 1 or why a particular sensory experience has an exponent close to .5.

An answer to the question of why there are so many power functions found in nature is mathematically complex, but one answer specific to the Zipf-type law has been offered by Abe and Rajagopal (2000). They noted that there are two types of central-limit theorems. Standard central-limit theorems prove that, for real-world conditions, the distribution of errors obtained in a given experiment will converge on a normal or Gaussian distribution for large numbers of samples. The generalized central-limit theorem relaxes some of the conditions for this convergence to include some situations that do not meet the strict conditions required for the standard version. The standard version had previously been used (Khinchin, 1949) to provide a formal axiomatic basis for some other kinds of mathematical systems.

The second, the generalized version of the central-limit theorem attributed to Gnedenko and Kolmogorov (1968), speaks directly to the sources and origins of power law distributions. The mathematical proof of this conjecture by Abe and Rajagopal (2000) are beyond the scope of this book, but their conclusion is clear—the basic property of certain number systems that is instantiated in the generalized central-limit theorem exactly predicts the Zipf–Mandelbrot power law distribution.[7]

Mandelbrot (1983) took a different approach to explaining the ubiquity of the Zipf-type functions. He relates the power law form of these expressions to the underlying scaling properties of tree-like structures of which language is but one example. Power laws also have interesting properties that relate them to fractal dimensions. The concept of the fractal dimension is a key idea in this whole story. The concept of fractal dimensions was probably (although, according to Mandelbrot, there were so many other influences that this is not entirely certain) originally suggested by a German mathematician—Hausdorff (1919). Hausdorff's suggestion was that even though we are used to dealing with the three dimensions of space as being integers, there remain other possible dimensions that are not integer.

Dimensions in general are denoted by D. Mandelbrot was concerned with two different kinds of dimensions—the Hausdorff dimension D_H and the topological dimension D_T. A fractal (an object or a form) is defined as any object in which $D_H > D_T$. Specifically, D_H is the dimension of an object determined by the expression:

$$D_H = \frac{\log N}{\log n} \tag{3.7}$$

where N is equal to the number of unit lengths along an irregular path between two points and n is the number of unit lengths along a direct linear path between the two objects. If D_H is not an integer, then the dimension is fractal.

---

[7]In point of fact, the Abe and Rajagopal (2000) proof goes in the opposite direction. They actually show that the Zipf law leads to the generalized central limit theorem, rather than the other way around. The question of whether this supports the point being made is problematical.

One of the most interesting properties of fractals is that they are *self-similar*. That is, they hold regardless of the scale of the process. Even if X in the preceding equation is examined at a smaller scale, the relation still holds. Only a scaling constant has to be changed. Thus, fractals are enormously general and represent the totality of a structure as well as any small portion of it.

Whatever the source, it is clear that the Zipf-type law and all of its close relations are more likely to be intrinsic properties of the mathematical structures we use or of the general properties of complex systems than of the particular universe of discourse within which it has been observed. Nothing about the nature of the underlying mechanisms in any of these universes can be inferred from the presence of Zipf-type descriptions since some simple fundamental mathematical principles, not the specific mechanisms being modeled themselves, are responsible for the form of these laws. The exact origins and conditions that generate these ubiquitous functions are yet to be determined. What is clear is that these descriptive laws do not provide an entrée into the inner working mechanisms of psychobiological or any other systems.

3.3   1/f NOISE

Zipf-type laws are not the only "universal" laws appearing throughout many different fields of science. Another class, which may be closely related, is designated by the rubric *1/f noise* and is used to quantify a wide variety of power spectra typically obtained with a Fourier spectral analysis. The 1/f noise measure is a relative newcomer on the scene compared to our century-old awareness of the Pareto-Zipf-Mandelbrot-type law. Although there were a few cryptic predecessors of 1/f processes observed in various fields, the concept did not emerge in psychological consciousness until the 1970s.

Just as Zipf's law originally related observations of ranks and frequency of occurrence, 1/f noise distributions were first observed empirically. Probably the earliest observations were in the first half of the 20th century as the new field of electronics blossomed. It took very little experience to observe that the output signals of some of the early devices sounded awful. They were filled with crackly sounds that greatly degraded the input signal. In addition, newly developed instruments like the oscilloscope visibly showed that, in addition to the information that was inserted into the "message" by the sender, random or noisy perturbations called "static" or "noise" appeared in the message. One of the earliest of the observations of this kind of random or "shot" noise in vacuum tubes was reported by Johnson (1925). Furthermore, this same kind of interfering "noise" also appeared in other domains. Mandelbrot alluded to the work of Hurst (1951) who observed a version describing water storage and discharge in the Nile River of what was close to a 1/f law. Mandelbrot (1967) himself published one of the earliest papers on the topic suggesting there was a direct relation between white noise and direct currents.

However, such papers were rare for the next decade. Halford (1968) was among the first to publish a possible model that he believed explained 1/f noise distributions. Voss (1978b) also noted that solid-state electronic devices exhibited two types of noise distributions. Transistors with p-n junctions could only be modeled by nonlinear mechanisms whereas resistors and field-effect transistors seemed to produce 1/f noise as a result of linear processes.

Despite the work of Halford, Voss, Hurst, and Mandelbrot that make specific references to 1/f-like processes prior to the 1970s, mathematical interest in this natural law has been slow in developing. Only a small number of mathematicians are actively at work on the problem currently. Those who are knowledgeable and to whom I have spoken state that only a few of their colleagues are aware of the issue at the present time. As we see later, it is only in the last decade that a few psychologists have become excited in this type of distribution.

The engaging fact about 1/f noise is that, like the Zipf-type law functions, it now appears in an enormous number and variety of applications across virtually the entire range of scientific fields as well as some interesting psychological functions. Therefore, it is important that we now clarify its nature and discuss how it fits in with other kinds of noise distributions.

1/f noise is also known as flicker noise or pink noise, but to understand any of these terms requires that we also understand the concept of a power spectrum. A power spectrum is a plot of the energy or power of the component frequencies (e.g., as determined by a Fourier analysis) of a combined (i.e., formed by superimposition of components) signal. A power spectrum will, therefore, have a vertical coordinate of power (or some other comparable measure of energy amplitude) and a horizontal coordinate of frequency as shown in the three plates of Fig. 3.2. Like the Zipf curve, if data exhibiting a perfect 1/f distribution are plotted on log–log coordinates, a straight line is produced.

"Noise" in this case refers to any distribution of different frequencies that are based on some random or stochastic process. Thus, the term denotes a much broader domain of energy distributions than just the obvious acoustic ones. 1/f noise is also called "pink" noise[8] because it is halfway be-

---

[8]The term *pink noise* has evolved from optical and visual nomenclature. Because noise of this kind will be more heavily loaded with long wavelengths (see later in this section) and long wavelengths of visible light are perceived by the human as being pinkish or reddish, such an uneven spectrum was analogized to the "pink" experience. If all of the wavelengths had been present in a visible spectrum, the experience would have been of a white light, whence comes the term *white noise*. *Brown noise* has a different etiology—it is named after Brownian motion, which is characterized by the function $1/f^2$.

A

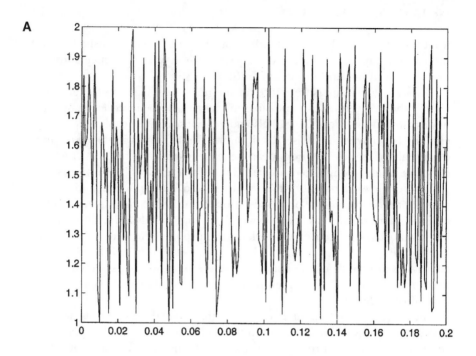

B

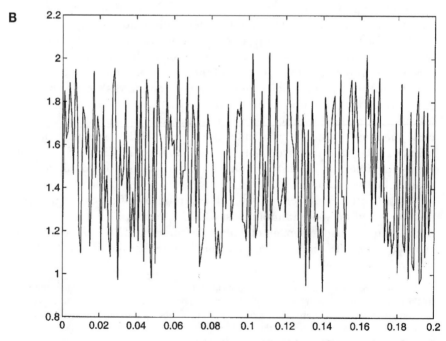

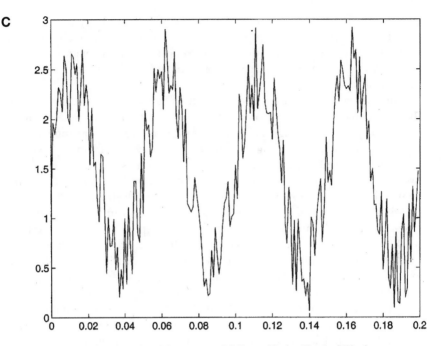

FIG. 3.2.   Three graphs of the spectra of different kinds of "noise." The horizontal axis represents an epoch of 200 msec. The vertical axes represents the relative amount of energy at each instant. Graph A (white noise) is of purely random noise centered on a frequency of 1 kHz. Graph B (pink noise) is the same random noise as in A with a small portion of a 20 Hz sinusoidal signal added to it. Graph C (brown noise) is the same random noise as in A with a much higher proportion of the 20 Hz signal added. The three graphs are on slightly different vertical scales reflecting the sequential addition of more and more energy to each graph, respectively.

tween totally random or "white" noise and "brown" or random walk noise. The three types of noise are related by the general expression:

$$P \propto 1/f^n \tag{3.8}$$

where P is the probability that a particular frequency f will be present at the standard power level. For completely random or white noise (also known as Johnson noise after the engineer who first observed it in early electronic systems), $n = 0$ and thus the expression reduces to $P \propto 1$. That is, all frequencies are equally represented—the powers of all noise frequencies are equal.

For brown noise (typically produced by Brownian motion—a situation in which each random jump of a given particle starts from [i.e., is constrained by] the position held at the end of each previous jump[9]) n is equal to 2 and, therefore, the power is inversely proportional to the square of the frequency of the component—an inverse square law. This relation specifies that higher frequencies will have substantially less energy than lower frequency ones.

The expression "1/f noise," on the other hand, suggests that n = 1, but this is not always so. The exponents for pink or 1/f noise are usually considered to be within the range 0.5 < 1.5. However, an even wider range of n values is obtained in psychological studies that may vary from only slightly more than 0 to nearly 2.[10] The fact that these values are intermediate between the white and brown noise means they will produce spectra relatively heavily loaded with low frequencies, less drastically than exhibited in a brown noise distribution, but more extensively than in white noise.

This relative abundance of low frequencies in pink noise compared to a white noise distribution can be seen visually. Indeed, even a cursory examination of running samples of the two types of noise distribution as shown in Figs. 3.2 B and C obviously indicates that there are many more low-frequency components than there are in a similar running sample of white noise. When visually compared to brown noise (see Fig. 3.2 C), the low frequencies are seen to predominate so strongly that there are only very small amplitudes of any high frequencies riding on the dominant low-frequency wave.

It is interesting to note the similarity between the formal expression of Zipf's law and 1/f noise. Although both are very much alike formally, both what they designate and their derivative origins are different as we see later in this section. Zipf-type laws are concerned with rank order–frequency distributions whereas 1/f distributions are concerned with the distribution of energies in a spectrum. Zipf type behavior, it has been suggested, may originate as an outcome of the central limit theorem; 1/f distributions have been attributed, as we see later, to quite different causal factors.

Like Zipf-type laws, however, 1/f distributions (as well as the other types of noise with different exponents) can be measured by a number of different metrics including the frequency of the component signals, distributions of variances, or even zero crossings, but they all seem to be equally plausible alternatives and all are characteristic measures of a spectrum. The important thing characterizing all 1/f distributions is that, unlike white noise they are either fully or partially (i.e., constrained) random processes and all reflect properties of generalized stochastic systems.

Because the basic idea of 1/f noise is that of spectral frequency and this is a basic measure of the properties of communication systems, it is not sur-

---

[9]According to Gardner (1978) Voss was the first to use the term *Brown noise.*

[10]The $n = 1$ idea was suggested early in the history of the study of this problem when this seemed to be the typical case and before the concept of fractal dimensions and other intermediate values were appreciated as much as they are today.

prising that electronic systems are the most frequent applications of this measure of noisy systems. The work of Voss (1978a) and Johnson (1925), presented earlier as an illustration of this kind of application shows how the noise properties of systems can be used as distinguishing measures. Indeed, Li's (2000) bibliography of 1/f articles has 180 entries of papers that deal with electronic devices and far fewer from other fields. The fascinating thing, however, is how broadly applicable 1/f noise measurements are in the non-electronic fields. Li's bibliography can be accessed to examine the range of articles showing the emergence of this ubiquitous relation for topics in the domain of ecological systems, physiology, traffic, astronomy, DNA sequences, number systems, optical systems, meteorology, and even one entry for "work related tardiness."[11]

3.3.1 1/f Distributions in Psychology and Biology

The particular concern in this book, however, is with the 1/f processes that are observed in the study of psychological and biological systems. Li's reference to work-related tardiness suggests, but does not do justice to, the variety of psychological processes that now appear to exhibit this same kind type of behavior. There is an emerging literature that describes the search for 1/f noise functions in human behavior. Not surprisingly, given that it expresses a fundamental natural law that must work in biological systems as well as in physical ones, this quest has been well rewarded; 1/f distributions have been increasingly observed in behavioral studies as well as in other fields. Of course, this fact must be tempered by the knowledge that, once again, the very ubiquitousness of the function raises certain questions about whether it is assaying some aspect of human cognition (as suggested by some of the researchers in psychology) or, to the contrary, whether it is simply reflecting an obscure and yet to be explained, but common statistical property of complex systems operating with various degrees of randomness. Before considering this question in detail, it is appropriate to review some of the situations in which 1/f functions have been discovered in psychology.

Some of the earliest observations that 1/f laws would also be observed in human behavior were published by Voss (1978a, 1978b; Voss & Clarke, 1975) the physicist identified earlier as one of the first to apply this kind of logic to electronic systems. Voss' contribution is described in eloquent detail and with popular lucidity by Gardner (1978). Gardner describes how Voss produced music that was based on white, pink, and brown noise selec-

---

[11]It is interesting to note that the one adjective repeatedly used by virtually every author who discusses 1/f noise is "ubiquitous." It appears so often that a vocabulary-poor reader might tend to believe that this word is synonymous with 1/f!

tion rules respectively. The interesting psychological aspect of the three types of music that were so generated was the aesthetic effect. Both white and brown music were unpleasant; pleasant sounding (but still somewhat uninteresting) music was produced by pink noise selection rules. According to Gardner, Voss interpreted this preference for pink noise as having evolved from the fact that we live in a world mostly composed of pink noise-type situations. This experience has tailored our nervous systems to "appreciate" and respond favorably to similar sequences. Voss was also, therefore, essentially suggesting that pink music might contain more information than white noise (which is totally unpredictable) and less information than brown noise (which is too predictable). Predictability, it should be noted, is an alternative hypothesis to the evolutionary one just mentioned as an explanation for human preference. Of course, as Gardner also pointed out, pink noise is not top quality music either. There are many other factors beyond just this bare statistic that make for a great piece of music.

Psychologists soon began to apply 1/f measures to the study of human cognition. In 1995, interest was stimulated in psychological studies of 1/f distributions in large part by the work of Gilden and his colleagues (Gilden, 1997; Gilden, Thornton, & Mallon, 1995).[12] In these seminal papers, they reported experiments that examined the variability of several different time-based tasks including the reproduction of spatial and temporal intervals and reaction times in mental rotation, as well as serial and parallel visual search and lexical decision-making tasks. Throughout these varied experimental protocols, Gilden and his colleagues observed that intervals and reaction times were often distributed in ways approximating the 1/f rule. This was particularly evident for longer intervals (i.e., for lower frequencies). Their interpretation of this observation was that it resulted from the underlying complexity of the various cognitive timing processes accounting for this behavior. As we see later in this section, the idea of multiple time scales (i.e., temporal complexity) is one of the recurrent themes in efforts to explain why 1/f distributions are so common in so many fields of science.

In recent work, Gilden (2000) extended this work to show that 1/f noise does not simply consist of random fluctuations conveying no useful information. Rather, it reflects long-term memory of a very special kind in an increasing variety of different experiment paradigms including choice and discrimination. He argues that it is not simply another way of encoding previous experience or priming, but rather is a property of the dynamical systems process that creates the internal representation of the state of the ob-

---

[12]It would be inappropriate not to note that Ward (1994) carried out a very similar experiment to the Gilden et al. studies. He also measured the same kind of distribution of estimated intervals. Ward's discussion, however, did not identify 1/f noise but rather was concerned with distinguishing between random and chaotic data.

server. It does, however, occur only in specific situations and under certain conditions. Although we do not know what these conditions are, Gilden (1977) considers these to be ". . . a central and open problem for physics" (p. 54) and, thus, presumably for psychology as well.

At about the same time as the first Gilden et al. papers, Clayton and Frey (1995) reported 1/f functions for a task in which observers were asked to specify whether an "X" or an "O" had been presented on a screen. Three different criteria were used: (a) Simple Choice—Was it an X or an O?; (b) Same–Different choice depending on what the previous stimulus had been; and (c) Same–Different choice depending on what the stimulus had been two trials back. Each of these tests progressively increased the demand on the memory capacity of the subject and slowed down the observer's response. Clayton and Frey found the resulting curves were composed of two components. On log–log plots, the Simple Choice task exhibited a two-segment component; low frequencies in the response time series seemed to be best fit by a 1/f distribution whereas the higher response frequencies seemed to be best fit by a $1/f^0$ (i.e., white noise) characteristic. The task in which the observer had to remember back two trials to make the comparison was characterized by a single 1/f plot, and the experimental protocol in which the subject had to remember back only one trial seemed to fall between these other two types of distributions. They believed this finding reflected the increasing role of memory as the observers had to look back in time to make their decision.

Others, for example, Brady, Bex, and Fredericksen (1997) took the idea a step further by actually manipulating the frequency distribution of stimuli.[13] Two classes of stimuli for an apparent motion detection task were used— white and pink noise respectively. Subjects were able to use the 1/f noise stimuli to make the detection but only the highest frequencies of the white noise stimuli provided adequate cues for the task. Brady et al. (1997) suggested, as had Voss previously, that the main reason for this difference was that the pink 1/f noise more closely approximated the realties of natural experience, whereas white noise contains useless extraneous information and only its high frequencies lead to the detection of apparent movement.

Subsequent applications in closely related fields reflected the excitement that 1/f distributions were generating. Neurophysiologists such as Ogawa (1998) observed that 1/f distributions were generated by the firing rates of olfactory neurons. He attributed the 1/f data to "self facilitation," in other words to the postresponse characteristics of the individual neuron.

---

[13]Pink or 1/f noise patterns had already been used as a type of stimulus in many psychological studies dating as far back as the mid 1970s. However, in most of these early studies it was merely one attribute of a stimulus and little attention was paid to its origins or to the fact that such a distribution might be generated by humans in behavioral tasks. The recognition of that fact was eventually to be the contribution of Gilden and his colleagues.

This result had not been unanticipated; Lundstrom and McQueen (1974) previously reported 1/f noise in neuronal cell membranes and Fujii, Aya, and Shima (1991) observed the same distributions in interspike interval fluctuations.

Closely related to the psychological applications was work in economics. Dooley and Van de Ven (1999) studied event time series in organizations and observed that the level of dimensionality (i.e. complexity) of the organizations was the key determinant of the nature of the observed time series. They stated:

> A causal system can be characterized by its dimensionality, and by the nature of the interaction between causal factors. Low dimensional causal systems yield periodic and chaotic dynamics, while high dimensional causal systems yield white and pink noise dynamics. Periodic and white noise dynamics stem from systems where causal factors act independently, or in a linear fashion, while chaotic and pink noise systems stem from systems where causal factors act interdependently, in a nonlinear fashion. (p. 358)

Again, the concept of complexity (here in the form of high dimensionality, nonlinearity, and interdependence) emerges as a potential explanation of the ubiquity of 1/f distributions. It is to this and other potential explanations of the phenomena to which we now turn.

3.3.2   Explanations of 1/f Distributions

Throughout the literature on 1/f-like distributions, there is a repeated refrain: We still do not know the exact reasons for the consistent reappearance of this and related distributions in many different arenas of science (see, e.g., Mandelbrot, 1999, p. 74, where he suggested "that a unique model was unrealistic all along"). As a result, there has been ample opportunity for a multiplicity of quite different theoretical explanations for the type of distributions we refer to as pink, flicker, or 1/f noise. As Mandelbrot (1999) so succinctly pointed out—explicit observation and visualization of the geometry corresponding to an analytic expression is also necessary. He said:

> Blind analytic manipulation *is never enough.*
>
> Formalism, however effective in the short run, *is never enough.*
>
> Mathematics and science are, of course, filled with quantities that originated in geometry but eventually came to be used in analytic relationships. In many cases, those analytic relationships *are not enough.* (p. 10; italics in original)

One may extend these aphorisms to argue that however successful any of these theories are in describing system behavior and proposing underlying components, they may create analytic entities that are, in fact, not present in the biological systems in other than a general or formal way. In other words, to reiterate what should by now be a familiar refrain in this book, mathematical models are neutral with regard to the inner workings of complex systems. Hausdorff and Peng (1996) stated it in another way, but the meaning is the same:

> This suggests the possibility that complex fluctuations and 1/f scaling observed in many biological systems does not reflect anything "special" about the mechanisms generating these dynamics. (p. 1)

Finally, it is important to at least note in passing that there simply may be no general or universal theory of 1/f noise possible. It may be that the very applicability it displays is so broad it will be impossible to do better than to identify some of the conditions under which the relations will hold. Mathematicians like C. Greenwood (personal communication, 2001) of Arizona State University are now hard at work in defining those conditions. That more than that could be accomplished in a way that would allow us to assay underlying mechanisms in psychological contexts is probably very unrealistic.

With these caveats and warnings in place, we can now proceed to explore some of the theoretical explanations that have been proposed to help us understand the origins of this surprising pervasive "inevitable" natural law. In the following section, I concentrate on the theories that have been proposed to explain 1/f distributions in psychology. Another, very extensive, list of potential explanations that have been forthcoming from engineers and physical scientists are considered here only in passing. Readers interested in sampling these nonpsychological physical and mathematical efforts to explain 1/f noise, in general, can read Milotti (1995), who attributed the kind of distribution to randomly varying relaxation times, Kaulakys and Meskauskas (1998) who attributed it to random increments of interpulse intervals, or to Alieva and Barbé (2000) who based their argument on the self-similar aspects of fractal-like objects. The very variety of possible alternative explanations suggests that a general answer to the question of the origins of 1/f noise is not yet at hand.

Nevertheless, a constant theme permeates all of these theories—that they incorporate some concept of the combination of many different components. That is, almost all theories of 1/f functions involved the addition or superposition of a family of component elements with different temporal or spatial scales. As we see later, this same theme has emerged in psychological theories of 1/f noise.

Before discussing 1/f functions specifically, it is important to digress to consider an important and interesting predecessor of many of these theories reported almost a half century ago by Cox and Smith (1954). They showed that if one mixed the output of a series of generators that produced sequences of perfectly periodic pulses, the result was a random sequence of intervals. That is, the deterministic and periodic origins of a sequence of apparently random intervals are lost in the combination process. Although Cox and Smith (1954) did not evaluate the different type of random patterns (e.g., white, pink, and brown noise) that might come from different mixing rules or different kinds of aperiodic generators (e.g., those that generated unequal, as opposed to periodic, intervals), their insight into the transition from periodicity to randomness as a result of combining and superimposing was an important step in helping to understand why the knowledge gleaned from mixed signals is necessarily so limited.

Their seminal article made the point that information (about the original periodicity of the component generators) is totally lost as the summation, pooling, or superposition takes place. The reason for this loss is that the initial pattern of periodic intervals no longer exists. It is not just difficult to reconstruct—it is completely gone from the final pattern of aperiodic intervals! The initial state of the system and its components is, therefore, no longer available to the analyst who may be searching for the original generators. Such a conclusion has much in common with the ideas of chaos and irreversibility of time and their implications for the neutrality of all analysis techniques. You can easily get from initial conditions to final state but it is impossible to go back to the initial conditions knowing only the final state. In other words, don't try to unscramble eggs or anything else! These topics are considered in detail in Uttal (1998). In the present context, the irretrievable loss of information as a result of combination should not be overlooked. This is also tantamount to the conclusion that underlying mechanisms of a complex system are generally inaccessible to any analysis technique.

However, the idea of multiple time scales percolated down through the years as a potential answer to the question of the origin of $1/f$ noise in behavior. Hausdorff and Peng (1996), for example, expressed the view that $1/f$ noise distributions occur as a result of the combination of processes having different time scales. Their mathematical proof definitively demonstrated that such a combination *can* produce $1/f$ distributions, but they also showed this would not happen unless the properties of the inputs are constrained and carefully chosen. Unconstrained systems of periodic processes do not necessarily produce the kind of pink noise that is of interest to us here.[14] In other words such a superimposition may be sufficient to produce

---

[14]It is interesting to note that Hausdorff and his colleagues went on to study $1/f$ noise distributions in a wide variety of other applications including heart rate dynamics, gait, and neurally controlled physiological time series. The range of applications of this type of description is very broad, indeed.

1/f functions in some cases but it is not necessary—thus leaving the door open for other potential explanations.

Pressing and Jolley-Rogers (1997) also studied the problem of the origin of cognitive 1/f functions, but from a more skeptical viewpoint than many of the proponents of the superimposition of multiple time scales hypothesis. Using a task in which the observer was supposed to respond in rhythm with a metronome, they obtained data they argued could not be explained by the summation of timing mechanisms hypothesis proposed by Gilden and his colleagues (see pp. 66–67). In its place, Pressing and Jolley-Rogers (1997) offered a theory based on a combination of cognitive and motor components, especially involving memorial functions. Their general approach, however, was much more eclectic than their predecessors. They suggested several different sources of behavioral spectral distributions. Their summary conclusion is of particular interest in this context:

> Overall, the spectra of cognition and skilled human performance show at least four types of behavior. First, when memory-less production with independent trials is involved, the data display no autocorrelation, and the spectrum is white (flat), as for example with iterated reaction time trials (Gilden et al., 1995). Second, when error correction variables based on successive synchronization to an external time template are treated, the error spectrum is reverse sigmoidal, normally arising from a first order autoregressive process, unless task demands of coordination and speed require greater accuracy. Third, estimation based on an internal reference and a sequential assessment process can produce 1/f-like behavior at low frequencies, due perhaps to medium- to long-term time fluctuations in attention. Finally, musical training can produce specific subharmonic peaks due to learned principles of cognitive grouping (phrasing). (p. 346)

Pressing (1999) went on to develop a theory of 1/f noise based on assumptions of multiple time scales arising from several different types of cognitive processes. In this recent electronic publication he suggested that virtually any combination of processes with different time scales could potentially produce behavior with pink noise properties. In particular he suggested that attention, long-, intermediate-, and short-term memory, control processes, as well as neural processes of all kinds, all operating with different rates, can combine by a moving average process to produce 1/f distributions. This can happen with as few as two different processes, Pressing argued, but the approach to a linear plot on log-log coordinates is enhanced when the number of processes is increased.

Although he seems not to have been particularly interested in psychological processes, it is clear that the best-known theoretician of 1/f distributions is the father of fractal geometry, Benoit Mandelbrot. In his two books, (Mandelbrot, 1983, 1999) and numerous articles, he led the theoretical discussion of the relationship between scaling, fractals, self-affinities, and distributions such as Zipf's law and $1/f$ distributions. In his 1983 book, Mandelbrot briefly related $1/f$ noise distributions to scaling phenomena. He merely suggested that they are simply exemplars of the kind of phenomena that appear to be invariant at different levels of scaling. In his 1999 book, however, $1/f$ phenomena play a much more central role as he reprinted some of the key papers and reflected on the history of the topic.

Mandelbrot (1999), although still asserting that a "unique" theory of $1/f$ noise is not possible, did specifically link it to the concept of self-affinity; that is, to the scale invariance typical of fractal systems that he previously demonstrated was ubiquitous in natural systems. Indeed, he suggested that $1/f$ and multifractals were simply different aspects of the same phenomena (p. 5). Mandelbrot further argued that many of the terms he has studied (e.g., fractals, scale invariance, self-affinity, self-similarity, Wiener spectra, etc.) are so closely related as to be essentially mathematical synonyms or recastings of each other (terms he did not, however, use explicitly). Much of the discussion in his book, however, was explicitly directed at showing the interrelationships among these various terms. For example, $1/f$ distributions were said to be operating in fractal time.

To summarize, the story of fractals introduced on page 59 is both mathematically complex and aesthetically pleasing. The figures that fill Mandelbrot's two books are fascinating and beautiful. It is, however, yet to be determined whether or not the kind of mathematics with which he was concerned (in which the interrelationships between a number of formalisms are just beginning to be understood) really offers much to psychology in the way of potential theoretical explanatory mechanisms. It may simply be one way of representing or describing human behavior. Certainly, a full explanation of the conditions under which $1/f$ spectral densities emerge is not yet at hand.

Beyond this mathematical incompleteness, there are several reasons why it is unlikely that psychologists will be able to access or identify internal mechanisms any better with this kind of mathematics than with any other formal or empirical means. First, like Fourier analysis, $1/f$ spectral densities can also suggest mythical entities that are actually mathematical fictions. Furthermore, if $1/f$ is necessarily based on Fourier or a similar frequency analysis, it would carry the baggage of artificial properties of that form of analysis as well as its own. In such a case, there is an increased danger of reifying some of the products of the analysis.

Second, as Cox and Smith (1954) postulated, much information about the underlying mechanisms of complex systems is lost when all we have to observe is the pooled result of combining different generators, processes, or time bases. However useful it may be to know that the summation or superposition of mechanisms at different time scales can produce random behavior, Cox and Smith's critical point was that there is no way to recover the properties of those original components from the pooled output simply from the interval pattern. Of course, if there is additional information available such as the height properties of the original pulses, then in some special cases the decomposition problem can be solved. Unfortunately, that is rarely the case in psychology.

Third, it must not go unremarked that a number of different subsystems can produce exactly the same noise distributions. It may be that there is no way to identify the particular types of processes that produce the overall behavior.

In conclusion, no matter how ubiquitous, how precise, or how universally observed $1/f$ noise distributions may be, they actually do not offer any better access to cognitive process than does any other kind of mathematical analysis or, for that matter, any behavioral finding. The best modern example of misunderstanding concerning the validity of this conclusion is found in the history of Fourier analysis, the topic of the next section. Perhaps, nowhere in perceptual psychology has a particular mathematical analysis led to the mistaken postulation of what are essentially psychomyths. As we now see, the mathematics led to an analytic series, which was converted, into the myth of specific frequency sensitive physiological channels.

3.4 FOURIER ANALYSIS[15]

One of the most popular means of representing images is to apply a two-dimensional Fourier analysis. Throughout the 17th century, mathematicians such as Brook Taylor (1685–1731) and Johann Bernoulli (1667–1748) showed that even very complex functions could be represented by adding up a series of simple *basis functions*. Bernoulli, in particular, proposed the following functional relationship between a function and one of the most common sets of basis functions—sinusoids.[16]

$$f(x) = \sum_{n=1}^{\infty} A_n \sin\left(\frac{n\pi x}{l}\right) \text{ for } 0 \le x \le l \qquad (3.9)$$

From these seminal ideas, came one of the most important developments in mathematical thinking of the millennium—Fourier analysis—the

---

[15]The material in this section on Fourier analysis is adapted from a similar discussion in Uttal (2002). It is included here because of its special relevance to the topic at hand in a revised and updated form to make this book self-contained.

[16]Sinusoids are not the only possible set of basis functions that can be added together to reproduce an original form. Virtually any other set of "orthogonal" functions (i.e., a set in which no member can be derived from a combination of other members) can be used including square waves, checkerboards, Gabor functions, and even sets of Gaussian functions.

development of J. B. J. Fourier (1768–1830). Fourier, an exceptionally talented and gifted mathematician and archeologist, was also active in solving practical engineering problems. He was particularly concerned with the measurement of the spread of heat on a surface. This work led him to enunciate the theory of what have come to be called both Fourier series and Fourier integrals in a classic mathematical document—The Analytic Theory of Heat (Fourier, 1822/1878). The impact of Fourier analysis went far beyond the study of heat, however. The wide-spread acceptance and enormous influence of the idea was based on Bernoulli's assumption that the sum of an infinite series of sinusoidal functions can be used to *perfectly recreate any function* as long as it met certain conditions of convergence, continuity, and, most of all, linear superimposition.[17] Indeed, one did not have to add all the terms in what might theoretically be an infinitely long series; even truncated sums of relatively few terms of a series could also approximate a function well enough for most practical applications. This was enhanced by the fact that as the frequency of the sinusoidal components in a long additive series increased, their respective coefficients (i.e., their magnitude) tended toward zero, and therefore, their influence and effect diminished.

Fourier went one step beyond Bernoulli to suggest it was possible not only to add together a number of selected sinusoids to represent a function, but also to solve the inverse problem—to let the function specify which sinusoidal (understood to include both sine and cosine components) functions had to be summed to carry out that representation. In other words, Fourier's theorem specified which components at which phase angles had to be added together to reproduce the original function. This analytic task was more difficult than the synthetic one of adding together an arbitrary set of sinusoids; it required that both the coefficients and the respective phase angles of an unknown set of sinusoids of varying frequencies had to be determined *from the properties of the original function.* As Fourier showed, this amazing inverse process could be carried out in a systematic and formal manner. This idea had a powerful influence on many areas of modern science.

Fourier proposed the following expression, essentially to generate the Bernoulli formula for a sum of a series of sinusoids, to represent a function $f(x)$:

$$f(x) = \frac{1}{2} a_0 + \sum_{n=1}^{\infty} (a_n \cos nx + b_n \sin nx) \tag{3.10}$$

---

[17]Superimposition means that the various components of the series must be capable of being added together in a simple (i.e., linear) arithmetic way.

The task of the Fourier analysis was then to determine the coefficients a_n and b_n *from the properties of* $f(x)$ *itself* rather than to just arbitrarily add a series of sines and cosines together—the basis of the Bernoulli equation. Fourier's efforts to solve this problem generated the following two equations:

$$a_n = \frac{1}{\pi} \int_{-\pi}^{\pi} f(x) \cos nx \, dx \qquad (3.11)$$

and

$$b_n = \frac{1}{\pi} \int_{-\pi}^{\pi} f(x) \sin nx \, dx \qquad (3.12)$$

By evaluating these two integrals, the coefficients needed to evaluate Equation 3.10 could be determined and a close approximation to any function meeting the criteria mentioned earlier obtained in the form of a series of a formally defined set of sinusoids. How close the approximation was is simply determined by the size of n; economy of computation time and precision always being balanced against each other at the hands of the investigator.

Fourier analysis works for both one-dimensional functions and those with two or more dimensions. The Fourier spectrum (the set of component spatial sinusoids) of a two-dimensional function such as a photograph is itself a two-dimensional array of what appear to be points in the *frequency space* defined by vertical and horizontal axes representing spatial frequencies. Indeed, not only do spatial sinusoids oriented vertically and horizontally have to be dealt with, but also the space in the quadrants between the axes represent a much larger collection of oblique functions. Furthermore, there are two such two-dimensional spaces defined when one carries out a two-dimensional Fourier analysis—one specifying the amplitude of each of the component frequencies and the other defining the phase angle of each of these component spatial frequencies. Figure 3.3 A and B show a sample of an original image and its frequency spectrum, respectively.

Because of the increased complexity of applying the Fourier analysis technique in two dimensions, the mathematics implementing the *Fourier transform* was designed to go directly from $f(x, y)$ (the original image space) to two functions in the (ω_1, ω_2) spatial frequency space.[18] These two functions represent the amplitudes and phase angles of the compo-

---

[18]ω_1, ω_2 represent the horizontal and vertical axes of a new space within which measurements are made in terms of the spatial frequencies of the sinusoidal spatial functions rather than the distance measures used in the more familiar x,y space.

A

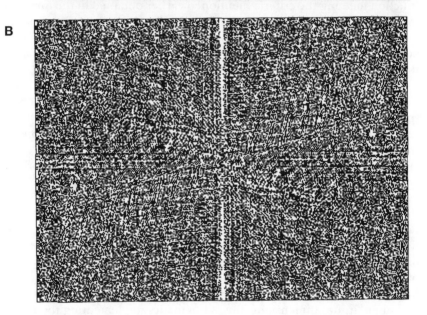

B

FIG. 3.3.   Fourier analysis breaks up an image into a spectrum of spatial frequencies. Figure A shows an original picture in the x–y space—"Trees with a View" (monochrume renditions of a watercolor painting by Susan Cohen Thompson, copyright 1991 from C. M. Thompson and L. Shure, 1995, *Image Processing Toolbox for Use with MATLAB*. Natick, MA: The Math Works, Inc. Used with the permission of S. C. Thompson). Figure B shows the frequency components in the (ω_1, ω_2) space. The phase diagram would have a similar appearance to B but the meaning of each dot would differ. In B the intensity of each dot designates the energy level at each particular Fourier spatial frequency component; in a phase diagram (not shown) the intensity of each dot would encode its phase angle.

nent spatial sinusoids, respectively. Equation 3.13 describes the Fourier transform into the spatial frequency space of a two-dimensional function—$f(x, y)$:

$$F(\omega_1, \omega_2) = \int \int_{-\infty}^{\infty} f(x, y) \exp\{-i(\omega_1 x + \omega_2 y)\} dx dy \qquad (3.13)$$

Each Fourier transformed function can be reversed back into the original function by a process called (not surprisingly)—*Inverse Fourier Transformation*. Thus, the representation of an image in terms of a sum of a series of basis functions is mathematically precise and unique as well as being nearly universally applicable, inasmuch as natural images almost always meet the required criteria. The challenge now faced is to determine whether this powerful mathematical method is psychologically relevant.

Although Fourier analysis has made many powerful contributions to science and engineering, its great mathematical power is, at the same time, its great weakness as a source of psychological theory. The problem is that this technique is so general that its suitability as a reductive explanatory theoretical model should have been questioned from the beginning. *This is so because it works (mathematically) to reduce a function to a set of basis functions regardless of whether or not the underlying processes or neural machinery are composed of mechanisms that correspond to that selected set of basis functions.* In other words, it is, too general and too powerful or, in another terminology, it is neutral with regard to the actual underlying mechanisms. It is another example, like Zipf's law or the $1/f$ distribution, of a nearly universally effective mathematical means of representing data that is totally insensitive to the actual mechanisms generating the data. Again, I must reiterate that what it does do is eminently worthwhile. In Aristotle's terminology (Killeen, 2001) *describing* the "formal cause" (that which is changed) is a nontrivial contribution to our understanding. It is not, however, a transparent road to understanding what the internal processes were that occurred as a thing changed from one state to another.

Furthermore, however satisfactory and convenient the sinusoid function-based (for example) Fourier transform may be as a means of uniquely representing a set of data, it is not the only analytic method or set of hypothetical basis functions capable of doing so. Stewart and Pinkham (1991, 1994), for example, have shown that all of the mathematical procedures (including the sinusoid-based Fourier analysis) that have been proposed as neuroreductive "explanations" of visual processing are actually equivalent to (i.e., duals of) each other and can be shown to be special cases of a more general form of mathematical representation called Hermitic Eigenfunctions. Each type of representation, however, is usually associated with distinctly different physiological assumptions that are quite separable from the mathematical ones. Any of the mathematical models is capable of modeling the actual biology of the nervous system equally well (Stewart and Pinkham's point) and none, therefore, is capable of discriminating between any of the neurobiological assumptions regarding internal mechanisms.

The point (once again) is that whatever the mathematical formulation and however successfully it may describe a form or a function, any method such as Fourier analysis, Hermitic Eigenfunctions, Gaussian modulated sinusoids (Gabor functions), or wavelets, is absolutely, fundamentally, and "in principle" neutral with regard to the specific underlying mechanisms. Any of these methods may perfectly describe any form or function and yet there may be nothing like the chosen set of basis functions actually present in the cognitive or neural domains. It should be pointed out, however, that this is an interpretive error on the part of psychologists. It certainly does not mean that Fourier or any other method of analysis is useless or necessarily misleading in psychology or any other science.

Similarly, if there is any sensitivity to the Fourier components evident in the psychophysical data, so too should one be able to demonstrate sensitivity to any of the other methods. The problem, to recapitulate, is that these analytical methods—Fourier (and similar) analyses—are too powerful! They work perfectly in a mathematical sense that is completely independent of the nature of the internal mechanisms. To summarize, this caveat is a frequent source of psychomythical mechanisms—in particular, the hypothesis that actual physiological frequency sensitive components are actually instantiated in the visual system.

Others have also raised similar caveats. Wenger and Townsend (2000) concerned themselves with the problem of the relevance of the Fourier model to psychological studies of face recognition. Their particular concern was with the popular idea that low-frequency information encoded the configurational attributes of faces. They raised three specific counter arguments to this hypothesis:

- First, and possibly most important for present purposes, the validity and coherence of the mapping between ranges of spatial frequencies and those aspects of the stimulus that support performance indicative of configural, holistic, featural, and so on, processing is compromised by a lack of definitional precision with respect to the latter constructs. . . .

- Second, the heuristic [of low spatial frequencies coding configurations] oversimplifies the distinction between global and local processing. . . .

- Third, in some applications it overlooks the degree to which various spatial frequency ranges might function to support performance in task-specific ways. (p. 126)

Wenger and Townsend concluded that their work cannot "answer the question of whether there exists *any* critical spatial frequency band for faces" (p. 138). Thus, they provide no support for either the low-frequency hypotheses or the high-frequency precedence hypothesis in face processing. Rather they argued for a task-dependency hypothesis (i.e., that those aspects of a stimulus used by the nervous system depended on the task at hand).

The analysis method proposed by Fourier adds an enormous amount of precision and quantification to anyone interested in studying or manipulating functions and databases. For obvious reasons, it is a precursor, at the very least, of our ability to examine what kind of noise (e.g., $1/f^n$) is being exhibited by a system since the power spectral density is the absolute Fourier transform, squared. What had been an arcane mathematical technique, useful only to engineers and physicists, became in the latter half of the 20th century a mainstay of both form perception and computer vision scientists, to note only two related fields of science. However, the practical utility and the indisputable power of the method also meant it could be misused in a psychobiological sense. The fact that mythical or artificial components could be produced by mathematical analyses led many unwary scientists to presume the components actually existed neuroanatomically. In conclusion, it appears that this false theory was another example of an inevitable consequence of a misapplication of a natural property of mathematics to produce a psychomyth.

3.5 CURVE FITTING AS PROTOTYPE THEORY

With surprisingly few restrictions and, in general principle, virtually any data set in any number of dimensions can be approximated with some kind of mathematical formulation. One simple and familiar set of examples of such curve fitting is to be found in the standard equations of two-dimensional (x, y) analytical geometry. Well-known algebraic expressions can represent familiar shapes such as straight lines (e.g., $y = mx + b$), parabolas (e.g., $x^{1/2} + y^{1/2} = k^{1/2}$), cubic functions (e.g., $y = ax^3$), cyclic functions (e.g., $y = \sin x$), as well as very unfamiliar shapes such as the "Cissoid of Diocles" represented by the unfamiliar expression $y^2(2a - x) = x^3$.

Three-dimensional or solid surfaces can also be expressed in the same way. For example, a sphere can be represented by the expression $x^2 + y^2 + z^2 = a^2$ and a hyperbolic paraboloids by the expression $x^2/a^2 - y^2/b^2 = cz$. It is difficult for us to visualize higher dimensional forms but it is no problem for mathematics to represent four, five, or even higher dimension data sets. For all practical purposes, therefore, it is possible, however excruciatingly difficult in some cases, to fit some kind of a mathematical expression to even the most complicated data sets. All you need are enough free parameters!

There are several key issues in representing data and shapes, however, that transcend this enormous mathematical power that have to be considered in the context of their role as prototype theories. First, what is the goal of being able to represent a function with an expression? Second, is the expression actually amenable to computation or does it represent an unrealistic shorthand that cannot be reduced to mathematical manipulation? Third, how does the description provided by the equation translate to explanations of the phenomena under study? Fourth, is the power of mathematics being oversold as a "royal" route to explanation?

I start this discussion by reference to two uses of mathematics that border on the fanciful and the unrealistic. The issue in both of these cases is: Does the mathematical expression add anything useful to a tabulation or graphical plot of the data? The first example was articulated in what had been for me a long lost article[19] (Nihm, 1976).[20] This insightful, but largely ignored, article was written intentionally as a satire on modern mathematical modeling. The title of this paper was innocuous enough—"Polynomial Law of Sensation"—but its content raised an exceedingly important point. In it the author suggested that *any* magnitude function in sensory psychology that could be represented as a function of one variable in terms of another could be "fit" by a power function expression of the form:

$$R = a_0 + a_1 \phi + a_2 \phi^2 + a_3 \phi^3 + \ldots + a_k \phi^k \qquad (3.14)$$

where R is the sensory magnitude and a_k is the set of coefficients of each of the ϕ terms. Thus, the expression represents a universal "theory" (i.e., as defined by the perfect fit of this expression for the data) of all magnitude functions if k is large enough. The author pointed out, in support of this contention, that this equation always works: "Correlations between the data and the theory are always 1.000" and "sensation is always a polynomial function of intensity" (p. 809). Indeed, these statements are absolutely true because of the enormous generality of the polynomial expression to fit a wide variety of functions and function types. Furthermore, as "Sue Doe Nimh" Birnbaum so accurately continued, no experiment could disprove the law. Because it is so general and so universal, Birnbaum argued further that it should replace both of the more limited theories known as Fechner's and Stevens' laws respectively.

---

[19]For years, I had been unable to recall the source of this article. After a considerable amount of help from my colleagues in the Society of Experimental Psychologists, I finally was able to locate it. I am especially grateful to Tony Greenwald and Dedre Gentner for their prompt and accurate reply to my request so that it could be appropriately cited.

[20]Sue Doe Nimh has now been authoritatively identified as Professor Michael H. Birnbaum of California State University at Fullerton, to whom I belatedly salute for his prescient and witty highlighting of a very important problem in psychological theory.

Of course, this tongue-in-cheek satire is an example of a *reductio ad absurdem,* but in its absurdity, it makes the same extremely important and valid point I have been arguing throughout this book, namely that mathematical models do not have anything explanatory to say about internal mechanisms—*no matter how good the fit*! Furthermore, everything that is said in this context about one-dimensional forms also holds for two-dimensional forms. The mathematics is a little more complicated, but the principles are the same. Thus, it is possible to perfectly represent complex three-dimensional surfaces with equivalent polynomial functions in x, y, and z without adding anything to our knowledge of the underlying mechanism. Like Fourier analysis, it is also possible to analytically expand functions or data into power series by use of such procedures as Taylor's method. In this way it is possible both to predict the future course of a function (extrapolation) and to infer some intermediate, but unmeasured value (interpolation).

The important point is that the polynomial expression, like many of the others previously mentioned, provides an analytic tool that allows us to express or represent information in terms of what are, in the final analysis, fictional mathematical components. Therein lies the difficulty! As the Sue Doe Nihm satire suggested, no matter how complex the function, one could always construct a polynomial of sufficiently high degree to exactly "fit" a curve to it. The power of this kind of descriptive mathematics is great enough to provide an expression for any curve of virtually any complexity from any domain of psychology.

To summarize once again, the point is that the representational power of mathematics is so great that an algebraic expression can be found for virtually anything, almost certainly including the generally continuous functions obtained from psychological experiments. Having enough free parameters or degrees of freedom or elements in the polynomial power function permits the experimenter to "fit" any curve. The problem is that the procedures used to fit any curve generate series of terms that themselves may have no concrete reality in terms of the underlying mechanisms and processes. Therefore, the best fitting polynomial is also as neutral as any other kind of mathematics with regard to actual mechanisms.

What then should be made of even the best fitting curves? The answer to this question brings us back to the issue of what the equations are intended to accomplish. If the intent is to use them to summarize charts and tables, they obviously fill an important role. If the intent is to predict or extrapolate from past observations to the future trajectory of the function, here, too, they can serve a very useful purpose. Past history does often provide very specific cues to the future course of events, unexpected discontinuities not withstanding. However, if the coefficients and exponents of a polynomial equation are taken literally as indicators of real underlying processes or mechanisms, then they, like Fourier components, run the risk of suggesting entities that are totally fictional or artificial and, thus, becoming psychomyths.

This then brings us to the next issue—the realistic computability of some proposed models of psychological performance. There have been a number of instances proposed in the psychological literature of mathematical models that, although correct in concept, are totally useless in practice. Although clothed in the formal dress of mathematical nomenclature, such theories actually offer little more than what words have to offer. There is, perhaps, no clearer example of this sort of pseudomathematics than in the model of "the organic world as a whole" proposed by Rashevsky (1948). Rashevsky started by suggesting that any organism can be "completely determined by n determining parameters" (p. 618), to wit:

$$x_1, x_2, x_3, \ldots x_n \tag{3.15}$$

in which each parameter can have the finite set of values:

$$x_n^{(1)}, x_n^{(2)}, \ldots x_n^{(m)} \tag{3.16}$$

He then defined two types of organisms in the world, designated by two applications of Equation 3.15. The total number of the first kind of organism is N_K and the total number of the second is N_l with K and l varying from 1 to n.[21] A coefficient of interaction between the two types of organisms is then defined as:

$$a_{k=1,\ldots,k=n,l=1,\ldots,l=n} \tag{3.17}$$

that I shorten to "a" for clarity. Rashevsky then defined I_0—"The total energy of interaction or total exchange in the whole organic world . . ." (p. 619)—as:

$$I_0 = \sum_k^n \cdots \cdots \sum_l^n a N_{k\ldots} \cdots \cdots N_{l\ldots} \tag{3.18}$$

Although this function appears to be a mathematical expression, in point of fact it is totally noncomputable and says nothing more than the phrase, "energy flow is too complex to be evaluated because it involves lots of organisms, lots of parameters, and lots of values for those parameters." The key to the deception is in the ellipses ". . ." used throughout this derivation and the actual, but hidden, enormity of the various values of n that are invoked for the several parameters.

---

[21]I have simplified Rashevsky's original notation a bit here with no harm to the present discussion.

Therefore, the ellipse-littered algebraic equations proposed by Rashevsky provide only an illusion of precision, prediction, and explanation. Not only would it be impossible to evaluate such a equation to actually determine I_0, but there is little hope of even estimating plausible numbers for the huge values of n or N, or determining the value of the constant a.

The caveat inherent in this analysis for the present discussion is that the conceptual organization provided by a formal expression should not be considered to be tantamount to a reductive explanation of the phenomena being described. Nor, it should be added from our previous discussion, should it be expected that even a perfectly fitting representation can open that door to explanation. Neither polynomial best-fitting expressions nor vague pseudomathematical formularizations can offer any insight into the underlying mechanisms. Each is likely to result in a cognitive model or theory that is, all too often, psychomythical.

3.6 DYNAMICAL SYSTEMS THEORY

3.6.1 Introduction

Among the most recent of new conceptual transfusions from mathematical thinking are ideas that have percolated into psychology from studies of dynamical nonlinear systems. The attraction here is obvious. Many fundamentally linear models and theories of the recent past were only gross approximations to cognitive or neural activity. Why this should necessarily be so, is clearly understandable. Both the brain (as observed by neurophysiologists) and behavior (as observed by psychologists) are almost always nonlinear in the formal mathematical sense. From the first time it was proposed, therefore, the analogy between some of the nonlinear mathematical ideas and psychobiology, was particularly enticing. However, it was not until the early and mid 1980s that psychologists began to take seriously this new metaphor for the brain–mind.

There are good reasons for this delayed acceptance of what seemed to be a very promising means of conceptualizing and representing psychobiological functions. Nonlinear systems are extremely difficult to analyze and most nonlinear mathematical problems cannot be solved except by approximation methods or by simulations.[22] Nevertheless, in recent years there has

---

[22]It is important to appreciate that although mathematics cannot cope with many of the complex problems encountered in nature, nature can and does solve them all the time. That we cannot predict the weather does not mean that such a complex system of atmospherics cannot occur. Nor does the difficulty in modeling the unfolding of a protein molecule mean that it cannot and does not happen uncountable times every moment. There is a host of other examples of natural systems that seem to function very well in spite of our inability to analyze them. The book to read on this topic is by Casti (1996).

been an effort to apply nonlinear methods to the problems of brain and cognition. Foremost among these new approaches is what has come to be called *Dynamical Systems Theory* (DST).[23] DST is a recent evolutionary development of what had previously been called systems theory—an idea that has percolated around science for many years in many different guises. In general, in both qualitative (i.e., prequantitative) and more or less quantitative versions, systems theory has emphasized the interaction of the components of complex "systems" and how they change over time. The primary advantage of such a conceptual approach is that it introduces a number of important concepts into the consideration of biological and physical systems that were largely ignored in conventional linear cognitive theory. Two modern texts introducing DST (Abraham, Abraham, & Shaw, 1990; Kuznetsov, 1998) are available and can be used to tutor oneself on the details of this kind of mathematics.

Although formulated in its ultramodern form as a revolutionary change in brain–mind studies, DST has roots that begin before the industrial revolution. DST can be seen as an extension of the kind of mathematical thinking that had originally been found to be useful in the classical Newtonian study of systems of moving objects. A rigorous study of the dynamics of physical systems became possible following Isaac Newton's (1642–1727) promulgation of his three fundamental laws in the 1660s:

1. Every particle continues in its current state of motion unless compelled by some force to change that state (i.e., to accelerate).
2. The rate of change of momentum of a particle (its mass times its velocity) is proportional to the magnitude and direction of the force acting on it.
3. Action and reaction are equal and opposite.

Newton's laws had the advantage of being expressed simply and specifically enough that they could be formularized in the language of mathematics. The particular mathematics used in both traditional dynamics and DST is the differential equation, a tool that is especially suitable for representing systems in which there is a high degree of interaction among the components and the states of each variable can change during the course of the process.

---

[23]My dictionary defines both "dynamic" and "dynamical" as synonyms with the joint meaning: "Of or relating to energy or to objects in motion." In the past *dynamic* has been the preferred term and *dynamical* has the connotation of a cruder neologism. I have not been able to find anyone who can explain this choice of terminology for the modern applications of this kind of mathematics. The best modern distinction I have encountered so far is that *dynamical* is an adjective referring to an entity that changes over time whereas *dynamic* refers to the governing rule that forces the change in the state of the entity.

Elaborations of the simple $f = ma$ relationship led to the development of calculus and, subsequently, differential equations, since position—x, velocity—the rate of change of position—$\dfrac{dx}{dt}$, and acceleration, the rate of change of velocity—$\dfrac{d^2 x}{dt^2}$ could all now be closely related to each other. Even more important was the fact that mathematical formulae could now be used to add together forces from different sources. Equations of the first degree such as expressed in Eqn. 3.19 (in which neither x nor any of its derivatives are cross-multiplied among themselves or each other) permit us to represent and analyze linear systems—a relatively easy task.

$$A\frac{d^2 x}{dt^2} + B\frac{dx}{dt} + Cx = D \qquad (3.19)$$

Thus, forces operating on a particle that were functions of the acceleration, the velocity, and the position could all be included in the analysis.

If, however, the problem attacked produces an equation exemplified by that shown in Eqn. 3.20, it is nonlinear (in this case, of the second degree) and can be very difficult, if not impossible, to solve. Consider the arbitrary equation:

$$A\left(x\frac{d^2 x}{dt^2} \right) + B\left(\frac{dx}{dt} \right)^2 + Cx = D \qquad (3.20)$$

In this nonlinear equation, x and its derivatives are multiplied by themselves or each other, thus identifying it as a nonlinear equation. Thus, some of the forces are joint functions of, as for example in this equation, position and acceleration or the square of velocity.

The essential fundamental concept embodied in the nonlinear differential equation mathematics discussed here as well as in its modern application to psychology, DST, is that the causes of the overall behavior of system are due to an complex interaction of many different forces mutually interacting with each other over time. The implicit hope with such an approach is that an appropriate kind of mathematics will allow us to specify the state of the system at some future time.

The invention of differential equations in both their linear and nonlinear forms was a magnificent achievement and, in a huge variety of instances, this kind of mathematics certainly revolutionized science. Differential equations have historically been and are currently used in an enormous number of applications; one would be hard pressed to envisage what science would be like without this powerful tool. One particular domain of science stands out as the prototypical application of differential equations—control systems. In the 18th century, engineers were confronted with the problems of centrifugal governors, originally invented by James Watt (1736–1819) to regulate steam powered mechanical equipment. Unfortunately, the governors did not always work and boilers had a very bad habit of exploding from time to time for unknown reasons. Those who were challenged by the problems inherent in these early "dynamical systems" turned to the great mathematical physicist James Clerk Maxwell (1831–1879) in the mid 19th century for a formal analysis and, hopefully, a solution to the problem. Maxwell used nonlinear differential equations to show that the behavior of a governed steam engine would depend on the parameters for which the governor was set. By adjusting those parameters, engineers were able to avoid the primitive boiler's explosively bad habits.

The rapid development of radio and television circuits in the 20th century led to other applications in which exactly the same mathematics could be used to model electronic in addition to mechanical systems. (This is another example of the neutrality of mathematics—completely different physical apparatuses could be modeled with the very same equations.) From there, it was only a short conceptual step to applying these same kinds of mathematics to biopsychological systems; in fact, however, it took almost another century for this small conceptual leap to occur.

However, control systems theory was not dormant during that century. The next relevant milestone in this brief history of the antecedents of DST was Wiener's (1948) introduction of *Cybernetics* as a tool for analyzing more complex control systems than Watt's simple boiler governor. Nevertheless, the metaphor of the steersman or the governor was basic to Wiener's subsequent formulation. Wiener delved into a number of then current mathematical developments including statistical mechanics, group theory, information theory, and the mathematics of feedback and oscillation to develop his integrated cybernetic approach. His contribution provided much more elaborate models of control systems theory than had been available until that time. Wiener (1948) was also one of the first to consider if control system ideas could be applied to human behavior. In doing so, however, he made it very clear that his cybernetic metaphor for psychopathology (his particular psychological interest) was a descriptive one and that he was not asserting that it was ". . . due to a specific defect in the organization of the brain as a computing machine" (p. 168).

The seminal ideas of control systems, sometimes with their related mathematics and sometimes without, have repeatedly been introduced into the biological and social sciences, although often in a nonquantitative manner. The idea of homeostasis or regulatory control by the body was introduced by Cannon (1932). Bateson (1972) introduced the cybernetic approach to anthropology, among other social and psychological systems. As another 20th-century example, the biologist and philosopher Ludwig Von Bertalanffy (1968a) proposed a mathematical approach to science called General Systems Theory and contemporaneously applied it specifically to psychology (Von Bertalanffy, 1968b).[24] Ackoff (1971) applied cybernetic systems to management systems. Finally, Miller (1978) developed a purely qualitative systems approach to the what he described as the full range of living systems (from societies to cells) emphasizing the common functions carried out at all biological levels. Miller suggested that since the cell and the society, for example, both ingested and excreted, that they could be described in a common systems oriented language that mirrored some of the control systems ideas.

Although none of these reconceptualizations of some portion of the physical, social, or behavioral sciences persisted in the form originally proposed, all contributed to a modern realization of the importance of systems, interactions, and, to a certain degree, to the idea that nonlinear mathematics (especially nonlinear differential equations) could play an important role in the study of real systems. The shared basis of the metaphor or model presented by each was the essential nonlinear complexity of most real systems.

As control system theory continued to develop, important contributions were being made by other kinds of mathematics. An important mathematical component of the current enthusiasm for DST is the incorporation of tensor mathematics. Tensors are expressions for more complex attributes of dynamic systems than either the single number representing the magnitude (a scalar) or a collection of numbers representing velocity labeled by a single index[25] (a vector). A tensor, which must be described by numbers labeled with two or more indices, can represent other more complex properties such as the moment of inertia of a rotating body. If two indices are used to describe a system, then that mathematical representation is referred to as a tensor of the second rank.

In summary, a scalar value (e.g., the mass of an object) is represented by a single number, m. (A scalar may be called a tensor of zero rank.) A vector, such as velocity v can be represented by v = ax where a is a constant relating velocity to x. x is also a vector, but in this case it represents the integral of the accelerations imposed on a mass. Velocity in this case will take on a number of values that can be labeled with a single index. (The vector v may,

---

[24]Von Bertalanffy had a much more ambitious goal than simply providing another theory engine for psychology. His overarching goal was to develop a universal system for all of science in which general principles could be applied to simplify the increasing isolation and specialization of the many "small" sciences. His emphasis on "wholeness" also reflects a behaviorist axiomatic base.

[25]The term "labeled by a single index" means that the terms in vector are values of a single variable or parameter. As discussed shortly, a tensor is labeled by two or more indices, indicating that the number in it are values of two or more variables or parameters.

therefore, be called a tensor of the first rank.) A tensor of the second rank is more complex and involves quantities that have to be ordered along two indices. A generalized tensor of the second rank (a matrix) would look like this:

$$\begin{pmatrix} T_{11} & T_{12} & T_{13} \\ T_{21} & T_{22} & T_{23} \\ T_{31} & T_{32} & T_{33} \end{pmatrix} \tag{3.21}$$

where each T_{ab} represents a term that has to be defined in terms of the two indices, a fact that indicates they are functions of two variables.

Tensors serve important function as multidimensional transforms that can relate the input and the output of a system when several dimensions, parameters, or influences jointly influence the outcome. Tensors, therefore, are especially useful in describing dynamical systems because, among other attributes, they help to express the parameters of system behavior in an invariant manner. Thus, for example, the interactive properties of an arm holding a weight can be held constant even though it is rotated by the shoulder through a substantial angle. The tensor acts on a vector to transform that vector in some way that is dependent on the invariant physics or geometry represented by the tensor. By analogy to the Newtonian formula $f = ma$ (involving only vectors), the general tensor action may be expressed as $v_2 = T \cdot v_1$ where T is the tensor, v_1 is the input vector, and v_2 is the output vector. Where the scalar m defined the simple relationship between the vectors f and a in the Newtonian equation, the more elaborate T defines the relationship between v_1 and v_2. Nevertheless, the principle is the same. The scalar m is a statement about an invariant property of the Newtonian equation just as the tensor T says something about the invariant properties of a more complicated system. The characteristic solutions or eigenvectors of the tensor equation

$$v_2 = T \cdot v_1 \tag{3.21}$$

represent the dimensions of a coordinate system in which certain of the properties of an object are nonarbitrary in much the same way that the mass of the object is not arbitrary in the classic $f = ma$ formulation.

The application of tensor type analysis in the physics of optics, electromagnetism, and, most notably, relativistic physics has long been established. Its applications in behavioral science are much more recent and represent a very novel way of thinking for most psychologists. A particular application of the tensor representation was reported by Turvey and Carello (1995) and summarized in Turvey (1997). They were studying the perception of a handheld object wielded about when the observer was blindfolded. The observer's task was to estimate the size and weight of the object. As a simple empirical fact, it is astonishing how extremely precise the appreciation of the size and weight distribution of the object can be to the blindfolded observer. It seems it is possible for the human observer to infer these properties simply from the physics of the interaction between hand and arm, on the one side, and object, on the other, as the object is manipulated. A description of this phenomenon is handled well by the tensor mathematics.

A tensor that is independent of time and gravity of the general form presented in Eqn. 3.21 transformed the temporal and gravitational varying parameters of the perceived haptic signals to a new representation that unambiguously represented the physical properties of the object in hand. In other words, the tensor permitted the problem to be analyzed in terms that were free of the constraints of the original coordinate system. This new invariant representation established a "nonarbitrary" coordinate system that permitted Turvey and Carello to determine the parameters and interactions that facilitated this almost magical ability to determine the length, width, weight, and, to a degree, even the shape of the wielded object by the blindfolded observer.

The currently popular version of psychological systems theory—DST— was presented as a mathematical alternative to the computational approach of contemporary cognitive psychology. A prime premise of DST is that mental and behavioral processes are characterized better by their dynamical behavioral properties than by their static properties. In essence, it should be noted, DST is a nonreductive approach, describing the behavior with mathematical formulations, but not making explicit attempts to reduce the behavior to neural or cognitive components. To the contrary, it is argued by DST proponents, that older cognitive models are still captured by the digital computer metaphor and the search for internal mechanisms. Indeed, one of the most profound differences between traditional cognitive psychology and the newly emerging DST is that the discrete, Boolean, digital computer metaphor is likely to be replaced by the continuous analog computer metaphor emphasizing the overall (i.e., wholistic) behavior of the system. In this regard, and perhaps to the expressed dismay of some of its proponents, DST seems to share many qualities with behaviorism, at least with regard to its finessing the problem of internal mechanisms.

One of the earliest and most specific challenges to the cognitive digital computer metaphor was articulated by Carello, Turvey, Kugler, and Shaw (1984). They list the following "failings" of contemporary cognitivism:

1. A misplaced emphasis on logic and algorithms.
2. The overvaluation of discrete operations as opposed to continuous processes.

3. Discrete computer models cannot be programmed to increase in power (i.e., it cannot make itself more complex because to do so requires "preadaptive foresight" of the direction in which it should be evolving).

4. Representations in a computer model are at best a reduced form of an organism.

5. Computer programs are intrinsically determinate but organisms are intrinsically indeterminate in the sense of chaotic sensitivity to complex initial conditions.

(Abstracted from Carello et al., pp. 230–237.)

In addition to these general principles, the neural net (i.e., the connectionist) model is seen by many contemporary theoretical psychologists as the most extreme version of the internal representational computational approach[26] championed by cognitive theorists. For mentalistic cognitivism, as noted, the major goal is reductionism to internal mechanisms and components. It is argued that DST, on the contrary, is largely unconcerned with the internal mechanisms but, instead, concentrates its attention on the interplay of forces that determine the molar behavior of the organism. From this point of view, the dynamical systems approach is a direct descendent of the control system and cybernetic constructs of previous psychological epochs. At the very least, the metaphorical instantiation of DST is obviously much closer to analog computing and the continuous mathematics of differential equations than to that of the discrete digital computer.

Proponents of DST (e.g., van Gelder & Port, 1995) emphasized the following positive properties of DST as it is applied to psychological processes:

- It deals primarily with nonlinear systems as required by the extreme complexity of most psychological processes and the huge numbers of interacting components.
- It concentrates on processes that change over time.
- It describes but does not "represent" internal processes.
- The mathematics of choice is differential and difference equations, well established and familiar techniques.
- The controlling metaphor is of a continuous control systems rather than a discrete connectionist neural net.

---

[26]Presumably it is the metaphor of mind cum computation rather than the use of computers themselves that is the basis of this criticism of cognitivism. The highly mathematical basis of DST obviously is going to require extensive computer power to manipulate some of the equations generated—regardless of the underlying philosophy. Of course, the digital computer can also solve the difference equation approximation to differential equations, therefore much of the dispute is really between one's respective choice of controlling metaphor.

- The state of the system varies from initial conditions to a final stable state. It is the goal of DST to describe this dynamical process and determine the governing rule or rules (i.e., the dynamic or dynamics) that govern the change in states over time.

(Abstracted from Van Gelder and Port, 1995)

In its current instantiation, DST has also been broadly applied to a variety of social and behavioral systems. It has now become the theoretical model of choice in several different kinds of psychology ranging from studies of motor responses (e.g., Thelen & Smith, 1994; Turvey, 1998) and their acquisition (e.g., Zanone & Kelso, 1992), perception (as is evidenced by the work of Amazeen & Turvey, 1996, on the size-weight illusion and Stroop, Turvey, Fitzpatrick, & Carello, 2000, on the perception of length from the dynamics of hand held objects), language (e.g., Elman, 1995), and even extending to psychotherapy (e.g., Hayes, Beevers, Kumar, & Winett, 2000). A good review of the full gamut of applications of DST up to 1995 can be found in Port and van Gelder (1996).

3.6.2   Chaos and Self-Organization

Many DST theorists have linked control system mathematics, a well-known and highly developed form of mathematics, to some new ideas from closely related domains. One set of new ideas comes from recent developments in *chaos theory*. Chaos theory is an outgrowth of the emerging appreciation that there are some kinds of systems that appear to operate in the peculiar world between totally random and totally deterministic behavior. Intermediate systems of this class are characterized by being extremely complex, nonlinear, and multidetermined. The term *deterministic* means that the system obeys laws and rules and can, in principle, be described with mathematical equations, albeit sometimes computationally intractable ones. It is, therefore, not assumed that there is any random or stochastic process involved at the most fundamental level, even if statistical methods are often used as a practical convenience to describe the complex conditions of chaotic systems. The other three characteristics of chaos theory all relate to the extreme complexity of such systems. Such characteristics are also among those that raised enthusiasm about DST; therefore, the linkage between the two approaches to studying complex systems is obvious. For example, dynamic systems may well be chaotic.

Chaotic systems are also characterized by a high degree of sensitivity to initial conditions. The classic folktale is that even the most minuscule change in early events (e.g., how a butterfly flaps its wings in the Brazilian rain forest) can produce drastic changes in the final system behavior (e.g., the weather in Midwestern United States). However accurate such a folktale may be, it would certainly be extremely difficult to validate. The reason for this intractability is that chaotic systems behave in the way they do because there is a huge number of different small causes contributing to the final global effect. In such a situation, as I have already mentioned, obscure initial conditions are long lost in the plethora of causal actions, reactions, and interactions. Although there is nothing inherently mysterious in such a system, the sheer volume of the actions precludes detailed examination of the causes. The situation is exacerbated by the nonlinear nature of the many interactions of the involved forces.

In principle, even though chaotic systems are considered to be deterministic, they display behavior that may be indistinguishable from randomness just because of this complexity. This quasi- or apparently random aspect of complex systems is due to the huge numbers of interactions and interactions, therefore, and is not to be taken as a sign of any fundamental indeterminativeness on the part of the system. It is a practical problem of numerousness and computability that leads to what appears to be an illusion of randomness and, thus, of an in principle insolvability. In a certain sense, it does not matter whether our models are stochastic or deterministic, the choice of the "best theory" is often better made on the basis of taste or convenience than on goodness of fit. What does matter is that neither point of view can ever completely exclude the other. Randomness may simply be the sheep's clothing over the wolf of complex determinism.

The study of chaotic systems has been graced by the work of a number of brilliant mathematicians. The early work by Christiaan Huygens (1629–1695) on the compound pendulum clock and its problems as well as Henri Poincaré's (1854–1912) analysis of the three-body problem (see also p. 98) set the stage for developments in the 20th century. Poincaré (1903) stimulated considerable later thinking in an oft quoted prophetic statement:

> If we knew exactly the laws of nature and the situation of the universe at the initial moment, we could predict exactly the situation of that same universe at a succeeding moment. But even if it were the case that the natural laws had no longer any secret for us, we could still only know the initial situation approximately. If that enabled us to predict the succeeding situation with the same approximation, that is all we require, and we should say that the phenomenon had been predicted, that it is governed by laws. But it is not always so; it may happen that small differences in the initial conditions produce very great ones in the final phenomena. A small error in the former will produce an enormous error in the latter. Prediction becomes impossible, and we have the fortuitous phenomenon. (p. 68)

Others also made significant contributions. Van der Pol and Van der Mark (1927), working with primitive electronic circuits, observed what has since been appreciated as chaotic behavior. Kolmogorov (1941) and Landau (1944) published significant contributions to the mathematical theory of turbulence—another classic example of a chaotic system. Although the word chaos had not yet been attached to this kind of fluid behavior, there is no question that they were pioneers in this yet-to-be born field of chaos studies.

Chaotic behavior was also observed, early on and not surprisingly, in an archetypical complex system—the weather—by Lorenz (1963). His discovery was based on a fortuitous observation that the outcome of his computer model was extremely sensitive to the initial conditions. Indeed, simply rounding off the inputs could produce totally different predictions. Other important early work was carried out by Stephen Smale who was the discoverer of strange attractors described in the subsequent discussion.

Because chaotic systems are fundamentally deterministic, some will have solutions or final states that can in principle be predicted. These final states are referred to as attractors and represent "solutions" or "outcomes" to the problem posed by the complex nonlinear systems. Attractors come in several kinds:

- Fixed-point attractors represent solutions to chaotic problems that are fixed once the system arrives at the final state. The system may go through indescribably complex behavior (i.e., intermediate states) but once it has arrived at the state defined by the attractor it remains there until perturbed.
- Cyclic attractors represent solutions to chaotic problems in which two or more solutions are possible. Rather than remaining fixed in one or another of these attractor states, the system is capable of jumping between them in what is often an oscillatory or cyclic fashion.
- Strange attractors represent solutions to chaotic problems that display neither fixed nor cyclic attractor behavior. Rather the system continues to behave in complex ways that are often very difficult to characterize even verbally. Another important property of strange, attractors is that they are *nonergodic*, that is there is no necessity that the system will return to any state through which it has already passed (although it may do so in the normal course of events). Although this behavior may appear superficially to be random, it, too, is considered to be deterministic and, therefore, in principle, if not in practice, predictable.

It is important to appreciate that even though the mathematics representing chaotic systems may not be solvable, the underlying assumption is that all such behavior, however complex, is determined by the initial conditions and the intervening states in which the system finds itself. The behaviors produced by attractors, for example, are determined by the various forces operating at any moment and the constellation of these forces changes from moment to moment.

Chaotic systems, although subject to some kinds of problem solution in relatively simple situations, have some implications that are important to both sciences in general and psychological science in particular. As already discussed, one of the inferences that has been repeatedly drawn by researchers is that chaos generally implies a lack of analyzability by virtue of the large number of interacting entities involved. The combinatorics of a realistic chaotic system suggests that it cannot be analyzed or reduced in any practical sense to the behavior of simpler components. A similar, but opposite, argument is made that even if we did know all of the initial conditions and all of the components, we would not be able to synthesize them into a coherent structure. For psychologists this pair of arguments places severe constraints on both top-down and as well as bottom-up theories of cognition and action. The implication, if these arguments are substantiated, is that a DST type or behaviorist type theory of wholistic psychology may be the proper form of a future psychology.

The thinking implicit in the concepts associated with chaos has been specifically applied to an increasing number and diversity of scientific endeavors. Lorenz (1963), as I noted earlier, was one of the first modern scientists to recognize its applicability, in his case, to meteorology. Goldberger and West (1987) described the chaotic behavior of the heart. May (1974) applied chaotic mathematics to describing the population dynamics of animals. There is an increasing number of applications of the ideas and principles associated with chaos theory to psychology. A representative sample of these is reported in Abraham and Gilgen (1995) and in Robertson and Combs (1995).

The important question that must be asked is how far have we gone beyond the metaphorical level in these varied applications. In some ways, chaos has provided a very powerful conceptual basis for thinking about brain and cognitive processes. It certainly adds to the vocabulary, but even more important, it has alerted psychologists to the true complexity of the problems they face. Even though it is unlikely that many of the posed problems can be definitively solved, at least we have a glimmering of an understanding about how very complex behavior can be produced by huge arrays of neural components. This intuition does not provide us with exact solutions or complete reductive answers. However, it does place psychological processes among the other natural events going on in the universe and helps to filter out ideas that invoke supernatural phenomena in place of natural forces. We have now arrived at another closely related question: Is it possible for complex systems to organize themselves into coherently functioning entities?

3.6.3   Self-Organization

The cybernetic metaphor of the self-controlled governor or steersman has, as we have seen, become closely associated with DST. The metaphor was originally based on the process of feedback—the ability of a system to control its own behavior. This property may be considered to be a primitive kind of self-organization. From this beginning, has come another major enthusiasm of modern complex systems behavior—system self-organization—a viewpoint that has had considerable influence in the development of this new approach (i.e., DST) to psychological theory.

Self-organization has occasionally been referred to as spontaneous. By this it is meant that it happens without apparent external cause. For example, we learn from neurochemistry that the lipid molecules making up the cell membrane of neurons have specific chemical properties that permit random distributions to organize themselves into continuous sheets of the membrane. This is accomplished without external forces (other than the presence of water) because the head of the lipid molecule is *hydrophilic*; that is, it is strongly attracted to water molecules, whereas the tails of this molecule, quite to the contrary, are *hydrophobic* (i.e., they are repulsed by water). The net effect of this dual attraction and repulsion is that the lipid molecules line themselves up into a bilayered membrane with the heads facing out toward the surrounding intercellular and intracellular aqueous fluids and the hydrophobic tails are hidden between the two layers of heads. In this case the property of the membrane is totally explained by the properties of the lipid molecules and the system may be fairly said to have self-organized itself. No external agent directed the alignment of the lipid molecules; it was their own properties that accounted for the emergence of the membrane.

Another much more complicated self-organizing system has been described by Karsenti and Vernos (2001). They were studying the extraordinary ability of the mitotic spindle—a structure in dividing cells responsible for distributing the genetic code "with stunning precision" (p. 543) to the two cells resulting from the division of the original cell. Their main point is that the spindle structures itself and carries out its function on the basis of a similar, albeit more complex, self-organization process compared to the lipid creation of the cell membrane.

The important point in both these cases is that either through primitive feedback mechanisms, chemical properties, or the interaction of other physical forces, certain systems have the capability of organizing their own behavior or structure. However, the metaphor has been expanded far beyond these primitive biochemical mechanisms to the study and design of much more complicated self-organizing systems capable of repairing or even reproducing themselves. Indeed, in the present context we see that both brain and behavior have become grist for theories of this kind.

In a more formal vocabulary, self-organization may be defined as the increase in the redundancy of a system without substantial intervention of some kind of external or environmental force. Heylighen (in press) offered another definition of self-organization when he said that self-organization was "the spontaneous emergence of global coherence out of local interactions" coherence being tantamount to redundancy. His article is a model of clarity as a nontechnical introduction to the field encompassed by the term self-organization.

There is, however, a critical controversy even in the context of these apparently straightforward definitions. Some students of self-organization theory (e.g., Von Foerster, 1960) have long argued that self-organization requires the interaction of the system with its environment and compare self-organization to evolutionary adaptation. In this context, the relationship of the lipid molecules with the watery environment, rather than the nature of the lipids themselves, is the key issue. Others have argued that the interaction among the component particles themselves can drive self-organization, for example in the alignment of individual magnetic particles to produce an ordered magnetic structure such as a bar magnet. In this case, it is the mutual repulsion of the respective poles of the tiny component magnets that ultimately accounts for their parallel alignment. From this point of view, the external environment plays little direct role.

In the lipid example, not only is the water present as part of the environment of a lipid molecule, but so, too, are the other lipid molecules. Where one draws the line between the thing unto itself and the external environment then becomes quite arbitrary. Whatever the details of one's interpretation of the metaphor, self-organization becomes increasingly possible and evident as the complexity of the system becomes greater. In my opinion, this debate is largely an artificial one depending more on one definition of "environment"; if you define your terms adequately, resolution of this controversy is immediate.

An excellent source of information about the self-organization concept is found in the work of Kelso (1995). Kelso performs a useful service by tabulating the conditions he believes are necessary for self-organization to occur. These include:

- Large numbers of components must interact.
- The interactions must be nonlinear.
- The components must not have achieved energetic equilibrium.
- The parts must influence the whole and the whole must influence the parts.

- Random fluctuations (noise) must constantly be perturbing the system so that it can self-organize toward a final stable state.
- Influences that control the self-organization need not be specific to a particular final state.
- Self-organization in complex systems can benefit from chaotic and random influences to produce complex behavior.

(Abstracted from Kelso, 1995, pp. 16–17)

Self-organization principles like these help us, at least in a qualitative sense, to overcome or rather finesse one of the great bugaboos of modern science—*emergence*.[27] "Emergence," to me, is the great copout; if one cannot explain the sources or origins of complex behavior from the primitive components of which it is obviously composed, an almost supernatural or mystical (and certainly inexplicable) emergence is postulated as an alternative to a complete explanation. But the use of this word adds absolutely nothing to the understanding of how wholistic properties arise from lower level ones. To state that macroproperties "emerge" from the microproperties of the system is simply to assert without further explication that the process happens. There is at least the hope, unrealized so far, that self-organizing principles will provide a foundation for understanding that which cannot be explained in terms of the simple laws and processes that control a system. This explanatory intractability arises from the tension that exists between the necessity for many, nonlinearly interacting components and the increasing difficulty of dealing with such ensembles analytically as the numbers necessary for the complex behavior increase. Whether the intractability of emergence is due to the combinatorics arising directly from simple numerousness or a lack of knowledge of the laws of combination almost does not matter: Both explanations represent impenetrable barriers to how something like intelligence could arise from the combined activity of myriad neurons.

The history of self-organization in psychology is relatively brief. Perhaps the first modern mention of the idea was by Farley and Clark (1954) in the context of a computer simulation. Later work (e.g., Amari, 1977) dealt with the problem of the self-organization of neural nets in learning situations. Amari argued that the weights of the synapses in a Hebb type neural net could be modified by the system itself. A few years later, Kohonen (1982) applied the self-organizing concept to the formation of two-dimensional arrays comparable to the retinotopic mapping in various regions of the ascending visual pathways and the brain. Kohonen's self-organization model, however, assumed a powerful influence of the stimulus pattern and thus is

---

[27]See also the comments on emergence on page 173.

slightly different in concept to self-organization theories proposed in other fields of study. Nonetheless, his model shows how a relatively simple array of unspecialized cells can reproduce the topology of the stimulus space by organizing itself in response to a stimulus form.

In the past 40 years the self-organization metaphor became extremely popular in psychological discussions of all kinds. PsycINFO, the information retrieval service of the American Psychological Association, responded with 518 citations to the phrase "self-organization" in the years 1967–2001. Although a few of them are technical studies of the behavior of computer simulations, in large part, the phrase is used meaninglessly to describe human behavior and adds nothing other than the vocabulary item itself. "Self-organization" theories of prejudice, of dreaming, of classroom organization, and of school achievement have all become metaphorical cousins, usually without any deep appreciation of the formal properties of the process. Self-organization is obviously a property of some complex systems and, if they are regular enough and the rules of interaction simple enough, analysis is possible. Most of the 518 applications to psychology, however, add little beyond the obvious intuition that our brains are likely to self-organize in some mysterious way. Here, too, an interesting idea has the potential to become a psychomyth.

3.6.4   Some Potential Problems With DST

Even from the beginning of the development of the mathematics that underlay DST there was awareness that some problems that could be easily stated in the nomenclature of differential equations might not be so easily solved. In the 19th century, Poincaré (1890) noted that the nine differential equations describing the interaction of three bodies could not be exactly solved. In recent years this conjecture has been repeatedly shown to be correct despite the many approximate and simulation solutions to the problem. In general, the behavior of such a system turned out to be chaotic and unpredictable rather than simple. It is only in a few special cases, for example, when the three bodies are positioned in an equilateral triangle, when one of the bodies is much smaller than the others, or in very special situations where nonlinearities deteriorated to approximate linearities that simple behavior was observed and the mathematics solved. Of course, as the number of bodies increases, both the mathematical problem and the difficulty of solving it increases up to the point that field methods may become relevant.

The classic case, with which Poincaré was dealing, obviously was the solar system in which the various planets exerted a powerful gravitation force on each other. From one moment to the next, the forces shifted as the objects moved about in space. The momentary state (i.e., the location and trajectories) of the planets and their exerted forces was assumed to be of secondary interest to the ever changing flux of potential and kinetic energy that was occurring. Furthermore, the initial conditions could strongly determine the final trajectory of the planets. Again, it must be noted, that explicit statements of this latter generality, however plausible, are not always subject to computational analysis.

Nevertheless, the concept of a host of forces interacting over time led some scholars in the last decade to extrapolate metaphorically, if not mathematically, from relatively simple gravitational forces to incomparably more complex dynamical systems of biological and psychological forces. At first glance, it seemed that the DST model could describe the complex operation of the human brain–mind system better than one based on nondynamical principles. The basic principles of this kind of mathematics seemed to map onto behavior in a particularly intuitive way.

However, there were practical problems. Just as Poincaré had discovered when he dealt with only three planets, the mathematical solution to the multivariate, nonlinear problems posed by human cognition and action was also extremely refractory. Like so many other instances in which mathematical procedures have been transformed from physics to psychology, DST may carry more weight as a convenient metaphor or means of describing actions than with its ability actually to solve the intractable problems of complex psychobiological systems.

Thus, just as quickly as DST appeared on the psychological scene, it became clear that it, too, was subject to some of the same criticisms aimed at its predecessors. Furthermore, the application of this novel theory was also capable of generating psychomyths in the same way they did. One of the most salient criticisms of DST is the one I made earlier in this book and elsewhere (Uttal, 1998). Namely, that the mathematics used to model the process is at best descriptive and is fundamentally neutral with regard to the underlying mechanisms. To be balanced in this account, it is very important to also note that many DST theorists see this constraint as an advantage. No DST theorists argue that their model is likely to "represent" internal mechanisms. Amazeen, Amazeen, and Turvey (1998) are very specific about this tenet of DST. They asserted:

> Characteristic of the dynamical model is its ability to describe coordination with concepts that are indifferent to the particular substrate (e.g., neural, physiological, psychological, computational, social) supporting the movement. (p. 237)

I have already alluded to the similarity of behaviorism and DST with regard to this nonreducibility constraint.

The same criticism was made by Ingvaldsen and Whiting (1997). They also pointed out that philosophers such as Ryle (1976) and Malcolm (1971) have long made this same argument. In Ingvaldsen and Whiting's words:

> ... to formulate a rule (mathematically expressed) for a kind of behaviour, does not in any way imply that the rule underlies (provides an explanation of) or improves our ability to carry out (control/learn) this behavior! (p. 722)

Ingvaldsen and Whiting go on in their critique to point out that DST is very limited in the sense that the applications to which it seems best suited are those that involve some kind of cyclic or repetitive behavior to which the mathematics (originally developed for such physical systems as a oscillating pendulum) can be most directly applied. This may explain why so much of the DST literature is concerned with motor skills and their development.[28]

In summary, the following list tabulates at least some of the concerns with DST that were previously expressed:

1. The general argument made by several authors that a mathematical model is actually neutral with regard to internal structure. At its best it can only describe and not reductively explain. Of course, as I already mentioned, this is generally accepted and, indeed, considered an advantage by many DST theorists. The point has been especially well made by Rosenbaum (1998) when he said:

> ... having an equation whose terms can be manipulated to provide a fit to data may be quantitatively elegant, especially if . . . the equation grows in a systematic fashion as additional data are accumulated. Still, if the terms' real world referents are opaque, questions may be raised about whether the enterprise amounts to sophisticated redescription rather than explanation. (p. 103)

Although Rosenbaum goes on to say that lack of reductive explanation may not be the worst thing that can happen (Is there another cryptobehaviorist lurking here?) he and many others now seem to have reached agreement, if not a consensus concerning the neutrality of mathematics.

2. Some of the models developed incur nonlinear mathematical challenges that cannot be "solved" in the sense that no results can be extracted and, therefore, are merely convenient descriptive vocabularies. The DST metaphor, however useful it may be as a quantitative theory in the simpler sciences, may not be useful in describing the highly interactive relationships of human cognition or, for that matter, of any truly complex system.

---

[28]Ingvaldsen and Whiting (1997) also argued that DST and Skinnerian behaviorism have a number of points in common.

The restriction of this and other methods to studying ultrasimple systems is no better served by DST than by the other approach restricted to "toy" problems, for example, connectionist neural nets.

3. The field is rather limited: Dynamical models are applicable only to repetitive, cyclic, or oscillatory systems such as human motor responses. Applications to other fields such as mental health depend on the usual loose kind of metaphor found in many other fields of psychology.

4. The introduction of DST is often proposed as a paradigm change in the sense proposed by Kuhn (1962). However, it may also be argued that it is ontologically indistinguishable from the other forms of mathematical theory applied to human behavior and cognition once stripped of some of its auxiliary axioms and assumptions and the particular kind of mathematics that is used. Although it may emphasize some aspects and ignore others that are stressed by other points of view, it is still incomplete. At the very least, it does not (by intent) incorporate the empirical knowledge obtained in neurophysiological laboratories. As such DST has been criticized for being too ambitious in claiming to be more "universal" than any other theoretical approach.

5. DST is often proposed as the kernel of a theory that will ultimately lead to the solution of the generic complex system problem: How does molar behavior emerge from the interaction of simple components? Simple toy systems aside, the evidence suggests a different prediction for future developments. That is, that the combinatorics of neural or other modular interactions are so horrendous that nothing will permit the neuroreductive explanation of emergent properties like mind and consciousness.

6. The most successful demonstrations have been those that are simulations rather than mathematical problems to be solved. Both Casti (1996) and Brooks (1991) pointed out that mathematics may not even be appropriate tools for the study of the complex behavior produced by even the simplest organization. Simulation may be the preferred approach when system behavior is difficult or impossible to formularize. In some cases it is possible to simply build a mechanical model to reproduce the desired behavior.

7. Eliasmith (1998) argued that the distinction made between the continuity assumption by the DST aficionados and the discrete computational theorists is a false one. Neurons (and, presumably, also logic gates), he argues, are discrete entities (at least in part; in addition to the on–off properties of the spike, they also have graded potentials) but can also be represented by continuous processes (i.e., differential equations) equally as well as can analog computers. There is no fundamental difference between the two points of view, just an emphasis on the language used in digital computers by one side and that used in control system mathematics by the other.

8. Eliasmith (1998) also noted that DST emphasis on chaotic attractors actually produces a "... tension between the dynamicist commitment to attractor dynamics and their rejection of discrete system states." The basis of this tension is that, on the one hand, a chaotic attractor implies an internal state and, on the other, the suggestion that it is internal implies it is "Boolean and discrete" presumably because of the discrete nature of the nervous system as an aggregation of individual neurons.

9. Although only infrequently raised as an advantage of DST, some authors (Borrett, Kelly, & Kwan, 2000) have gone that far in proposing that DST permits us to reproduce the phenomenology (i.e., the experience itself) of human experience. Such an assertion is patently absurd. We cannot even answer the most basic questions of the accessibility of human or animal cognition, much less argue that we have reproduced it. All that has been done is to simulate the behavior in this particular application just as it is done by every other form of psychological model. To suggest otherwise, and conjure up implausible tools for making consciousness accessible does ill to whatever good there is to be found in DST theory.

10. Finally, in all-too-many instances the metaphors associated with dynamical systems, chaotic behavior, and self-organization add nothing to the discussion beyond a very general set of ideas or a convenient vocabulary with which to deal with complex systems. From one point of view, these general ideas are almost certainly valid descriptors of the kind of nonlinear system behavior that must be present in organisms as well as machines. However, as some of their most vocal supporters have asserted, most applications of this particular metaphorical language have not gone beyond simplistic nominalism. The error they make is not in trying to use the concepts or the language, but in overstating their progress.

3.7   SUMMARY AND AN INTERIM CONCLUSION

In summary, mathematics is a powerful tool and has many wonderful applications. However, just as the mathematics is neutral with regard to the underlying mechanisms of physical systems, so, too, can injudicious analogizing suggest false psychological mechanisms. The examples of superpowerful mathematics that can attach their own properties to those of the systems being analyzed are constant reminders of the conceptual dangers one faces when attempting to extrapolate from description to reductive explanation.

In the context of the overall goal of this book, it is important to appreciate that at least some of the phenomena that are quantified by these formal expressions are not necessarily attributable to transformations carried out by the cognitive system. In many cases they can either reflect causal actions of general properties of nature or of misinterpretations of the super-powerful mathematical analysis techniques themselves rather than actions or transformations attributable to the brain–mind. It is these latter behavioral transformations of the stimulus that, I argue, should be the salient topics of psychology.

The wonderful conclusion on which any application of mathematics to psychology must converge is that mathematics is a powerful descriptive tool. Clearly, however, as shown in this chapter, it is a serious mistake to seek reductive explanations of these phenomena in the mathematical models. Mathematics is neutral in terms of internal mechanisms. The result of ignoring this dictum is the inevitable proliferation of psychomyths.

Measurement, Counting, Magical Graphs, and Some Statistical Curiosities

Not everything that can be counted counts and not everything that counts can be counted.

—Attributed to Albert Einstein

4.1 INTRODUCTION

In this insightful and penetrating statement, the great physicist summed up one of the great problems faced by psychology as he implicitly asks three questions:

- What can we measure?
- What can we not measure?
- What of that that we can measure is important for understanding natural reality?

and also leads us to ask several more:

- What exactly do we mean by the term *measure*?
- Can precision be generated from imprecision?
- Do physics and psychology operate by the same laws of quantitative measurement?
- Does correlation imply causation?

Indeed, there are a number of fundamental questions like these that lie at the very heart of the scientific psychology enterprise that are usually overlooked in our headlong rush to collect data, test for significance, and construct hypothetical entities and theories. All of these questions, in one way or another, are concerned with the nature of our measurement processes. They involve the measures we use to quantify the attributes of cognition, the validity of even the most familiar and well established data manipulation methods, and perhaps most important, how we interpret these measures.

It is important that we understand the powers and weaknesses of current measurement and analysis techniques to appreciate the role they play in our attempts to unravel the nature of cognitive processing. As we see in this chapter, understanding of the basic nature of measurement is fundamental to distinguishing between psychological reality and some artifacts that differ little in principle from the psychomyths or other effects of inevitable "laws" introduced in previous chapters.

Furthermore, there is a string of assumptions, that when critically considered, should alert us to some obvious limitations of many of the most popular data analysis techniques now in use. What is to be avoided is the same kind of conceptual error discussed in previous chapters—the mistaken attribution of causal responsibility for perceptual and other cognitive processes to the mind–brain when, in fact, they should more properly be attributed to exogenous causes. In this additional sample of cases, the interpretive errors could well be introduced by the inappropriate application of an imperfect measurement or statistical methodology.

Psychology, in particular, is beset with both concern and controversy concerning the measurements we make and the analyses that we perform on them. At its most immediate level, the concern is mostly with reliability and validity: Do the measures replicate when the same test is reapplied? As well as its familiar partner: Do the measures so obtained dependably and truly describe or represent the process or mechanism with which they are associated? In my earlier books (Uttal, 1998, 2000) I discussed validity, albeit clothed in other terms, and viewed from the viewpoints of "reduction" or "accessibility." My conclusion was that validity was unverifiable, that, at best, a relation between a measure, a model, or behavior and an internal mechanism remained a hypothesis or a theory that could not be confirmed no matter how well it described the observed phenomena. I concluded that confirmation of validity was very often an unobtainable "will-o'-the-wisp" that was, for matters of deepest principle, beyond the pale of psychological inquiry.

Reliability, on the other hand, is a much more mundane and practical matter. It seems so trivially obvious how one should go about seeking confirmation of earlier findings: Just repeat the experiment. However trivial and obvious this idea may seem to be, it may also be profoundly misleading;

I now argue psychology is not simple enough to be subject to this naïve test. The dynamics of time and situation suggest that in more situations than we wish to acknowledge, psychologists are shooting at moving targets. Verification by simple replication, therefore, cannot be obtained except when the investigator is using anything other than the bluntest of measurement tools. It is often pointed out that even the most reliable measure need not be valid: This is a truism. We may also have to acknowledge the most valid measurement may not be reliable.

Only a few psychologists (compared to the much larger number who continue to blithely "measure" cognitive processes) have had the temerity to deal with the deeper issues that underlay the superficially simple act of "applying" numbers to attributes of human cognition. Concern is even less frequently raised about the most basic issue of all: Can a quantitative mathematical system be applied to the questionably quantitative attributes of cognition that we believe we are measuring in the laboratory? In the instances in which they are raised, the arguments are vigorous simply because there is so much vested interest riding on the outcome. It would be devastating to the deepest presumptions about modern scientific psychology if it were established that mental processes were not quantifiable in the sense required for measurement and mathematical analysis. For this reason alone, this topic deserves detailed scrutiny.

The intensity of the modern version of the debate was epitomized in the response to Gould's (1981) well-known book, *The Mismeasure of Man*. Gould struck out largely against the factor analysis movement and its generation, in a formal manner, of such "hypothetical" cognitive attributes as *intelligence* and even more specifically the attribute called "Spearman's *g* factor," otherwise known as general intelligence. It is not the place here to reiterate the details of the arguments presented on either side. Rather, it is the very existence, as well as the persistence, of the debate itself that is relevant here. The controversy was characterized by extremely strong opinions, held by the proponents on one side who argued against the quantifiability of mental activity. Much of this side of the controversy has been simply ignored because such arguments usually seemed to have been molded by personal, theological, societal, or political positions that had little if anything to do with the scientific issues that were being raised.

However, the scientific community on the other side of the debate was not innocent of similar prejudices. Proponents of the measurability and mathematization of human cognition were equally driven by their own vested interests and commitments to positions that were often equally difficult to justify on a sound scientific basis. For example, Carroll (1995), a distinguished researcher in the field of intelligence, concentrated his counterattack to Gould's book on the strengths and weaknesses of the factor analytic technique interpreted purely as an analytic tool. He did so without consideration of the fundamentals of accessibility and quantifiability that really were the core issues raised by Gould. It seems to me that Carroll missed the point. It is not technique that is the issue, but the more basic epistemological uncertainties of the quantifiability of human behavior and cognition themselves that motivates this debate.

It is, therefore, important to look at the debate in a slightly different way. All too often, controversy of this kind has been carried out at the wrong level—merely recapitulating the a priori hypotheses and judgments of the respective protagonists. Whereas social pressures or methodology are typically predominant, it is clear that many of the scholars and citizens on either side may be beating a herd of dead horses rather than attacking the elusive but relevant live one. The issues that should have been joined exist at a different level on which neither the socially concerned nor the methodologists concentrated. It would be far better from a scientific point of view to ask questions such as: Are cognitive attributes measurable? Are cognitive dimensions quantifiable? What is the role of mathematics if they are? What are the powers and limitations of statistical analyses? The search for answers to questions such as these is the purpose of this chapter. In it, I consider some of these issues in search of a more satisfying answer to the question of the measurability and mathematical analyzability of cognitive processes. If some clarity can be brought to such matters, then some of the irrelevant aspects of the debate may be reduced in stridency, if not resolved. If, on the other hand, the measurements we make in the laboratory of cognitive attributes turn out to be inadequate or even suspicious, we may have to reconsider some of the theories that psychology has generated to explain them.

4.2　MEASUREMENT

Although the basic issue of the applicability of measurement to mental processes is usually finessed, the practical details of measurement have long been of concern to at least a few psychologists and other social scientists. I now consider aspects of the measurement problem including the twin questions of what is measurement and what can be plausibly measured. Indeed, the very meaning of the term is typically not a part of our current scientific consciousness nor do efforts to define it exhibit any precision. For example, a typical modern dictionary[1] defines it as:

meas-ure-ment　**1.** The act of measuring or the process of being measured. **2.** A system of measuring: *measurement in miles.* **3.** The dimension, quantity, or capacity determined by measuring: *the measurements of a room.*

---

[1]The American Heritage Talking Dictionary For Windows 95 (1995).

Obviously this definition is totally inadequate; all three definitions are circular involving the words "measuring" or "measured" in their effort to define "measurement." To more precisely characterize the scientific meaning of the word we have to go elsewhere.

One thoughtful source of lexicographic illumination can be found in the work of Wright (1999). He has much more deeply and in a much less circular manner operationally defined the term in a way that enormously clarifies the muddiness of previous attempts. Figure 4.1 (from Wright, 1999) compares four different systems of scientific thought in a way he suggested might help to define what we mean by this surprisingly complex word "measurement." The first column is made up of the latter six steps in Charles S. Peirce's "set of signs" (the previous six steps being prescientific to such a degree that Wright choose not to include them in his chart); the second column shows the four kinds of scales proposed by Stevens (1939); Kinston's (1985) five steps in science compose the third column; and the last column is Wright's (1999) own classification of six steps of creative thought. Clearly, there are differences in the thoughts of these four scholars, but the chart does help us home in on a deeper and more useful meaning of measurement.

C.S.Peirce 1903	Stevens 1939	W.Kinston 1985	6 STEPS TO SCIENCE
5. possible ICON			FANCY qualitative
6. possible INDEX		Entity real idea	THOUGHT qualitative
7. factual INDEX	Nominal	Observable existent	OBJECT qualitative
8. possible SYMBOL	Ordinal	Comparable quantity	SCORE quantitative
9. factual SYMBOL	Interval Ratio	Measurable unit	MEASURE quantitative
10. arguable SYMBOL		Relatable process	RELATION quantitative

FIG. 4.1. A comparison of the "six steps to science" providing insight into the nature of the measurement process. From Wright (1999). Reprinted by permission of Lawrence Erlbaum Associates.

Most informative is the fact that a distinction is drawn between two kinds of entities in this table by all four authors. All agree that to "score" or "name" an attribute is not the same thing as a quantitative evaluation (i.e., a measurement) of it; a score (i.e., a nominal value or an index) is not the same thing as a measure, ratio scale, or other related quantitative unit. Herein, we see the germ of a key property of the elusive term *measurement*; it must be "quantitative" and the attribute it measures must itself be "quantifiable." Intermediate operations such as developing the order of values or simply assigning numerals to some attribute are not "measures" in the sense for which we are searching. This is an important distinction, as we shortly see, because such an idea is contrary to the pronouncements in the extremely influential handbook chapter by Stevens (1951b).

Exactly what is meant by the central concept of *quantitative* is dealt with later in this chapter. Even at this point, however, it should ring clear that for an attribute to be measurable, it must exhibit certain special properties that make it quantifiable. Briefly, and in preview, quantifiability requires that attributes exhibit such properties as additivity and orderliness or ordinality. Also in preview, it should be noted that it is not clear that all cognitive attributes do exhibit such properties.

Wright (1999) provided a much more precise and meaningful definition of measurement when he describes it as a step beyond counting involving:

> . . . an imaginary variable along which we can define and maintain an ideal of perfectly equal units which, while abstract in theory, are, nevertheless approximable [*sic*] in practice. (p. 67)

Here, the ideas of "equal units" and a "variable" begin to broaden our idea of what we mean by a measurement. Properly, they should be added as additional descriptors of the word "quantitative." The notion of equal units was particularly important to Wright (1999). Indeed, he argued for the additional property of "linear measures" as a *sine qua non* of quantitative reasoning. Many others have adhered to the necessity of measurement being a linear process. Wright quoted Thurstone and Chave (1929) as saying that, "The very idea of measurement implies a linear continuum of some sort such as length, price, volume, weight, age" (p. 11).

According to Wright (1999, pp. 73–74), in addition to linearity, other properties that true measurement should possess are concatenation (another word for additivity), sufficiency (the idea that a statistic must be able to "exhaust" the information in a data set), and divisibility.

Obviously, consideration of the most fundamental aspects of measurement suggests that the process is not as simple as just applying numbers to some observations as suggested by Stevens (1951b). Certain conditions must be met that transcend such a minimal form of nominal numerics. This issue is considered in detail in subsequent sections of this chapter.

4.2.1 On Psychophysical Measurement

In this section, I argue that there are two ways in which measurements have been applied in experimental psychology and, in particular, in psychophysics—one way is arguably appropriate and the other is arguably inappropriate. The appropriate types of measurements are those that deal with boundary conditions (i.e., thresholds). The inappropriate types are those dealing with the suprathreshold continua or scales of psychological dimensions. The difference between the two can be found in the strategies used by each to produce their respective findings.

Psychophysics has had its greatest achievements when it used very simple, discriminative responses types that minimize judgmental demands on the part of the observer. An early clarification of the importance of this strategy of responding is attributed to Brindley (1960). He distinguished between two kinds of "observations" (i.e., response types) in a psychophysical experiment. The first, which he designated as *Class A*, are simple decisions of identity or difference. In his words, an observer is asked only to judge whether:

> the stimuli α and β under conditions X, Y produce the same sensation OR the stimuli α and β under conditions X, Y produce different sensations. (p. 145)

Class B observations or responses, on the other hand, are more complicated and are characterized by Brindley as:

> observations [that] include all those in which the subject must describe the quality or intensity of his sensations or abstract from two sensations some aspect in which they are alike. (p. 145)

In point of fact, Brindley was thus distinguishing between two kinds of judgments—one simple and requiring little in the way of cognitive processing beyond a judgment of equality or inequality and the other so much more complex that it was arguably tapping into a level of cognitive processing that was qualitatively different. In the first (Class A observations), the observer is only being asked to serve as a nulling instrument; two stimuli are evaluated on the simplest basis: They are either the same or they are different. In this case any intrusive high-level cognitive processes are minimized to a degree that is probably the maximum possible extent in any study of human cognition. In the second (Class B observations), the observer is typically being asked to make much more complex evaluations of the extent and values of some suprathreshold scale by judging ratios or relative ranks or values.

I now argue that these two strategies actually lie on either side of a boundary that not only distinguishes simplicity from complexity but, also, appropriate quantification from inappropriate quantification. It is at the interface between these two types of observation that some of the most fundamental issues in psychological measurement should have been engaged. I now propose some Gedanken experiments that should help to clarify the enormous conceptual differences represented by findings obtained with Class A and Class B experiments respectively.

Consider a prototypical experiment in which only Class A observations are used. The archetypical example in this case is the determination of the energy threshold of visible light as a function of its wavelength. An observer is presented with a sample stimulus condition of a particular wavelength at a particular energy level and asked only to report if the sensation is different from a condition in which no stimulus is presented. The amount of photic energy necessary to have the observer reliably indicate a perceptible difference between the two conditions is determined at each wavelength and a curve plotted of these values. Given that the psychophysical method[2] and the control of criterion levels were adequate, the sequence of physical energy values at different wavelengths plot out what has been now come to be appreciated to be mainly due to the absorption spectrum of the photochemicals in the receptors of the eye. Slight corrections must be made for certain other optical properties such as the absorption of light by the lens, but these are generally secondary perturbations.

The essential property of this archetypical experiment is that there are no judgments made by the observer other than the simplest possible ones of "same" or "different." In this case, same means that the response to the stimulus condition is no different from the situation when it is absent. Different means that the response to the stimulus condition differs from the nonstimulus one; in other words, "I see something" says the observer.

As described, the observer is performing a simple nulling operation to indicate if two conditions were or were not the same. Critically important is the fact that both the dependent (the energy level at which a difference is detected) and the independent variable (the wavelength of the incident light) of the resulting graphs are measured with values obtained from the physical instruments that were used to generate the stimulating light. Another critically important characteristic of this type of experiment is that the functional relationship between wavelength and sensitivity is predomi-

---

[2]These days, this almost always means that a forced choice procedure (typically a two-alternative version) must be used. In such a test, the observer is required to say "yes" to one of two alternative stimuli and cannot equivocate with the criterion polluted response "no."

nantly unidimensional.[3] That is, the dependent variable is well specified by changes in the independent.

Now consider the other kind of experiment, one in which Brindley's Class B response type is used. The archetypical example in this case is the determination of the change in subjective estimates of perceptual magnitude with changes in stimulus intensity—for example, in the determination of psychoacoustical "loudness."[4] The method of magnitude estimates is superficially the most direct way (as well as the easiest) to map this kind of suprathreshold function. It provides loads of data in a very economical manner. However, regardless of what psychophysical technique used with Class B responses, the observer is always required, in one way or another, to compare the subjective magnitude of one *suprathreshold* stimulus with another and make what are assumed to be quantitative estimates, not just to say if they are the same or different. This involves a much greater requirement for and intrusion of cognitive processes than in the Class A paradigm. The end product of this type of experiment is a plot of subjective values or amplitudes, *not physical values*, measured in what are sometimes fanciful and arbitrary psychological units. Indeed, psychoacoustic units of subjective intensity have been proposed many times. The most famous is Stevens' (1939) definition of a "sone" as a psychophysical loudness of a 1000 Hz tone 40 db above threshold.[5]

Clearly, the two types of experiments entail two very different types of cognitive manipulations—one requiring the observer to do very little other than to distinguish between equality and inequality and the other requiring the observer to make quasi-quantitative evaluations of subjective scales that have not been shown to adequately exhibit the properties required for quantitative measurement. That these two archetypical experiments are fundamentally different is clearly evident in the resulting relationships between their types of dependent variables. This difference highlights a profound difference between the ways in which the two kinds of response mode are interpreted. The experiment using the nulling or Class A response type uses a dependent variable that is a physical measurement—the energy of the stimulus; the experiment using the more complex Class B response results in a dependent variable that is assumed to directly reflect a

---

[3]Again, it is possible to show secondary effects, but in sufficiently simple experimental designs, when very narrow bands of light (functionally monochromatic) are used and that all stimulus amplitudes are close to threshold, secondary effects (such as the effect of purity and intensity) do not detract from the basic simplicity and unidimensionality of the relationship between wavelength and threshold.

[4] This method was popularized by Stevens (1956).

[5]Scales of visible perceptual magnitudes also exist. Subjective brightness also has had artificial units associated with it but they are even less familiar and had even shorter longevity than did the "sone."

property of an internal cognitive dimension inferred from a long line of indirect steps, assumptions, and, most seriously, penetrated by a substantial number of cognitive intrusions. The former dependent variable is well anchored to an observable physical entity; the latter is "measured" in the inferred units of a hypothetical perceptual dimension.

Two questions arise: First, is this internal dimension (subjective magnitude) produced by the Class B observation actually quantitative or at least quantifiable to a degree that is comparable to the intensity or wavelength of light? That is, are the attributes of this subjective dimension sufficiently quantifiable to allow us to apply the principles of measurement and mathematics in a valid manner? Second, are we actually measuring a real psychobiological property of the visual system? That is, does the magnitude estimate really "measure" the perceived magnitude of the perceptual experience?

Let us dispose of the second one first. Arguments about the inaccessibility of mental processes suggest this question cannot be answered. It can be further argued that the underlying property purported to be measured is at best only a hypothetical construct inferred from the measurement. Therefore, even the concept of a "perceived magnitude" may be nothing more than a convenient fiction.

The currently most popular answer to the first of these two questions, on the other hand, is derived from one of the milestone articles in modern scientific psychology. As things were settling down after World War II, chaotic prewar psychology was brought to order by the publication of what probably has to be considered the most influential scientific psychological handbook of the 20th century, *The Handbook of Experimental Psychology* (Stevens, 1951a). In the opening article (Stevens, 1951b), he spoke out vigorously about his view of the meaning of measurement. His definition had profound and persisting conceptual influences on psychology. However, it contained some cryptic underlying assumptions that were not completely appreciated at the time. Specifically, Stevens stated:

> In its broadest sense measurement is the assignment of numerals to objects or events according to rules. (p. 1)

And

> It seems safe enough to say that measurement involves the process of linking the formal model called the number system to some discriminable aspects of objects or events. (p. 22)

Stevens then asserted that these two definitions are synonymous with Bertrand Russell's (1937) statement that:

> Measurement of magnitudes, is in its most general sense, any method by
> which a unique and reciprocal correspondence is established between all or
> some of the magnitudes of a kind and all or some of the numbers, integral, ra-
> tional, or real, as the case may be. . . . Measurement demands some one-one
> relation between the numbers and magnitudes in question . . . a relation that
> may be direct or indirect, important or trivial, according to circumstances. (p.
> 176 in Russell, 1937; quoted on p. 22 in Stevens, 1951b)

The cryptic aspects of these definitions have to be teased out very carefully to understand their underlying assumptions and the potential difficulties they engender for modern psychology. First, despite Stevens' careful attempt to define different kinds of scales, there is an a priori assumption in
these definitions of the idea that the cognitive (i.e., experiential) dimensions are "quantitative" in the same sense that physical dimensions or number systems are. However, as Michell (1999) discussed and as I review in the
next section, this is not now, and was not then, quite as self-evident as these
persisting definitions seemed to imply.

Furthermore, the concept of measurement proposed by both Russell
and Stevens is based on the additional assumption that both the number
system and the subjective experiences are "quantifiable" in the same way. If,
for example, subjective experiences are not *ordered* in the same way as is the
number system, then the number system could not be mapped on a "one-
one" basis (in Russell's words) on the experiences. A *number* larger than another one might represent an *experience* smaller than an experience represented by the larger number. The possibility of emerging irreconcilable
paradoxes and mythical psychological theories would be non-negligible in
such a situation. Indeed, consideration of some of the paradoxical visual illusions such as metacontrast and apparent motion suggests that this is exactly what happens. In these cases times seems to run backwards as effects
precede causes.

Clearly, Stevens and Russell's superficially simple, yet profoundly influential, definitions of measurement leave many deep issues unresolved. Not
the least of them is the very idea of what we mean when we say that a property is quantifiable. Narens (1996, 1997) attacked this problem directly by
suggesting the conditions that are necessary for observers to make valid ratio estimates, the conceptual core of Stevens (1956) method of magnitude
estimates, are insufficient to justify the method. Narens argued that both
commutative and multiplicative properties[6] (as well as some other second-

---

[6]Commutativity is defined as the property of insensitivity to the order in which conditions
are presented. Multiplicativity is defined as the property such that if a × b = c, then the effect of
sequentially presenting a and b is equal to the effect of presenting c. Neither of these properties are always characteristic of psychological phenomena!

ary properties) must be established before the magnitude estimates can be considered to be valid measures of the psychophysical states of the observer. Ellermeier and Faulhammer (2000) have carried out empirical tests to see if commutativity and multiplicativity actually hold in psychophysical studies of loudness. Their results indicated that although commutativity does seem to hold generally, there were many instances in which the multiplicativity criterion simply did not hold. They interpreted this finding to mean that even though the observers were using some kind of a ratio scale, the numbers they were generating were not "scientific numbers" (p. 1509). By this phrase, I believe they meant that the numerals resulting from a magnitude estimate experiment should not be used to develop a scale of loudness. In other words, the numerals that the observers produced, were not the same as numbers to which could be applied the conventional rules of mathematics.

4.2.2 Michell's Critique of Quantification in Psychology

One scholar who broadly challenged the traditional approach to quantification and measurement in psychology is Joel Michell (1999) of the University of Sydney. His penetrating analysis of the situation was carried out at the most fundamental level of the meaning of the terminology and the nature of mathematics. He dealt with many of the questions just highlighted, but also in terms of some of psychology's most basic axioms. Michell was particularly critical of the casual way in which Stevens' definition of measurement has persisted with virtually no consideration of what this classic statement meant and the assumptions on which it is based actually implied. Indeed, he calls our attention to numerous articles as recent as 1995 in which measurement is still defined in Stevens' (1951b) exact words (Michell, 1999, p. 16).

Michell (1999) further noted two major discrepancies between Stevens' canonical definition of measurement and what Michell referred to as the "traditional" one—by which he (Michell) was alluding to the definition prevalent in ordinary mathematics. He argued that both couldn't be correct if these discrepancies are valid. The first discrepancy is that numbers or numerals are not "assigned" or "linked" to objects in other fields of science. Rather, according to the "traditional view" of the physical sciences, he argued that numbers *are* properties of the objects that must be "discovered" instead of assigned. In other words, for physics, mathematics is a reflection of nature and not something imposed on nature by an observer—the latter being implicit in Stevens' definition for psychological attributes. The role of measurement in psychology, therefore, is quite different from that of physics, according to Michell, especially as Stevens and Russell had so influentially defined it.

The second major discrepancy between psychological and physical measurement lies in the fact that, according to Michell, Stevens (as well as Russell) spoke of the measurement of objects or events when, in fact, the attributes of the objects or events are what is actually being measured.

This then brought Michell (1999) to the crux of the issue at hand: How do we know when a dimension is quantifiable as opposed to being merely qualitative? (The obvious corollary, of course is: Are psychological objects quantifiable?) Specifically he asked: ". . . how the presence of quantity can be detected. What are the marks of quantity?" (p. 19). Michell's answer to this question was an empirical one (which he attributed to Helmholtz). To be quantitative, an attribute must be tested to determine if it contains two kinds of properties—ordinality and additivity. Ordinality is determined by demonstrating that the measure used is characterized by values that always are arranged such that if a > b and b > c, then it must follow that a > c. Not too surprisingly, this is not always the case with psychological dimensions, pleasure and pain being among two of the most obvious exceptions to such an ordinal criterion.

Likewise, according to Michell (1999), additivity must be determined by "the [empirical] discovery of a method of connecting or concatenating the objects that indicates the additivity of the attribute" (p. 69). He continued on to discuss some of the methods that have been used to "discover" additivity. One of the least useful, of course, is quasi-exhaustive measurement—simply carrying out a sufficiently extensive, if not completely exhaustive, series of measurements. Michell pointed out that the proposed alternatives to exhaustive measurement are sometimes arcane and include the classical work of Hölder (1901) and the modern classic of Luce and Tukey's (1964) conjoint measurement theory. Hölder's suggestion was based on the idea that:

> What is true of intervals within a straight line must also be true of differences within any quantitative attributes. (Michell, 1999, p. 200)

This is another way to say that "equals plus equals gives equals." It is also a necessary property of a quantifiable attribute. Luce and Tukey's (1964) contribution extended this idea to two attributes and their "conjoint" effect on a third attribute. The task of conjoint theory is to determine how the two attributes combine and how they trade off.

Michell also pointed out that several other conditions must previously have been met to justify the assumption that an attribute is quantifiable. In addition to the "equal plus equals gives equals" stressed by Hölder, it is also necessary to show that the differences within the attributes cannot be "infinitely large or infinitesimally small" and that there are comparable differences between the two attributes, the effects of which are being compared.

The important point of this brief abstract of Michell's (1999) thorough and very important discussion is that quantifiability cannot be a priori assured for any system—as psychologists seem all too prone to assume. To establish that an attribute is quantitative and subject to the laws of ordinary mathematics, one must, of necessity, carry out an empirical research program that consists of two tasks. First, as described earlier, it must be demonstrated that the dimension is actually quantitative and, then and only then, can the second—actual measurement of the dimensions and measures of the attribute—be successfully carried out. Michell's main message in his constructively iconoclastic book was that psychology has gone full steam ahead on the second of these two tasks without adequately engaging the first. It was his conviction that in many, if not most, psychological instances, the answer to the question of quantifiability may well have been a negative one, Therefore, we psychologists may have, to a considerable but unknown degree, been fooling ourselves that we are actually taking part in a quantitative science. Regardless on which side of the argument one stands, this is a very serious matter and deserves careful consideration. To disregard it may cost us dearly.

4.2.3   Shifting Standards

One of the formidable measurement problems faced when an observer is asked to perform a Class B operation (Brindley, 1960) is that the psychological attributes or dimensions are not adequately anchored to a stable standard. Numbers can be, in Stevens' (1951b) words, "assigned" to the attribute. However, as Michell so compellingly argues, if the underlying attribute is questionably quantifiable, then arbitrary number assignments may be virtually meaningless. The problem appears most obviously when a researcher is using a magnitude estimate scale in which the reported numbers are based on internal estimates and introspective reports of the strength of a sensation. Beyond displaying a common asymptotic trend in sensory experiments, the data for individual observers typically vary enormously, one from the other. Obviously, the numbers used as estimates of the strength of an experience do not mean the same thing to each of the observers and perhaps not even to the same observer at different times or in different contexts.

It should have been even more obvious, in a situation in which observers use quasi-quantitative words such as "more than" as their "measures," that the process was even more questionable. However, history tells us that it was not obvious; in fact, until very recently it was completely overlooked. Psychologists have been using rating scales with such categories as "less than average," "average," or "more than average" with a kind of blasé slap-happiness for a period that may literally be measured in generations.[7]

The key to understanding the seriousness of the problem is that the words used in these rating scales, even more so than assigned numerals (which, at least, have the advantage of superficially appearing to be both ordered and additive) are enormously variable in their denotative significance for each observer and arguably at each moment in an experiment. This variability is a compelling additional piece of evidence of the fundamental barriers to our understanding the inner workings of human cognition. Even some of what appear to be the simplest measurements are grossly distorted or even made invalid by cognitive penetration of Class B type responses.

In this section the idea is carried one step further by asserting that one can make an even stronger statement: Not only can we not determine the structural interrelationships of cognitive processing, in many cases it may also be impossible to properly measure the behavior supposedly related to those processes using techniques based either on numbers or words.

Bartoshuk and her colleagues (Bartoshuk et al., 2000; Fast, Green, Snyder, & Bartoshuk, 2001; and Carpenter, 2000) have recently brought to our attention a very serious problem that can occur with careless use of rating scales. The work of Bartoshuk's group is centered on taste perception; one of the main goals of research in this field of sensory science is to quantify the relative "strength" of the gustatory experience produced when chemicals of different concentrations are applied to the tongue. One tradition in this field has been to simply ask observers to rank order their experiences by using words such as "weak," "moderate," and "strong."

Bartoshuk and her coworkers were mainly concerned with the use of adjectival words as measures in their critique of the scaling methods used in a wide variety of fields. However, the problem is clearly not limited to just these verbal descriptors. Other researchers have used magnitude estimate techniques to assign numerical estimates to the strength of a taste experience (see Stevens, 1971) and have observed power functions with exponents of about 1.3 for sucrose and salt, respectively. However reassuring that numbers, rather than vague adjectives, are used in magnitude estimation experiments, both means of scaling intensity are subject to the same criticism—namely, that the subjective strengths indicated by either the words or the numbers mean different things to different observers and may not even mean the same thing to the same observer on different days or even in different trials!

---

[7]I don't discuss the problems associated with the role of question design in survey research on attitudes. That is, in itself, a hugely complicated topic that transcends even the difficulties encountered in simple rating scales.

A part of the problem is that previous experience and their effects on the current state of the observer influence judgments of all kinds. Everyone is aware of this truism: The Gestaltists called this state of the observer "Einstellung" long ago. A sequence of trials in an experiment leaves a trail of effects that can strongly influence each subsequent response. The history of psychophysics has been a continual search to develop methods that minimize these sequential effects without paying too high a cost in terms of the number of trials required to obtain a particular quality of data. The effect of this experiential history is to momentarily develop within the observer implicit standards that vary in what must be considered to be virtually an uncontrolled manner.

The impact of this misunderstanding of the rating scale technique can be profound. Bartoshuk and her colleagues (Bartoshuk et al., 2000; Fast et al., 2001) demonstrated how insidious the effects of such free-floating standards can be. They pointed out that when the different rating scales of a group of observers are pooled it can actually lead to what they refer to as a "reversal artifact." Such an artifact can completely reverse the conclusions drawn from even the best designed experiment; furthermore, a conclusion of "no effect" can result from the erroneous assumption that such a judged scale value as "very strong" means the same thing to all observers.

The ultimate effect of this variation or floating standard on the meaning of the words (or, for that matter, even of numerals when they are used qualitatively[8] rather than quantitatively), therefore, is that comparisons between observers can be totally meaningless. According to Bartoshuk and her colleagues, highly sensitive "tasters" may rate even a low concentration of some substance as having a very strong taste. Furthermore, following adaptation with one kind of taste, the entire scale for another may change drastically. If accepted uncritically, Bartoshuk made it clear how this could lead to absurd and paradoxical results. For example, very sensitive tasters could rank a given chemical concentration as tasting less strong than a much less sensitive taster.

There is a further complication resulting from the shifting standards used to produce rating scales by observers—the problem of *quantifiability* discussed in the previous section. Even if the implicit standards were stable and had not been subject to the criticisms of Bartoshuk and her colleagues, there still is uncertainty concerning the fundamental quantifiability of the attribute of the hypothetical taste dimension. No tests have been made of its orderliness or of its additivity—the two central criteria necessary for assuming that such a dimension is quantifiable in the sense raised by Michell. Considering how tastes can change qualitatively as concentrations increase,

---

[8]Stevens' (1951b) suggestion that measurement is the "assignment of numerals to objects or events" is the exact instantiation of the qualitative use of quantitative measures.

it seems likely that no matter what kind of a psychophysical method is used, it may well be subject to a profound error in attempting to measure the unmeasurable. This may be an inevitable conclusion of a violation in the orderliness criterion for a subjective dimension.

It is very important to appreciate that even specialized techniques for anchoring the scales at both their upper and lower ends, as suggested by Bartoshuk, will not overcome this fundamental problem for what could ultimately turn out to be nonquantitative attributes.

The esoteric sensory topic of taste with which Bartoshuk was concerned is certainly not the only exemplar of the difficulties encountered when one uses shifting adjectival descriptors to describe psychological states. Social psychologists (e.g., Biernat & Kobrynowicz, 1997; Biernat, Manis, & Kobrynowicz, 1997; Biernat, Vescio, & Manis, 1998) have also shown that the same problem can occur and that it may have more profound immediate social effect than the esoterica of taste sensation. For example, racial stereotypes lead observers to use significantly different scales of accomplishment and capabilities for different racial groups. Furthermore, gender stereotypes also lead to different performance scales for men and women. The classic example, according to these social psychologists, is the U.S. Navy's evaluation of women in pilot training programs. More seemed to be demanded of women than men in a manner that seems to be a direct result of shifting scales based on gender-based prejudices and stereotypes.

The reversal artifact effect can also be catastrophic if it leads to incorrect diagnoses of behavioral patterns. For example, Fred Baughmann, Jr., is quoted in Goode (2001) as making the following very reasonable argument:

> However, it is invalid to assume that ratings on a rating scale by (1) two separate teachers of the same child, (2) by a teacher and a parent, or (3) by a teacher and a school counselor, are comparable. This is why raters so often vary—with one judging the child "ADHD" [Attention Deficit Hyperactivity Disorder] the other "normal." Such differences of opinion, being entirely subjective, are the rule. (p. 1)

In this case, the clinical diagnosis is so potentially destructive to the misdiagnosed youngster that practitioners would be well advised to become and remain scrupulously aware of the frailty of the decision process behind it. The possibility that such diagnoses represent an artifact of rating scales identical to the ones observed in studies of the chemical senses and racial prejudice and stereotypy cannot be overlooked.[9]

---

[9]Baughman goes on to argue against assigning such behavioral disorders as may exist to chemical or anatomical causes. This is an important additional point because of the propensity on the part of too many of our colleagues to diagnose organic brain disorders on the basis of observed behavior in the absence of any objective signs that such is the case. I have previously argued (Uttal, 1998) against this kind of false reductionism.

4.3 STATISTICAL ANALYSIS

Because of the adaptability of the human observer, the many different factors that influence decision making and responding, and the virtual impossibility of controlling all of these factors, human behavior is characterized by enormous variability above and beyond that observed in most inorganic systems. Not only do individuals differ from other individuals, but an individual's responses at one time can also differ from those emitted at a different time. Indeed, differences in even well controlled experimental situations may be extremely slight and yet still produce huge qualitative as well as substantial quantitative differences from one experiment to the next. In fact, one may plausibly propose and defend a psychophysical law of the form—*Slight changes in experimental protocol can and usually (often? sometime?) do produce large changes in behavior*! One does not have to delve very deeply into the literature to see instances of diametrically opposed results among experiments intended to be replications of each other.

For this reason data pooling and analysis of variability using highly developed statistical methods, which were originally developed in agriculture, have come to be the methods of choice in much of scientific psychology. Averaging or pooling individual observer's responses has been a mainstay of psychological research since the idea of the "personal equation" was first proposed by the astronomer Friedrich Wilhelm Bessel (1784–1846) in the 19th century.

Because there is such variability and because of the overlap of response distributions, it, therefore, became necessary to establish estimates of the "truth" of pooled data in the form of "tests of significance" or "analyses of variance." The standard protocol for psychological experiments of most kinds then became repeated measures, pooled measures, and comparisons with "neutral" control groups matched as well as possible for all variables other than the one being studied.

Another way to look at statistics is to consider that it is a quest for the "true" distribution of data of an unexamined total population by examining only a small sample of that population. In most instances it is not possible to sample the entire population (censuses notwithstanding) and, therefore, a small sample must, for practical reasons, be examined in its place. The task for the scientist, whether agriculturalist or psychologist, is to determine how large a sample must be collected in order to adequately estimate the properties of the total population.

Because of the fluctuations and variability in behavioral responses, this quest had to be tempered with what is known about randomness and probability, and eventually had to be based on some assumptions of the ways in which scores, data, or responses might be distributed. Some of these assumptions are well known to the users of statistics; others, however, are subtle and not completely understood even by the most technically sophisticated. Some of these assumptions create constraints on the situation in which statistics are used; others provide opportunities for misunderstanding, misuse, fallacious applications and misinterpretations, and, persistent but meaningless controversies. Surprisingly, some of these controversies have long histories, largely unknown to those who are practitioners but not to students of the statistical methods themselves.

Some psychologists, because of the rarity of individual cases or for ethical reasons, cannot use the standard statistical approach and have to deal with individual observers. Thus we see the "case history" developing as a putative psychological investigative procedure in fields such as clinical psychology or psychophysiology—the specialized study of the behavioral effects of brain injuries. Many, however, consider these individual cases to be outside the pale of good science—the pejorative "anecdote" all-too-often being quite appropriately applied to such singular observations.

Even within domains in which multiple data points and relatively large samples are available, it has long been appreciated that raw statistics of a data set may be deceptive and lead to incorrect interpretations. In fact, commenting on the misuse of statistics has almost become a cottage industry since the 1950s. Three popular books, in particular, exemplify this tradition. The first (Huff, 1954) was blatant in title (*"How to Lie with Statistics"*) and humorous in content. Huff demonstrated an interesting aspect to this criticism of statistical analysis: Many of the fallacies are fraught with the same kind of irony and unexpected twists that make for a good joke. This sense of the humorous seems characteristic of many other books of this kind that have been published over the years. Huff's book set a standard for later ones in which flawed statistical logic was combined with whimsical cartoons. Huff was one of the first to point out problems with unqualified averages, inadequate sample sizes, and post hoc explanations of meaningless numbers.

The second popular book (Campbell, 1974) also demonstrated that statistical interpretation could be misused for the most elementary reasons and result in "Flaws and Fallacies" in ways that were of practical consequence—sometime serious and yet in many situations also quite humorous. Campbell (1974) pointed out that either by intent or by foolishness many statistics are patently ridiculous. Poor definition of what is being designated (e.g., what does the term "a bag of potatoes" mean?) can also lead to what will ultimately turn out to be a useless or even a seriously misleading piece of information. Campbell also suggested that a spurious illusion of accuracy could drastically mislead a reader. One example of this kind of fallacy is the classic one of the paleontologist who claims that a fossil is 3,000,004 years old. When queried on this suspiciously precise value, the response is "Well, I was told that it was three million years old when I got it four years ago." Another is that the population of the United States is 275,329,041, a number that is hardly accurate to the precision suggested by its last seven or eight digits.

Other statistics cited by Campbell were equally "meaningless," "far-fetched," or "unknowable." He went on to list any number of other causes of misused statistics including a general ignorance of probability, in particular a lack of understanding of how several probabilities are combined.

Campbell (1974) collected a large number of sources of fallacious statistical thinking in his book. Some were obvious once we were confronted with them; some were not so obvious. Most, however, were due to a kind of naïve misinterpretation of the underlying assumptions, laws, and methods of statistics. In subsequent sections of this chapter we deal with some much subtler and much less naïve kinds of misinterpretations by scientists who should have known better. Again, they are all-too-susceptible to the parody of a cartoon or a joke.

The third book (Best, 2001) is brand new, but continues this same theme. Best emphasized how even the best numbers forthcoming from a statistical analysis can be mutilated or misunderstood. Best was also very concerned with the meaninglessness of some numbers. There is, he asserted, an all-too-compelling power of numbers to mesmerize the reader, especially when we tend to use them out of context. One of the most discouraging things he said in a recent interview when asked if people would ever respond to the kind of criticisms he and his colleagues have made about the misuse of statistics: "Bad statistics are harder to kill than vampires." The same expression may also be applied to psychomyths.

The fact that the results of statistical analyses are so often attacked in the popular press, as well as in scientific controversies, is both a demonstration of their vulnerability and a justification of the central role they play in our everyday lives and in modern behavioral and social science. Clearly, statistics is critical to scientific psychology given the huge variability and the multifactorial causation of virtually any response. No one can deny the magnitude of the contribution of statistical thinking to the development of knowledge in this field. We would be hard pressed to think of psychology, or for that matter any other social science, without it. If nothing else, it has played a critical role in controlling the wildest kind of speculation and standardizing some of the decision making that ties psychological findings together into at least a limited form of coherence. As formally standardized as the methods may be, however, there are many pitfalls in the application of these methods. Some of them are universal and have to do with the epistemological issues of measurement and quantification to which I have already alluded. On the other hand many are specific to esoterica of statistical methodology. This is the topic of the next several sections of this chapter.

It should also be noted, before beginning a discussion of some of these more arcane topics, that additional problems arise when one attempts to interpret the meaning of data forthcoming from even the most rigorous and most accurate statistical methods. Errors of logic or interpretation are sometime heaped on top of impeccable statistics that distort or mislead what are otherwise meaningful numbers. Logicians warn us of such errors as "*Petitio principi*" (begging the question), "*Argumentum ad ignorantiam*" (accepting a conclusion because there is no contradictory evidence), "*Post hoc*" (assuming that something that occurs prior to something else is the cause of the latter), "*Ad hominem*" (attack the person, not the ideas), and "*Ignoratio elenchi*" (drawing a conclusion that is totally irrelevant and unsupported by the statistics).[10] Logical fallacies of this sort are committed by laypersons and scientists alike and are surprisingly pervasive. This is not the place to consider such logical fallacies in depth, the point only being that they are also likely to be the source of incorrect conclusions in the chain that goes from data to final interpretative explanation.

In the following sections I look closely at some statistical fallacies that are particularly relevant to psychological research itself in ways that are sometimes quite unappreciated by even the most sophisticated of our colleagues.

4.3.1 Yule's Admonition—"Correlation Does Not Imply Causation"

Perhaps nothing could be more important for those seeking to build an explanatory theory of nature than a crystal clear expression of a long known, but under appreciated, rule of statistical inference—namely, that *correlation does not mean causation*! Correlation in its simplest sense is defined as the relationship between two variables usually expressed as the dispersion of data points about a graphed line relating the two variables. The correlation coefficient r can be estimated directly from the following formula (Pearson's product moment correlation) among many other similar forms:

$$r = \frac{\sum XY - \frac{(\sum X)(\sum Y)}{n}}{\sqrt{(\sum X^2 - \frac{(\sum X)^2}{n})(\sum Y^2 - \frac{(\sum Y)^2}{n})}} \qquad (4.1)$$

where X and Y are the individual scores obtained for the two variables and n is the number of pairs of scores collected. As easy and precise as it is to de-

---

[10]The interested reader is directed to Downes (2000), a Web site that lists many additional kinds of logical fallacies.

fine this formal kind of correlation, causation is much harder to define, as I have suggested earlier (see page 14).

The problems with suggesting causation from even the strongest positive or negative correlation coefficients (+1 and −1 respectively) were definitively discussed by Yule (1926). He pointed out that third factors could jointly determine the course of two highly correlated ones. Therefore, any assertion of causation between correlated variables would be nonsensical. Others have pointed out that causation may be complex and be defined by interactions among many different variables. It has been suggested by some statisticians (e.g., Blalock, 1971; Wright, 1921) that it is possible to use multiple correlation studies or path analyses to disentangle the causal forces in such a complex system. But, it seems likely that the caveat originally expressed for a two-variable correlation is even more important when one is considering a more complex system. That this misunderstanding continues to recent times (e.g., as critiqued by Granger & Newbold, 1974 and Hendry, 1993) is sufficient proof that this point must be repeated and repeated until it is driven into the heads of some of our more insensitive and/or reluctant colleagues as well, of course, as the general public.[11] The irrefutable point remaining, however, is that it is never appropriate to assume that correlation does support a causal relationship between two variables. Nevertheless, the number of popular myths violating this dictum is legion. For example:

- Because ice cream consumption and shark attacks go up in the summer, ice cream causes shark attacks.
- Foot size is correlated with test performance. Therefore, larger feet account for higher intelligence.
- Experience studying Latin and taking IQ tests are correlated. Therefore, studying Latin improves the mind and raises IQ scores.
- There is a strong correlation between stock prices and women's skirt length. Therefore, skirt length determines stock prices (or vice versa).
- Asian rice prices are correlated with Canadian teachers' salaries. Therefore, increased rice prices are caused by teachers' salaries (or vice versa).
- Life expectancy and the number of people per television sets are inversely correlated. Therefore, TV kills you if you watch it in groups!

In fact all of these "causal" conclusions are obviously incorrect and unjustifiable in spite of very high correlations. Even the introduction of additional criteria such as temporal precedence (i.e., the cause must precede

---

[11]Mueller (1998) refers to a Gallup poll I have not been able to independently locate that found 64% of a sample of the American public believes that correlation does imply causation.

the effect in time for it to be a cause) falls victim to paradoxes of psychological time such as apparent motion or the uncertainty of whether one stimulus actually preceded another.

Another often suggested criterion for using correlations to demonstrate causation is that one must eliminate any possibility of a third, common causal factor. This is, of course, a practical impossibility: Who knows what third factors might be lurking in the data from even the best-designed experiment. On the other hand, it is also important to appreciate that Yule's (1926) admonition can also be misused in the opposite direction. Some correlations do expose or at least hint at putative causal relations. Correlations were the first kind of data to link cigarette smoking to lung cancer. However, it took other kinds of studies, beyond simple correlation, to prove that there was, in fact, such a causal relationship.

In the context of the dangers of statistical inference, one of the most important issues is the role of statistics in resolving and identifying differences between conditions within an experiment. In the next section I concentrate on the particular issue of hypothesis testing using tests of significance following Nickerson (2000). Another critical issue is the problem of resolving controversies between theories in general. In the following section I deal with the problem of distinguishing between competing theories highlighting the critical comments of Roberts and Pashler (2000).

4.3.2 Nickerson on Significance Testing[12]

For the last several decades there has been increasing concern in psychological circles about what is arguably the most used analytical approach in experimentation—significance testing. The main goal of such tests is to determine whether or not it is appropriate to reject the null hypothesis—for example, the suggestion there is no difference between the results obtained in two experimental conditions. Gregson (1997) reviewed the emerging controversy between traditional null hypothesis testing and the new approach to evaluation of results obtained from experiments based on Bayesian inference and entropy methods. He argued that what is still taught in psychological statistical courses and used in all-too-many laboratories is obsolete in light of the new techniques developed in modern statistics. To highlight the backwardness of "modern" experimental psychology, he called our attention to three critical comments by some important scholars in the field:

> . . . much of psychological investigation is bogged down in more or less mindless applications of techniques that are eminently suited for discovering what type of fertilizer to employ. (Townsend, 1994, p. 321)

---

[12]This section on Nickerson's work and the next one on Roberts and Pashler's work are adapted and expanded from some similar material in my earlier book (Uttal, 2002).

And,

> ... at the very least we should stop the practice of using p values to sanctify data merely to appease the Simplicios and put some effort into using data to sift through theories. (Gonzalez, 1994, p. 328)

And,

> The principles of significance testing and estimation are simply wrong, and clearly beyond repair, they are the phlogiston and alchemy of twentieth century statistics; and statisticians in the next century will look back on them in sheer wonderment. (Howson & Urbach, 1994, p. 51)

To which Gregson (1997) himself added,

> Why psychologists have seemingly been untouched by these criticisms [of null hypothesis testing] is a question about the sociology of science and scientists, not a question about statistics at all! Professor G. A. Barnard (in England) recently commented [at a discussion at the Royal Statistical Society] that significance testing was something that survived in statistical backwaters, like the Journals of the American Psychological association, ... (p. 63)

Pithy and acerbic though these comments are, they all reflect an emerging awareness of the problems with the conventional significance testing research paradigm in modern scientific psychology.

The most recent and perhaps most persuasive voice to be heard on this issue is that of Nickerson (2000). He has heroically reviewed the controversy surrounding the role of null hypotheses significance testing. He noted that, in spite of the continuing awareness of the difficulties with such an approach and the fact that it has historically been subject to contentious controversy from it earliest origins, significance testing is still frequently misused. The problem, according to Nickerson is, as usual, that the barefoot uses of tests of significance are based on some hidden assumptions that are not generally appreciated. One, for example, is the false "Belief that rejection of the null hypothesis establishes the truth of a theory that predicts it to be false" (p. 254). Another is the false "Belief that statistical significance means theoretical or practical significance" (p. 257).

These two closely related "beliefs" are closely related to the neutrality of behavioral data about which I have spoken earlier. A related point being that even if a statistical test assures one there really is a difference between two curves, that "real" difference has nothing to say about the "cause" of that difference, about its internal mechanisms, or that it even matters. There are innumerable possible alternatives that could account for a "significant" finding, not just the single theory the experimenter originally used to explain whatever phenomenon was being studied. This is not to say that data differences should be a priori assumed be to be incorrect measurements, but rather that a given explanation of the data is not uniquely assignable to any particular theory as a result of a passed test of significance.

Nickerson (2000) also pointed out some other criticisms that have been directed at significance testing including:

- The a priori unlikelihood that the null hypothesis is true. (In other words, it is always likely there will be some measurable difference between the outcomes of two conditions.)
- Null hypotheses significance testing is sensitive to sample size. (In other words, you can always collect more data until significance is obtained.)
- All-or-none decisions regarding significance are inappropriate. (In other words, rejection or acceptance of the null hypothesis may camouflage deeper issues.)
- The decision criteria are arbitrary. (In other words, what is so holy about .05?)
- The ease with which the assumptions underlying any statistical test can be violated. (Read further about the assumptions underlying statistical analysis.)

(Abstracted from Nickerson, 2000, pp. 263–273, parenthetical comments are those of the author of the present book.)

The question of how far one should go in letting statistics dictate our interpretations of experimental results was foremost in Nickerson's article. Most of us have seen reports in which two curves appeared to be very similar yet the author concluded on the basis of a test of significance that the very small differences obtained actually reflected a real difference and, thus, confirmed the presence of an experimental effect by rejecting the null hypothesis. Fortunately there seems to be some consensus appearing in the psychological literature that statistically significant differences do not necessarily mean real effects. Nickerson referred to the American Psychological Association's Task force report (Wilkinson & the Task Force on Statistical Inference, 1999) in which it was recommended that statistics should be used to "guide and discipline" experimental design instead of dictating conclusions.

Tests of significance are, as I have noted, designed to evaluate the probability that a null hypothesis is correct. There is a simple logic followed here. (a) The null hypothesis assumes there is no difference between two conditions in an experiment. (b) The null hypothesis can be rejected if the difference is greater than an arbitrary criterion value. (c) If one rejects the null hypothesis, then one can accept the high probability there is a real difference. This logical chain, as simple as it seems, leads, according to Nickerson, to insidious misunderstandings about the result of even the best-designed experiment. These misunderstandings are acerbated, according to him, by the use of packaged computer programs by scientists inadequately prepared in the subtleties of statistics.

Nickerson (2000) also raises another point: Perhaps the most egregious situations in which null hypothesis significance testing is abused can be observed among graduate students whose careers depend on a successful "positive" result in their dissertations. The smallest significance becomes justification for rejecting the null hypothesis, accepting the result as a real effect, and, thus, verifying some pet hypothesis or theory. This would not be unacceptable if dissertations were mainly meant to be pedagogic tools and these students went on to understand the limits of what they had done and correct their scientific behavior later in their careers. Unfortunately, having attended my share of conventions, I am now convinced it is unlikely this self-correction takes place often enough. To make the point even sharper, Nickerson (2000) quoted an acerbic comment by Rosnow and Rosenthal (1989) that bears repeating.

> It may not be an exaggeration to say that for many Ph.D. students, for whom the .05 alpha has acquired almost an ontological mystique, it can mean joy, a doctoral degree, and a tenure track position at a major university if their dissertation p is less than .05. However, if the p is greater than .05, it can mean ruin, despair, and their advisor's thinking of a new control condition that can be run. (p. 1277)

How perfectly eloquent an expression of the situation that so many academics have encountered!

The other side of the coin is that it is also widely misunderstood that the failure to reject the null hypothesis does not mean the experiment failed. It is important also to understand when a treatment had no effect, especially in proposed therapeutic situations. Of course, as Nickerson also noted, articles describing the results of such "no significant difference" experiments are very hard to get published.

Although Nickerson proceeded to wisely advise his readers the conditions under which a significance test can and should be reasonably used, the caveats he raises concerning the interpretation of this kind of test for hypothesis testing and theory testing are very germane to the discussion in this chapter. I feel that his comprehensive review of the situation is among the most important papers published in the last few years. Like many other penetrating critiques of the standard mode of operation in psychology, it is unlikely it will have the impact it should.

4.3.3   Roberts and Pashler on Goodness of Fit

In a related vein, but pertaining generally to theories of all kinds, was a recent analysis by Roberts and Pashler (2000). Their concern was with the goodness-of-fit criterion used as a means of choosing among competing theories. They argued that too much credence is given to mathematical models involving several free parameters.[13] Roberts and Pashler criticize this line of thought in much the same way that Nickerson challenged the significance test as an argument for supporting a particular hypothesis. There also are, they argue, some hidden assumptions embedded in the use of goodness of fit that result in three serious problems for any theory. There are several steps to their argument.

First, goodness-of-fit criteria are not specific concerning what the theory predicts. Specifically Roberts and Pashler (2000) asserted:

> Theorists who use good fits as evidence seem to reason as follows: If our theory is correct it will be able to fit the data; our theory fits the data; therefore, it is more likely that our theory is correct. However, if a theory does not constrain possible outcomes, the fit is meaningless. (p. 359)

Roberts and Pashler further argued that an important aspect of a theory is its ability to predict what cannot be as well as what can be. In other words, a satisfactory theory must constrain the behavior of the system under study. A simple fit of the data does not justify accepting a theory particularly when there are enough free parameters to permit virtually an infinite number of functions or processes to be modeled.

Second, variability is ignored. Roberts and Pashler assert that a satisfactory theory should be able to account for variability in the data. Sometimes a theory can be so general as to represent a very wide range of variable data and, thus, actually may be accounting for almost nothing.

Finally, the third problem with goodness-of-fit criteria noted by Roberts and Pashler is the ". . . a priori likelihood that the theory will fit—the likelihood that it will fit whether or not it is true—is ignored" (p. 359). The real test of a theory, they argued, is its ability to predict unlikely events. It is only when one compares theories that have different predictions that one is in the position of choosing between them in a valid way.

Roberts and Pashler (2000) listed several examples of theories that depended only on goodness of fit and were subsequently forgotten or shown to have serious empirical or conceptual flaws. They also performed a useful service by showing how the three problems they identified can be over-

---

[13]Recall the discussion on page 80 about the supposed universal theoretical power of the polynomial power series.

come in an idealized environment; the first by specifying the predictions; the second, by dealing with the variability by always including it in the definition of the theory; and, finally, the third, by identifying some predictions that the theory cannot fit. This latter criterion provides a means of constraining the model to a reasonably restricted universe so that one does not have to deal with such absurdities as a universal polynomial that can account for all magnitude estimate data or for Rashevsky's (1948) equation for the "organic world as a whole," to mention only two examples of the most egregious (see p. 82). However, the world is not ideal. It is not always possible to predict or to specify variability. It is even more psychologically difficult for the usual researcher to think of instances in which his or her theory would fail.

Roberts and Pashler (2000) wax a bit philosophical when they ask the rhetorical question, "Why has the use of good fits as evidence persisted?" (p. 365). Their answers to this question are a fascinating mirror in which to hold up any kind of psychology that seeks to determine the underlying mechanisms of some behavioral response. Their list of forces that have led and continue to lead us down the slippery slope of an addiction to "good fits" includes:

1. The previously mentioned desire to imitate physics ["physicophilia"].
2. A tendency to test beliefs in a way likely to confirm them.
3. Sheer repetition [perpetuating a bias or belief].
4. The complexity of theories sometimes overcomes our ability to really understand their implications.
5. Neglect of basic principles concerning the falsifiability of a theory. A good theory requires strong tests of plausible alternatives and this is not always appreciated nor are the necessary tests actually carried out.

(Abstracted from Roberts & Pashler, 2000, p. 367)

Perhaps if psychologists had truly modeled their science after physics and appreciated the significance of the black box constraint or of Moore's (1956) theorem, these profound conceptual and paradigm errors might have been avoided. Unfortunately, it requires an omniscience that is rare among mortals—including psychologists.

Both Nickerson's and the Roberts and Pashler's articles are thoughtful contributions to our understanding of theory development. Such ideas should be considered and attended to by every generation of psychologists, particularly the next one. Both of these articles are compelling arguments against both reductive psychological theories and any attempt to claim uniqueness or validity of one theoretical formulation compared to another. They also add support for the contention that mathematical models, at best, are neutral and can only describe (but not expose the inner mechanisms of) cognitive activity any more than can behavioral observations.

4.3.4   Sample Size and the Law of Large Numbers

One of the faults with significance testing to which Nickerson (2000) alluded is worthy of some additional discussion. He correctly noted that the value of a significance test that should be accepted as affirmative is dependent upon the sample size. The problem inherent in this remark is that whether or not a Type I error (i.e., rejecting the null hypothesis when there is, in fact, no difference between the results obtained from two experimental conditions) will be committed does not change as the sample size gets larger. Only Type II errors (i.e., not rejecting the null hypothesis when there is a real difference between two distributions) are committed with less frequency when the sample size gets very large. The sample size difficulty, therefore, lies with the Type II type of error. When a sample size gets very large, virtually any small difference will ultimately become significant and the null hypothesis will be rejected. However, these very small "significant" differences may be meaningless in terms of the scientific issue being studied. It is just that the sample size became so large that a mathematically significant (i.e., ever smaller) difference would appear between what were for all practical purposes identical distributions.

On the other hand, if the sample size were too small, then a real difference between what, in reality, are two quite dissimilar distributions would not be statistically significant. Thus, the actual nature of a difference between two distributions, an experimental one and a control one, depends in large part on the sample size used in an experiment. Research psychologists handle this problem in different ways. Some experimenters start off without a predetermined sample size and simply continue collecting data until a particular level of significance is obtained. Given the sensitivity of the test of significance to sample size, it is almost certain that at some point a very slight difference will be considered to be significant. If, to the contrary, practical considerations, such as the cost of collecting data limit the amount collected, a real, albeit small, difference may go unrecognized.

Indeed, in a world in which relatively small samples are drawn from very large distributions, the most unlikely things are likely to happen. Such sampling errors can produce acceptable "significant differences" even though their sources are quite coincidental or improbable and should not have obtained unless the sample had been larger. Consider, for example, precognition, the totally unrealistic ability to predict the future attributed to some "gifted" people. Once in a while even an unlikely prediction comes true and the myth is perpetuated. Statistical thinking concerning sample size suggests that although precognition may appear to work once in a while, the many instances in which predictions are made and are not fulfilled suggest that accepting it as a real phenomenon is a classic case of a Type II error due to inadequate sample size. Similarly, the fact that a pair of dice can be rolled and come up with a "7" five times in a row does not correctly establish the true randomness of the distribution for dice rolling that would emerge with more rolls. Sample size is everything in these two examples. Unfortunately, the potential for errors of this kind is not quite so obvious in experiments in which sample size floats on the whim (or the budget) of the experimenter.

Hidden in the details of significance testing are formal sensitivities to sample size that are not always obvious. For example, consider the F test of significance. The value of the F ratio that can be deemed to be significant depends on the sample size as reflected in the measure called *degrees of freedom* (df). Degrees of freedom are calculated for both the number of groups and the total number of samples in all of the groups. The larger the number of within group samples, the smaller the F ratio that must be used to ascertain statistical significance. For a four-group experiment (between group $df = 3 = 4 - 1$) and 8 samples in each group (within group $df = 29 = 32 - 1 - 3$) an F ratio of 5.28 must be achieved to substantiate the claim that this difference would have occurred by chance in less than 5 out of 100 times the experiment was carried out. However, if only 5 samples had been in each group the within groups degrees of freedom would have been equal to 16 and an F ratio of 6.30 would have been required to claim the same level of significance. For smaller or larger sample sizes the level at which the F ratio becomes significant at this .05 level would vary correspondingly.

The sensitivity of significance tests to sample size arises out of a fundamental law of statistics known as the *Law of Large Numbers* or *Bernoulli's theorem*. This law expresses the fact that the mean value of a random sample drawn from a larger population will approach the mean value of the total distribution closer and closer as the sample size increases. In fact, there are two such "laws." The first or the "weak" law of large numbers says that the convergence of the sample mean to the distribution mean will occur with a higher and higher probability as the sample size increases. In this case, there is a measurable probability that a small residual difference exists between the mean of a very large sample and that of the entire distribution. The second or "strong" law of large numbers goes beyond that and states that the convergence of the sample mean to the population mean is absolutely certain to happen with a probability of 1. In either case, the larger the sample size, the surer one can be that one's "estimates" are approaching a true measure of the total population being sampled.

It is interesting to note that the law of large numbers is not the most primitive step in the logical chain. Rather, its proof depends on another famous relationship known as *Chebyshev's Inequality*. This theorem has the form:

$$P\left\{|X - \mu| \geq e\right\} \leq \frac{\sigma^2}{e^2} \tag{4.2}$$

which states that the probability of the absolute value of the difference between a score (X) and the population mean is greater or equal to e is less than the square of the standard deviation σ divided by the square of e. For the law of large numbers to hold, Chebyshev's Inequality must also hold. Thus, a chain of logic from primitives is built up from ideas and theorems which themselves must be proven. It is unlikely that most users of statistical package programs are aware of this logical basis for the two laws of large numbers.

The point of this discussion is that fundamental laws of statistics and the nature of random distributions guide the interpretation of experimental results. A serious problem is the arbitrariness of the choice of sample size. Choosing too few samples may lead the experimenter to miss a real difference. Choosing too many may lead the experimenter to interpret a meaningless statistical test of significance as a real and meaningful difference. This arbitrariness is heaped upon the fact that in the final analysis the most robust test of significance could simply be wrong for reasons associating with an incorrect sampling procedure. It may be improbable, but it is not impossible that the result was due to the vagaries of random sequences where even the most unlikely events or sequences are occasionally encountered.

This brings us to the next peculiarity of statistical analysis: Most statistical tests are dependent upon the assumed normality of the total distribution. This assumption can also lead to incorrect statistical assumptions and the enunciation of false psychological theories—psychomyths. This is the topic of the next section.

4.3.5   The Normality Assumption

A distribution is said to be "normal" or Gaussian if it is symmetrical and the probability of small deviations from its mean or average are more likely than of large deviations in a very particular way. Formally, a normal distribution is defined by the following expression:

$$p(x) = \frac{1}{\sigma\sqrt{2\pi}} e^{-[(x - \mu)^2 / 2\sigma^2]} \tag{4.3}$$

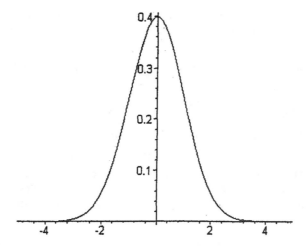

FIG. 4.2.   A sample of the normal distribution. This is only one of a very large family of similar curves differing in their means and standard deviations. The horizontal axis is measured in standard deviations; the vertical axis is measured in the probability of occurrence of a sample drawn from such a distribution.

where $p(x)$ is the function describing the relative likelihood of a score x over a range $-\infty < x < \infty$, μ is the mean of the distribution, and σ is its standard deviation. The familiar normal distribution curve is shown in Fig. 4.2.

There is no question that many sets of real-world data fit the normal or Gaussian distribution very well. Nevertheless, like the law of large numbers, the expectation of normality is an outgrowth of another mathematical theorem—the *Central Limit Theorem*, a close relative of the Law of Large Numbers. The distinction between the two is that the Central Limit Theorem adds the concept of normality to the concept of convergence to the total population distribution. Mathematically, the central limit theorem states that, given certain conditions, as the sample size increases, its distribution will be better and better fit by the normal equation (Eqn. 4.3). Indeed, in many practical situations this is exactly what happens: Increase the sample size and eventually you will end up with something that cannot be distinguished from a normal distribution if that was characteristic of the original population distribution. This is a critical assumption given the dependence on the normality assumption of so many different statistical techniques including significance tests as well as other important analytic tools such as the standard form of Signal Detection Theory.

However, a bit of caution is warranted. The clue that we had better be a little careful can be found in the phrase "given certain conditions"! It turns out that the central limit theorem will work as specified only if certain properties of the processes being examined are present. These properties have been expressed in several different ways including:

- The sources of variation that dictate the shape of a distribution must be independent.
- All of the sources of variation must be relatively small so that one does not dominate.
- That these sources of variation be random.
- That the sampling procedure truly be random.
- We agree on what we mean by large. That is, that the theorem only works if the numbers are, indeed, "large." Theoretically, *large* means infinite! In samples of practical size, there is also the implicit possibility that the normality assumption will not hold.

The important fact is that this list of properties suggests the central limit theorem is *not* universally applicable to cognitive properties, attributes, and dimensions. Nevertheless, many, if not most, statistical tests depend on the presumed normality of the underlying distributions. However, in many cases even large samples of data do not necessarily converge on normal distributions: Unfortunately, nature is not quite so compliant as is typically assumed by psychologists. There are innumerable examples of non-normal distributions including some surprisingly familiar ones. The height of a mixed sample of humans is not normal—it is bimodal. The weight of a random sample of adult human males is not normal; some very heavy fellows out there at several standard deviations skew it. Thus, tests of statistical significance that are based on the assumption of normality may be misleading.

A rule of the thumb for the suitability of statistical tests can be summarized as follows:

- If the data being analyzed is normally distributed, then any of the usual tests (F, t, and χ^2) can be used with confidence for relatively small samples.
- If the data is approximated by a normal distribution, then a z-test is preferred for reasonably large samples (e.g., greater than $n = 50$).
- If the data is not normal, then a z-test is appropriate, but only with very large sample size. Furthermore, the more skewed the data, the larger the sample size required.

Obviously, normality, the law of large numbers, and the central limit theorem are all closely related. The point being made here is that it may be naïve to make the a priori assumption they are all true for every set of results from every experiment. Careful consideration is required to assure data from any given experiment meet the conditions required to make the application of any particular statistical test justified. Blind application of cookbook or computer methods may lead to some misconceived conclusions about the nature of human behavior. Even if all these caveats are kept in mind, it may be necessary to reconsider what are acceptable confidence limits for psychology given the probabilities of random events.

Psychology, with its multivariable subject matter and its usual small-scale experimental design is particularly susceptible to incorrect conclusions drawn from tests of significance that are based on the assumption of normal distributions. However, it is hardly unique. Even the largest scale science is subject to the same problem, particularly when the data being sought must be extracted from noise of similar dimensions. Seife (2000) discussed the same problem as it occurs in a slightly different form in the field of particle physics. The conclusive demonstration of the existence of a new particle in an accelerator laboratory, it has been generally agreed, must be based on a criterion standard deviation of 5 σ. That is equivalent to a random occurrence of one part in 3.5 million, a much stricter criterion than the one part in 20 (.05) generally accepted by psychologists. However, even at this extraordinarily severe and strict level of confidence, there have been repeated instances of "confirmed" observations eventually being shown to be spurious—particles being "identified" that ultimately turned out to be phantoms! These physical "facts" included such items as the still unconfirmed discoveries of the long sought Higgs Boson and of other very heavy new particles. The problems faced by psychology are no different in kind, but it is illuminating in the context of the very high levels of confidence required in physics, some of which have been shown to be incorrect, to consider just how many of the reported .05 effects in psychological journals may be incorrect.

Furthermore, there are some coexisting nontechnical considerations. As Nickerson (2000) pointed out, there is a cultural tendency for articles that reject the null hypothesis to be accepted for publication to the exclusion of those that find little difference and accept it. The net effect of such a bias is to proliferate mythical laws, concepts, and conclusions that in all to many instances have little if any relationship to psychological or any other kind of reality.

4.3.6 Some Other Statistical Problems

In the previous pages I have considered some subtle and not so subtle ways in which statistics can mislead even the most sophisticated user. Most of the issues raised are based on the most fundamental nature of statistical analysis itself. Obviously, the discussion presented is far from complete. Many other potential hazards exist when one uses methods based on the laws of probability: Some are deeply conceptual; some others, however, are simple errors of logic or method that should not happen. The following list briefly summarizes some of those not treated in detail in earlier sections.

1. Data from two different populations should not be averaged, pooled, or mixed unless it has been previously established that the groups do not differ with respect to the treatment. It is clear for example, that simply pooling data from male and female populations can in some cases lead to a misunderstanding of the effects of a medical treatment.

2. Averaging percentages is fraught with problems. Percentages ignore sample size and, for that matter, lead to major errors in the specification of the number of degrees of freedom required to evaluate the scores of most tests of significance.

3. It is important to be sure that a variable has been precisely enough defined to avoid statistical nonsense. For example, the unemployment rate in Turkey has been asserted to be both 4% and 50%. The problem is that the term *unemployment* is not well defined. Many people who do not have regular jobs still earn a living (or close to it) by individual entrepreneurship that would otherwise classify them as unemployed.

4. Not every variable that produces a "significant" difference is necessarily the source of the variability. As noted earlier, correlation is not the same as causation.

5. Data from populations selected according to different rules cannot be compared directly. One of the most egregious examples of this kind of error was the comparison made of academic achievement in the United States and China. In China, only a very small proportion of the total population goes on to higher education. These are among the most talented and represent a small portion of the remote tail of the distribution of intellectual ability. In the United States, a much larger proportion of the population goes on to higher education and this sample, therefore, includes a much larger portion of less capable students. Obviously, in this case the highly select Chinese sample population was being erroneously compared against a much less select American population.

6. Data that has previously rounded should not be subject to statistical analysis, particularly if the difference between comparison groups is relatively small.

7. Standard statistical tests should be applied to rating scales or multiple-choice tests with great care. The problem in this case arises from the fact that the intervals between steps in a rating scale may not be uniform. Thus the difference between a 1 or a 2 may be vastly different than between a 3 and a 4. Assuming that uniform intervals actually exist can lead to nonsensical conclusions.

8. Inadequate randomization or subtle biases can often creep into sample selection. Many political surveys select subjects in a biased way. For example, a survey of political opinion conducted over the Internet draws a sample from those who use the Internet, a sample population whose opinions may be very different than those of the total population.

9. Although it is often possible to distinguish the effect of a test condition from the effects of "noise" in the system, it is not possible to make precise estimates of some parameter from even a very large number of imprecise ones. Precision cannot be generated from imprecision.

10. Extrapolation of statistical trends is a very risky operation. The future is determined by extremely complex interactions of many variables. Discontinuities of many kinds can completely alter the actual course of events. Major corporations have found that their 6 month or 5 year plans are usually wildly inaccurate. Population trends seem never to reach Malthusian catastrophes because of famines or wars or some other unexpected discontinuity. Many predicted catastrophes are, thus, self-limiting even when the trends seem inescapable.

11. The superstitious belief that randomly occurring rare events constitute proof of some outlandish theory of nature is a constant problem for science.

12. Finally, there are a host of opportunities for statistical errors to occur that are based on drawing premature conclusions before sufficient data has been collected to assure that a statistical test will adequately represent the true situation. "Jumping to conclusions" may be the source of some of the most dramatic examples of the misuse of statistical analysis.

The examples given in this list are only a few of the many interpretive and methodological problems that can occur in the application of statistical thinking. There are many other potential errors and opportunities to misconstrue the meaning of even the most careful application of well known and mathematically impeccable tests and measures.

Even worse, from some points of view, is the fact that well designed and well executed experiments are often ignored because of political or vested interest positions. Certainly, every one of the criticisms made here has a mirror image in which solid statistics are rejected for what are often very poor reasons. The worst of these reasons are based on vested interests from the political, financial, therapeutic, theological, or personal domains.

4.4 MAGICAL GRAPHS

Experimenters can sometimes proceed with their statistical analyses with all cautions accounted for and all methods properly applied and yet still present their results in a manner that ultimately leads to drastically wrong conclusions. Given that a substantial amount of statistical analysis requires us to compare the results of our experiments or surveys, pictorial and/or graphic displays of what are often complex data sets becomes highly desirable and sometimes essential. The presentation of statistical data in the form of charts and graphs can, however, exert a powerful influence on what meaning is to be drawn from any particular experiment. Graphical misrepresentation, therefore, has been one of the most persistent criticisms of the application of statistics.

One of the most important and creative scholars of charts and graphs is Edward R. Tufte (1983, 1990). His elegant and informative books on the visual display of information are models of wisdom in this field and should be a part of any statistics course. Tufte argued that even if the calculations and computational algorithms had been perfectly executed, there is still ample opportunity to mislead one's audience inherent in the way the data is graphically presented.

Tufte was concerned globally with the problem he referred to as *graphical integrity*—the degree to which a pictorial representation of data adequately represents the outcome of a statistical analysis. He argued that a poorly designed graph could distort data to the point that the word "lie" leaps to mind. But he went on to make an important point when he said,

> data graphics are no different than words in this regard, for any means of communication can be used to deceive. There is no reason to think that graphics are especially vulnerable to exploitation by liars. (p. 53)

This is an important caveat; it reminds all of us, and especially this writer, that although the critical comments presented in this chapter are largely negative warnings, the power and utility of these techniques are so great that all we really can hope for is that we psychologists temper our enthusiasm with an awareness of the problems that may be encountered in their application.

One of the best ways to do this is to make explicit exactly where the pitfalls are in this area of information display. Huff (1954), Campbell (1974), Tufte (1983), and Best (2001) as well as others have repeatedly pointed out some of the presentation errors that can intentionally or inadvertently make a chart or graph "lie." One of the most egregious errors of statistical chart making is what we may call the "floating ordinate." In the simple Cartesian coordinate system, the x- and the y- axes are linearly scaled and the coordinate system starts at a point at which the both the abscissa and the ordinate are set to zero. In this simple example, the step sizes along each axis are equal to each other and the natural range of the variable being examined determines the maximum value. For example, in a "percent correct" experiment, the maximum value is set at 100%. In a reaction time experiment, however, the maximum value is determined by the results of the experiment. Here, the maximum value might be 800, 1000, 2000, or more milliseconds.

But, not everything is quite so simple; injudicious (or unscrupulous) selection of the origin values of scale values may grossly distort the message intended to be carried by the data. For example, suppose that we conducted an experiment in which the independent variable is stimulus luminance and the dependent variable is reaction time. Suppose that we found there was a linear decrease in reaction time with an increase in luminance, but that the range of this variation was only from 600 to 650 msec. If plotted in the standard linear coordinate system, ranging from 0 to 1000 msec, for example, the data would plot as a nearly flat line exhibiting a relatively small amount of apparent variation. The obvious interpretation would be that there was only a small effect of luminance.

Suppose, on the other hand we plotted the same data on a graph in which the y-axis started at 550 msec and ended with 700 msec. If the physical size of the graph were the same the plotted data would appear to represent huge relative differences. The two modes of graphical presentation could lead to vastly different conclusions even though there had been no difference in the plotted numerical results per se. Selection of coordinate ranges is a classic means of accentuating differences in data in which there are, in fact, only very modest differences, or vice versa, of hiding differences that are real.

Of course, this is the problem that significance tests are supposed to handle by factoring in the variance of the data. Unfortunately, as we saw earlier in this chapter, there are major problems with significance tests. "Significance" can often be achieved by using large numbers of samples or trials even though a visual examination shows very little difference between the findings from two different conditions. This becomes a particular problem when there is any possibility of sequence effects (i.e., when prior trials can alter the criteria or physiological status of the observer). I have always been particularly perplexed by the presentation of stimulus evoked brain potential data—two rather noisy curves being designated as "different" even though this particular technique requires extensive blocking of the trials over extended periods of time to compute the averaged response.

Another problem with graphical presentation is the use of coordinate scales that are not systematic—in which the values of the intervals between tic marks are not identical or vary in some noncontinuous manner. (This problem is quite different from the one discussed later that deals with unequal intervals defined by a specific functions, e.g., a logarithmic compression, which, at least, is orderly.) Rather, it is a fundamental error for data to be presented in a way that arbitrarily mixes two different units. One example given by Tufte (1983, p. 54) is the use of both annual and semiannual values on the same graph.

Several critics, Tufte among the most eloquent on the topic, have commented on the absurdity of using two-dimensional pictures as indicators of numerical values. The true change in a one-dimensional dependent variable is not well depicted, for example, by the size (i.e., area) of a two-dimensional rectangle. The relative "apparent" size of a set of such areas is not closely linked to their actual area. If, therefore, that two-dimensional attribute (area) is intended to be used to indicate the numerical value of the one-dimensional dependent variable, misinterpretations are almost certain.

Similarly, also according to Tufte, artistic fillips of one kind or another, however well intentioned, can often make it difficult to interpret graphically presented data. A clear-cut example of this is the use of perspective in three-dimensional charts to represent simultaneously the effects of two independent variables on a single dependent variable. Although extremely attractive and economical in terms of the amount of data presented on a single graph, a price is paid because of the difficulty in comparing the heights of the various dependent variable columns on a chart that involves substantial amounts of linear perspective.

Next, we must consider the problem of graphics with precisely defined but unequal scale intervals. There are many examples in psychophysics why the presentation of data on a nonlinear scale is advantageous. The classic example is Weber's Law, which states that (to a reasonable approximation) the size of the just noticeable difference (ΔI) in amplitude between a stimulus with intensity I and another similar stimulus intensity is equal to:

$$\frac{\Delta I}{I} = K \qquad (4.4)$$

where K is a constant. However approximate this equation has been shown to be over the years, it is clear that the larger is I, the larger, too, must be ΔI. Thus the psychophysicist is faced with the problem of depicting both very small and very large values of ΔI on the same graph as I is varied. To accommodate the large values on a linear graph would squash together the small values and to accommodate the small values would require an enormous vertical coordinate.

The solution to this is to use a "compressed" coordinate system. That is, one in which the intervals between tick marks are not equal. The most frequently used compression scheme is one based on a plot of the logarithms of the coordinate values rather than the values themselves. Since logarithms are essentially power functions, that is:

$$\log_B y = x \qquad (4.5)$$

where B is the base and x is the power to which B must be raised to make B^x equal to y.

Since the logarithm does not rise as fast as the raw values, the intervals between tick marks at the upper end of a logarithmic scale must represent a much larger difference in the raw values than those at the lower end. The result is that a much wider range of values, both large and small, can be accommodated on the same graph. This can be done on a single axis (semi-log plot) or on both axes (log-log plots) as, for example, is done in Zipf-type plots.

Logarithmic scales, as noted, offer some important advantages in plotting data, but they do so at some cost. The main disadvantage is that they minimize the absolute size of the larger values and overemphasize the apparent size of the smaller values. Thus, the convenience gained in using them may impact on the interpretation of the actual effect of data. A further problem for continuous curves plotted on a semi-log coordinate system is that they distort the area under the curve when visually inspected. The underrepresented larger values do not reflect their major impact on the total energy of the system. Similarly, a fraction, say half, of the scale does not visually represent half of the total range of the variable.

We have already encountered another difficulty with logarithmic plots in chapter 2 in the discussion of Zipf's Law and the $1/f$ noise problem. Because they tend to minimize the apparent size of larger values, they also tend to obscure any variations in those values. Therefore, what may appear to be a smooth curve with little variability may actually be quite irregular.

Another means of systematically altering the value of intervals on a graph is to use a power function. Made famous by the psychophysicist S. S. Stevens, power functions have the additional advantage of permitting both compressions (as accomplished by the log function) and expansions (not possible with log functions). An expanded graph is one that emphasizes the high values at the expense of the low values. Indeed, power functions can also represent linear functional relationships. This makes them capable of representing a much wider range of different monotonic relationships that may be obtained in psychological experiments than are possible with logarithmic plots. Furthermore, they can do this with a single index number. These are very important properties since sensory magnitude functions have been measured over wide ranges of compression and expansion. Whereas brightness and loudness are typically compressed (i.e., exponents less than one), other sensory magnitude dimensions such as taste and proprioception typically are expanded (i.e., exponents greater than one). Thus, a power function with an exponent n greater than 1 describes a psychophysical function in which a small change at the higher levels produces a larger sensory effect than the same small change at a lower level.

This type of expansion is most clearly exemplified by the effect of electrical stimuli where a small change at a low level may have a minimally appreciable sensory effect, whereas an equally small change at a high stimulus level may produce an enormous differential psychological effect.

Power functions are represented by the following expression:

$$\Psi = K(I - I_0)^n \qquad (4.6)$$

where Ψ is the perceived magnitude of the sensory experience, K is a scaling constant, I is the stimulus intensity, and I_0 is the threshold stimulus intensity. Another advantage of the power function representation is that any such function will plot up as a straight line on a log-log graph; the slope of the straight line in this case being equal to the exponent or power n.

As convenient as the power function is in representing a wide range of sensory experiences, it also shares the fundamental disadvantage of the log compression—the intervals represented on the graph are not equal in meaning. However convenient this may be as in squeezing a graph to emphasize either high or low values of sensory experience or wide ranges of stimuli, it is a potential source of misunderstanding.

In conclusion, no matter how accurate the calculations and how robust the statistical analysis, it is possible to misrepresent the outcome of an experiment by violating the integrity of the means by which the outcome is visually presented. Tufte (1983) suggested six principles that, if followed, could help to enhance the integrity of a graph or chart:

1. The representation of numbers, as physically measured on the surface of the graphic itself, should be directly proportional to the numerical quantities represented.
2. Clear, detailed, and thorough labeling should be used to defeat graphical distortion and ambiguity. Write out explanations of the data on the graphic itself. Label important events in the data.
3. Show data variation, not design variation.
4. In time-series displays of money, deflated and standardized units of monetary measurement are nearly always better than nominal units.
5. The number of information-carrying (variable) dimensions depicted should not exceed the number of dimensions in the data.
6. Graphics must not quote data out of context. (p. 77)

Finally, it should be pointed out that graphs used to summarize data are only good as far as the data goes. A recent news article in *Science* (Gewolb, 2000) reported a very important reminder that had been posed by a biostatistician Yen-Hong Kuo. Kuo observed that in a broad sample of medical journals, 60% of a sample of examined articles displayed graphs in which straight lines fitted to sample data points went far beyond the range of the actual data. If one used the extrapolated values on these lines, one was making a serious graphical error of the kind considered here. The extrapolated portions of the curves were actually based on no data at all and, should there be any surprising discontinuities in those regions, serious consequences could occur.

4.5 SUMMARY AND AN INTERIM CONCLUSION

First, let me clarify once again that the application of statistics to subject matters that are beset with high variability and multifactorial causal factors, psychology being only the current example, is one of the most important developments in the history of science. Because of the much greater complexity and the more numerous variables determining the behavior of organisms, our ability to examine issues such as randomness, variance, and means, and to introduce ideas such as population sampling and significance of differences is not just advantageous, but may be essential for any kind of rigorous progress. It is quite clear that the scientific study of individual and social systems would have descended into a morass of unverifiable speculation had it not been for developments in statistical thinking.

Nevertheless, statistical methodology and theories are replete with potential pitfalls and hazards. As we have seen some of them are obvious and some are subtle, some are ridiculous and some are of serious import. It is a testament to its role that from the time statistics first became a mainstay of modern science, criticism of it has become continuously forthcoming. Fisher (1960), one of the giants of statistical experimental design, alluded to this tendency to criticize statistics throughout the many editions of his influential book. He made an important point suggesting that the application of statistics is a powerful example of inductive reasoning. As such it can be characterized as arguing "from a sample to the population from which the sample was drawn, or, as a logician might put it, from the particular to the general" (p. 3).

Statistical analysis, Fisher went on, does differ from the usual kind of mathematical rigor in that there is in the former the ever present possibility that the conclusion drawn may be accidental even when it is not intentionally or inadvertently misinterpreted and even when the analyst has scrupulously followed all the rules. Mathematical logic is quite different; ignoring the possibility of a technically incorrect step, the logic leads from premises to inevitable conclusions. For statistical analysis, however, the specter of possible error, although remote, is always lurking on the horizon. This residual degree of uncertainty provides the basis for many of the controversies and clouded conclusions drawn from statistical thinking.

However, it is not these philosophical musings that raise questions about the use of statistics these days, but rather an increasing appreciation of the interpretative errors resulting from perfectly good data obtained in experiments for which there is no possible alternative than working with a sample of the total population. This is the point made by many of the critics of the field. It is not so much the limits of statistical logic as a result of the residual formal uncertainties, but rather that formal training procedures, either in classes or in texts, do not include a sufficient level of admonitions, warnings, and caveats to prepare users of these otherwise powerful techniques for the situations in which errors of statistical interpretation can occur. Instead the mechanics of the methods and procedures are all-too-often presented in a critical vacuum. Little about potential misinterpretation is discussed beyond the ideas of Type I and Type II errors, themselves dictated by the frailties of the formal methods rather than by fallacious interpretive logic.

There are many other sources of error, a few of which have been discussed in this chapter. Just how widespread erroneous conclusions are in the scientific literature of psychology is not known. There are some indications, however, that it may be much wider than is often appreciated, particularly as attacks are made on more and more complex cognitive functions. In an earlier work (Uttal, 1988) I expressed frustration at my inability to find a stable set of conclusions and results as I reviewed the scientific literature of visual cognition beyond the most basic demonstrations. Widely disseminated and highly respected articles were refuted shortly after their publication because the original experimental design had used too small a number of trials, did not fully explore the range of a critical parameter of the stimulus, or had violated (usually inadvertently) some aspect of the selection of sample subjects. There were also some results that did not replicate for which there was no clear-cut violation of the methodology but only an interpretive error that occurred as the conceptual bridge was constructed from the data to the conclusion. In some cases, I suspect the authors simply had been "stung" by the .05 demon: They were the victims of the improbable, but actual, instances in which their sample population did not reflect the real population distribution.

It is, I believe, in the extrapolation and inference stage of the development of a theory that the most serious damage is done. When a scientist goes beyond the data to infer what are internal mechanisms or to draw exclusive conclusions about the nature of cognition, even the limited anchor provided by a rigorous statistical analysis is lost. It is in this context that much more fundamental issues of the accessibility, reducibility, and analyzability of cognitive processes return to attract our attention.

The point in this chapter is not so much a matter of whether the causal explanation of a psychological phenomena are external or internal, but rather if such a question can be resolved. That is, given the frailty of experimental design, statistical analyses, and interpretations of the forthcoming data, it just may be that some of the conclusions that are a traditional part of the psychological corpus of knowledge may simply be incorrect. From such a point of view come other kinds of psychomyths—theories, conclusions, observations, and phenomena that are figments of our technology, extrapolations from flawed theories, or misinterpretations of statistical analyses.

Note added in proof: Another lucid discussion of how experimental results can be statistically misinterpreted can be found in the work of Michael H. Birnbaum (Birnbaum, 1999, How to show that 9 > 221: Collect judgments in a between-subjects design. *Psychological Methods, 4,* 243–249). This study makes it clear that different standards used by different groups of subjects can produce absurd results as a result of their respective contexts. What greater psychomyth could there be then to conclude the subjective size of 9 is greater than 221!

Chapter 5

Erroneous Assumptions and Conceptual Errors

5.1 INTRODUCTION

Because of its central importance to all humans and the complexity of the subject matter of cognition, psychology has been particularly susceptible to siren songs that lead to mythical processes, components, and misunderstandings about the nature of our cognitive world. In previous chapters I showed how inevitable mathematical and physical laws, superpowerful mathematics, statistical misunderstandings, and errors of measurement, among others, could be sources that produce erroneous causal attributions of a variety of phenomena to psychological processes and mechanisms. Psychology is also, however, beset by conceptual errors that transcend these essentially methodological and technical issues. In some instances, the flaw is in the succession of ideas from one link in the logical chain to another. However, other psychomyths are based on the most fundamental axioms and initial assumptions held both by scientists and lay persons. This chapter examines some of these foundation assumptions, particularly those that have led to incorrect conclusions about the causal origins of mental phenomena or the properties of cognitive activity. My goal is to strengthen the argument that a psychological theoretician–experimentalist can do everything right and still end up with what must in the long run eventually be considered to be a mythical construct, an erroneous conclusion, or an incorrect theoretical explanation. Indeed, it is both possible and arguable that much of the controversy and effort expended in psychological research are, in reality, attempts to reify nonexistent entities and processes emerging from theories based on such flawed assumptions.

148

Of all the targets of criticism at which this book is aimed, this will probably be the hardest to discuss. The assumptions underlying a particular scientist's research program are, at once, the least well articulated and the
most deeply ingrained. Indeed, in most cases, investigators do not identify
the specific assumptions guiding their research program and, even when
queried, are often unable to specify their axiomatic roots. These roots are
typically deeply embedded, implicit, and not always accessible.

This inability to appreciate ones own assumptions and logic is not
something limited to the scientific enterprise. As Nisbett and Wilson
(1977) pointed out in their very important, but currently underap-
preciated, report, most people are not capable of describing the logical
processes or the assumptions driving their behavior. This empirical admonition, originally expressed for observers in their experiments, also holds
for scientific thinking.

How could such a state of affairs arise? The answers are obvious. For example, many of the premises and assumptions of a science are deeply embedded in the Zeitgeist within which a particular individual was trained.
These "schools of thought" are often based on ideas that are never made
explicit, but that may exert an enormous influence on the details of experimentation and theoretical construction. A perusal of the literature offers
little hope that most scientists know and understand the powerful forces
that can be exerted by the basic assumptions underlying their research programs. It is often not until much later in the development of a science that a
few more philosophically oriented scholars look back in an effort to tease
out the basic roots of a trajectory of scientific thinking.

It must be noted at the outset that this absence of insight into the intellectual roots of a scientific theory is not necessarily bad. Indeed, it may even
be a necessary stage in the early exploratory stages of a science. To make
any progress it is often necessary to take as givens some of the foundation
ideas in the field of research in which one is involved. Most scientists work
at the frontier, the cutting edge so to speak, of their field and cannot and
probably should not go back to question every fundamental assumption or
the origins of every useful technique. To do so would jeopardize the hope
of making any progress into the unknown.

Nevertheless, it should not go unremarked that there is some risk in such
conceptual "shortcuts." Entire sciences can go wildly astray if what is generally and unquestionably accepted is, in fact, incorrect in some important
way. Therefore, it is critical for at least a few people to eschew laboratory exploration and work to discover what is embedded in the "mud" at the bottom of the well of ideas. This may be especially important for psychology, a
field in which the logical flow of ideas may be totally sound, and yet erroneous conclusions obtained exactly because the foundation axioms and assumptions on which a theory were based were inappropriate. In short,

enormous amounts of human energy can be wasted because of incorrect and unexamined foundation assumptions. This chapter examines a few of these questionable assumptions.

5.2 THE FALSE ASSUMPTIONS OF ANALYZABILITY AND ACCESSIBILITY

Throughout all of modern psychology there are certain widely accepted assumptions that serve as the basis for conclusions that are of questionable validity. Among the most generally accepted and perhaps the most invalid of all—for psychology as well as for other closely related endeavors—are the twin assumptions of analyzability and accessibility. The assumption of analyzability asserts that mental activity can be parsed or subdivided into components, modules, parts, or subsystems by appropriately designed experiments. Indeed, this axiom, more than any other, can be considered to be the principle foundation assumption of modern cognitive mentalism. Whatever other divisions and competitive theories may exist among cognitivists, the ability of experiments to parse mind into modules seems to be widely accepted. The classic applications of this assumption were the attempts by Donders (1868/1969) and Sternberg (1969) to divide reaction time experiments into a set of isolatable components. Pachella (1974) wrote specifically about the frailty of this idea and I have raised my voice about it in earlier work (Uttal, 1998). However, the ideas are so important to the present argument they will be briefly reconsidered here. Indeed, the idea of analyzability of mental activity is so fundamental to so many different fields of psychology that examining the basis of its validity or fallaciousness is much too long delayed.

The second assumption of prime importance to this discussion is the equally arguable one of the accessibility of mental processes. This is not just a matter of concern to experimental psychology but to the many areas included within the rubric "psychology." Therefore, there is perhaps no more contentious assertion in the face of the enormous vested interest in psychology that mental process are, to the contrary, inaccessible to even the best designed verbal and experimental assay tools. The position taken regarding this particular foundation assumption is the key differentiating factor between modern behaviorism and cognitive mentalism. It is also the singlemost important factor justifying the enormous human expenditure of time, energy, and money spent on most kinds of psychotherapeutic procedures.

In this light, it is obvious just how important the twin assumptions of analyzability and accessibility are to many different kinds of psychology—scientific and applied. I argue here that both these assumptions are unjustified and misleading for matters of deep principle as well as matters of empirical fact.

Perhaps this point of view can be introduced most effectively by particularizing it to a special, exemplar case. Recently I was discussing the problem of the mechanisms underlying emotional "systems" with a prominent social psychologist. He told me about an ongoing controversy in the field concerning the nature of the mechanisms underlying pleasant and unpleasant affective states of mind. On the one side were those who argued that a single "system" controlled our affective states. The principle being expressed here was that there was a balance between positive and negative affective experiences; if we were positive, positive affect counterbalanced any negative feelings, for example. The bipolar psychotic state is assumed to be an extreme expression of this balance. The logical conclusion of this line of thought is that there is a limited pool of both positive and negative affective states and that the total amount remained constant. Thus, if one emphasized positive to the exclusion of negative emotions, a presumptive pool of affective energy would be drained. "The power of positive thinking" school of thought (Peale, 1952) is based on this assumption.

On the other side of the debate were those who argued there were two separate and independent affective "systems," each of which was endowed with its own capacity for positive and negative emotional states, respectively. Therefore, having pleasant experiences would not diminish the unpleasant ones, perhaps only repress them for a while, but they would return in full force once one's attention was redirected back to the conditions that led to them. Each alternative theory was deeply held by their respective proponents. However, on another fundamental matter they did not disagree at all: the jointly held assumption that experimental techniques are available to determine which of the two models of internal mechanism is, in fact, correct.

Clearly, the two basic assumptions—analyzability and accessibility—on which the entire argument should be based are all-too-often simply finessed or ignored. Both analyzability into the mechanisms called affective states (whether they be singular or multiple) and accessibility (that the issue can be resolved) are taken for granted. The first assumes that, at the very least, some kind of analyzability is possible and that there are two distinguishable mechanisms actually present. Accepting this assumption leaves one only with the task of determining the exact nature of the modules. Indeed, contemporary discussions of the nature of this emotional system go into great detail attempting to scale the positive and negative forces that are presumably to be balanced against each other.

The second assumption asserts that the structural (i.e., modular) nature of these systems, whatever it is, is accessible to well-designed experimental procedures. Social psychologists, apparently, accept both assumptions and move on from there to debate the actual structure of emotions. The residual problem, however, is that neither assumption may be correct.

If one rejects the two assumptions, the resulting antithetical view would make the emotional system component controversy almost meaningless (and certainly a waste of time). Here it would be argued that there are no such separable systems for either of the two affective emotions any more than there are for any other cognitive process. That is, not only can the components of emotionality not be separated from each other, but also emotionality cannot be separated from the sensory, perceptual, learning, and other cognitive processes by any conceivable research technique.

Even worse, according to the inaccessibility hypothesis, if such modules existed, they would not be accessible. Rather, these "systems" must, if this antithetical view is correct, be considered to be hypothetical constructs, attributes, properties, or just behavioral manifestations of the action of a fundamentally unanalyzable and inaccessible cognitive system. Whatever side of this controversy one comes down on, it is clear that that decision to accept or reject these two basic assumptions will have an enormous impact on the work done in the laboratory and the theories that will develop.

Given at least the possibility of the correctness of the inaccessibility and nonanalyzability assumptions, a related question has to be asked: What kind of an experimental result could resolve the emotional systems controversy as posed by my social psychologist colleague? It is not at all clear that a definitive experiment could be carried out to unravel the dual emotional module from the monolithic emotional system controversy. Rather, because of the extreme adaptability of the human cognitive system, virtually any kind of system organization could exist that would be reflected in some experimental result, a result that itself would be neutral with regard to the actual underlying mechanisms. Indeed, like many of the other situations described earlier in this book, superficially contradictory experimental findings may both be correct. Choose one set of conditions and one kind of result obtains. In this case, the particular result would support the idea of a single emotional system. Choose another set of conditions and another kind of result would obtain, leading the experimenter–theoretician to exactly the opposite conclusion. Whether a single definitive experiment could be designed that conclusively distinguishes between the alternative hypotheses is problematical. Indeed, if analyzability is rejected as a fundamental assumption (or denied by experimental results), the idea of a critical and definitive experiment becomes chimerical. Only the acceptance of an initial assumption of analyzability (i.e., cognitive modularity) makes the experimental effort to resolve this issue of alternative emotional subsystems at all meaningful.

The twin assumption, widespread throughout all fields of psychology, is that cognitive processes are accessible to well-designed methods of psychological experimentation. In my earlier book (Uttal, 2000), I discussed the assumption of cognitive mechanism accessibility and concluded it was not, in general, justified. This conclusion was based on a wide variety of logical as well as empirical arguments and led me to a renewed appreciation of the behaviorist tradition—one that emphasizes interpersonally observable observations and eschews any attempt to study the inner cognitive processes connected to behavior. Among the most salient arguments against mental accessibility identified there were:

- The Black Box argument. It is impossible to distinguish among alternative internal mechanisms by means of input–output type experiments (e.g., Moore, 1956).[1]
- Empirical evidence shows that people have no insights into their own cognitive processes and introspective verbal reports, therefore, are worthless reporters of how and why they arrived at a particular decision (e.g., Nisbett & Wilson, 1977).
- The discovery that much of human behavior is controlled by automatic behavioral mechanisms, sometimes going contrary to our own interests (Bargh, 1997; Wegner, 1994).
- The ease with which false, but convincing, memories can be introduced (Loftus, 1996a).
- The continuing capability of the human to learn in an essentially passive and unconscious manner by implicit learning (Neal & Hesketh, 1997; Watanabe, Náñez, & Sasaki, 2001).

It is clear, without any commitment to which side of the accessibility argument one comes down on, that the early decision in favor of one point of view or the other will fundamentally affect the theoretical and experimental programs, techniques, and conditions one pursues. The a priori acceptance of either one of the assumptions of analyzability or accessibility can lead to the development of mythical and fictitious hypothetical constructs possibly including such ideas as centers or modules of positive and negative affect.

In the final analysis, however uncertain the actual resolution of this particular debate may be, it is clear that the implicit assumptions underlying work in this field do dictate how and what kind of research will be done, and thus ultimately what kind of explanatory theory will be developed. To

---

[1]I particularly enjoyed the following quotation from Dennett (1997) in which the same point is made. "Not just any structure can realize the functions that we determine must be realized, but the step from functional constraints to structural constraints is treacherous, and takes a philosopher quite far from home" (p. 163). In other words, behavior and mathematics are neutral with regard to underlying mechanisms.

have a science so dependent on its as yet unproven or even unexamined assumptive starting points rather than the nature of the psychobiological system under investigation is an unsatisfactory state of affairs for any science.

5.3 REDUCIBILITY

A closely related assumption guiding a substantial portion of the psychological research and thought is the assumption of reducibility—in particular of high level cognitive processes to neurophysiological mechanisms. There are two levels at which this kind of neuroreductionism is currently being carried out. The first assumption is that cognitive functions can be localized to particular areas of the cerebral mantle. This persisting assumption of traditional physiological psychology has been revitalized by the availability of modern imaging equipment such as the PET and MRI scanning devices. Despite the undeniable power of these essential machines, the classic difficulties that emerge in an effort to localize a vaguely defined cognitive phantom in the brain remain as germane now as they were in the days of classical phrenology. I considered this problem in Uttal (2001) and raised the following counterindications that cognitive components can be so localized.

- The difficulty of defining exactly what is the nature of the mental or cognitive entities that are to be localized.
- The prevailing evidence that cognitive process (other than well-known sensory and motor activities) are encoded by widely distributed and complexly interconnected components of the brain.
- The idiosyncratic nature of neuropsychological findings.
- Methodological difficulties with the double dissociation and subtraction methods.
- The arbitrariness of criterion levels of brain activity.
- Fragile and contradictory data. For example, some cognitive functions have been localized in many different cortical sites and some brain regions respond during any cognitive process.
- A convoluted chain of logic from cognition to localization.
- Technical misunderstandings and sources of error in imaging equipment and its application.

The second assumption underlying a modern neuroreductionistic approach is that it is possible to attach cognitive significance to either single neurons or complex nets of neurons. I argued that this kind of reductionism is also questionable (Uttal, 1998) because of the following counterindications:

- The behavior of individual neurons does not really track cognitive functions very well outside of the sensory and motor systems (despite the protestations of many cognitive neuroscientists). At the very least, individual neurons are relatively broadly tuned and perception and other kinds of cognitive systems are very finely tuned.

- The individual neuron is unlikely to be the critical level of psychoneural identity. Cognitive functions are most likely to be instantiated by vast and complex networks of neurons. Simple numerousness acts to preclude understanding of the way cognitive activity emerges from these networks by virtue of the combinatorics of the problem.

- Some successes with the analysis of simple, repetitive neural networks systems are misinterpreted as harbingers of a future ability to deal with complex networks. In fact, these exemplar systems in invertebrates and in the periphery of the vertebrate nervous system are part of the relatively simple communication aspects of the nervous system and do not represent the most likely locus at which neural net activity becomes cognitive activity.[2]

- The complexity and nonlinearity of even the simplest neural nets, much less those instantiating cognitive functions, is so great and the resulting computational problems so profound they are beyond analysis.

- Chaos theory, thermodynamics, and other kinds of complexity and computability theory suggest that it is not possible to either use a top-down approach (cognitive processes cannot be parsed to unique neural nets) nor a bottom-up approach (understanding the emergence of cognition is equally intractable from the details of neural net organization).

- Behavior and mathematical and computational theories are all neutral with regard to internal mechanisms. Many different internal structures can produce the same external behavior.

- The feedback and feed forward between higher level processes (i.e., cognitive penetration) and lower level processes (i.e., the action of

---

[2]I am fully aware of the fact that the word "becomes" used in this context is ill defined. Like many other words in psychological science, it is a frail attempt to express a kind of monistic and naturalistic identity theory. Somehow, in some way that we do not yet understand and may never be able to unravel, the activity of many neurons becomes instantiated in awareness, consciousness, mental states, of which only we have indirect evidence. The assertion made here is that such an "emergence" (another equally ill defined term) is not supernatural, just complex, and is limited to some kind of corresponding activity in the brain. To suggest that the physical basis of the "mind" is distributed outside the nervous system is a kind of spiritualistic nonsense. Such an idea ignores the simple straightforward fact that the nervous system is stimulated, activated, and constrained by external (to it) forces including both internal and external (to the body) events. Such "stimuli" may direct and guide but are not the psychoneural equivalents of cognitive processes.

neurons) stipulates that the brain is a system of enormous complexity that is probably unanalyzable by any known methods of science.

In summary, the assumption of reducibility also leads to mythical constructs in psychological theory. The now defunct "grandmother" or the "face" neurons are examples of what can happen when one assumes a simplistic theory of neuroreductionism based on distant analogies or misinterpreted events occurring at the tip of a microelectrode. Neural net "models" aiming to mimic cognitive functions are, likewise, based on assumptions that comparable behavior implies comparable underlying mechanisms. This is an example of a fallacious misidentification of analogies and homologies, a topic discussed later in this chapter.

5.4   CLASSIC SCIENTIFIC ASSUMPTIONS THAT MAY NOT SERVE PSYCHOLOGY WELL

Science and the philosophy of science have provided an enormous positive influence on the development of our understanding of the natural world in which we live. But even science is confronted with uncertainties, ambiguities, and constraints that make it necessary to lean on some "rules of thumb" or guidelines to resolve issues that cannot be adjudicated by empirical methods alone. In a sense these guidelines are extrascientific matters of taste departing greatly from a hardnosed approach to research—a hardnosed approach, it may be noted in passing, that exists only in the ideal world. Science has always been guided by the priori hunches, unjustified explorations, fantastic dreams, preexisting theories, as well as by unexamined and possibly incorrect assumptions. It is absolutely necessary to fall back on these guidelines and criteria when direct observation is impossible or when not enough is known to provide more rigorous guidelines. Extrapolations, prediction, theoretical explanation, and meaningful coherency can all arise from these extensions beyond the purely empirical. To assert a historical fact, this is the way it has always been. To make a value judgment, this is the way it should be. To adopt the role of a futurist, this is the way it will always be.

Nevertheless, it is important to understand the role that these extraempirical assumptions and concepts play in science. Some of the classic criteria or guidelines proposed over the years to assist science have become the foundations of progress and have brought not only wisdom but also wealth and, without doubt, health to vast numbers of people. Nevertheless, some of these criteria are so ingrained in scientific thinking that it is exceedingly difficult to even raise questions about their suitability to serve as guides for other fields of science than the ones for which they were originally invented. As difficult as it may be, it is necessary, regardless of their noble past contributions to the physical sciences in particular, to at least ask about their relevance to scientific fields such as psychology. That is the purpose of the following sections.

5.4.1   The Principle of Parsimony

Perhaps the hoariest and most frequently alluded to of the classic criteria assumptions or guidelines for science is the *principle of parsimony*—the admonition to stick to the simplest explanation of an observed phenomenon. Long associated with the writing of William of Ockham (1285–1349),[3] the principle asserted that "the simplest explanation is the best" or "What can be done with fewer assumptions is done in vain with more." Indeed, this criterion for resolving disputes between otherwise indistinguishable alternative theories in science is now known around the world as *Ockham's razor*. In his words, contemporary documents assure us that William stated *"Pluralitas non est ponenda sine neccesitate"*; in translation—"entities should not be multiplied unnecessarily."

As important as William's "razor" is to modern science, there are two aspects of it that should be considered in this discussion of possibly irrelevant fundamental assumptions. The first, something that is true for all sciences, is that it is not at all clear what is meant by simplicity. Efforts to define this elusive term have engendered other seemingly endless philosophical dialogues, most of which usually end with an appreciation that *simplicity*, whatever it is, comes in many guises and types. Philosophers and mathematicians both have been involved in the discussion; mathematicians often describing simplicity in terms of the formulation with the fewest unprovable axiomatic statements whereas philosophers often speak of the number of alternative possible outcomes or the portion of the universe that can be explained as an index of simplicity. (See Lloyd, 1967, for a more complete discussion of various meanings of "simplicity.")

The close association with axiomatic numerousness as a criterion for simplicity may, however, be misdirection for complex systems like the brain and its product—the mind. The quantitative connotation of the term suggests it should be used only in those situations in which attributes of the problem can be enumerated. For the brain and other complex nonlinear systems, however, enumeration may be difficult or impossible.

Just as it is clear that simplicity comes in many guises, it is also obvious that the proposed alternative definitions of it often stress wildly different

---

[3]However, historians have now made it clear that a number of predecessors and contemporaries of William were also promulgating the idea. These anticipators included the French monks Durandus de Saint Pourçain (1275–1334) and Nicole d' Oresme (1323–1382), the latter of whom it was said that he also invented coordinate geometry long before Descartes.

connotations of the term. Thus, it is sometimes applied as an *ex post facto* criterion to justify that that has already been settled. Even then, as Lloyd (1967) said, the parsimony admonition is honored more in the breach than in adherence. Specifically he notes, alluding to its most common use as the "criterion of choice between scientific theories," that the razor is not absolute or predominant:

> Of course, there are other criteria for satisfactory theories, some of which may take precedence over simplicity—for example, logical consistency, past confirmation and absence of refutation, coherence with wider domains of theory, intuitive plausibility, and so on. (V. 7, p. 445)

The second problematic aspect of the simplicity criterion lies in its relation to the biological sciences in general and to psychology in particular. The most explicit restatement of Ockham's razor for psychology was suggested in 1894 by Conway Lloyd Morgan (1852–1936), a distinguished English comparative psychologist. His rephrasing of the principle of parsimony came to be called *Lloyd Morgan's Canon.* Here he urged that when examining animal behavior, the simplest explanation was by far the best. By this, it was long assumed that he meant that one should not *anthropomorphosize* (i.e., ascribe conscious decision making) to explain the behavior of animals that might better be explained in terms of simple conditioning or other kinds of innate reflexive behavior. Indeed, the entire current interest in the study of animal consciousness reflects a lack of adherence to Lloyd Morgan's cannon as well as a rejection of the fundamental assumption of the inaccessibility of thought processes. It is still a wonder that we strive so hard to determine if subhuman animals have consciousness when there is still so much residual doubt about whether or not we can access it in humans. It is still the case, many of us would argue, that the only direct evidence for consciousness is the first-hand experience each of us has of our own awareness.

Indeed, it seems obvious that psychologists have not honored the spirit of the simplicity or parsimony criterion as proposed by either William of Ockham or Lloyd Morgan throughout their history.[4] In the face of these admonitions, hypothetical constructs are endlessly created and each experimental outcome seemingly leads to a new theory or a reification of a new cognitive entity rather than convergence onto a unified, if not universal,

---

[4]It requires no extensive comment that the lay public at large has also largely ignored any idea of simplicity in popular (i.e., nonscientific) culture. The many manifestations of theological explanation, astrology, ill documented UFOs, superstitions of all kinds, fads, charlatan medical panaceas, and a host of other "demons" stand as monuments to the general ignorance about simplicity and the admonition not to multiply entities unnecessarily. For the reader interested in pursuing this topic, there are no better resources than Evans (1946) and Sagan (1995) for clearheaded surveys of these and other kinds of extrascientific myths and nonsense.

understanding of the problems of cognition and behavior. Anti-parsimonious proliferation rather than simplification has been the archetypical characteristic of all-too-much of modern psychological theorizing. There has been little effort to classify the hypothetical modules of psychology into some orderly taxonomy or to constrain wild conjectures by not needlessly "multiplying entities." However useful the principle of parsimony has been in the physical sciences (even though specific instances of it being the final arbiter are arguably rare even in those simple sciences), its application in psychology is even rarer.

There is, however, an even more severe criticism of the role of the principle of parsimony in psychology than its rarity of application. That is, it may be totally inappropriate as a criterion for psychological theory selection, not just a vague one, an imprecisely defined one, or an infrequently honored one. Considering the close relationship between quantity and simplicity, what do we make of the need for simplicity (and, by implication, small numbers of entities) in a system where the number of components (neurons) is, quite to the contrary, astronomically high? A simple-minded application of the Razor to the problem of psychoneural equivalence would add enormous weight to the theory that single neurons are the representatives of complex cognitive processes. That is certainly the "simplest explanation." Indeed, this oversimplification is unfortunately buttressed by other trends such as the single microelectrode methodology that dominates so much research in neurophysiology. A naïve application of Ockham's razor, therefore, supports what is becoming increasingly obvious is an incorrect model of mind. Parsimony, even if only implicit in the thinking of mind–brain theoreticians, probably was a major factor in leading recent theories wildly astray from the idea that vast networks of neurons are responsible for cognitive functioning. The implicit acceptance of the simplicity criterion with its emphasis on the smallest number of components forced us toward psychomythical ideologies of modularity and elementalism that seem incompatible with modern ideas of complex system representation.

The point is that neither simplicity of structure nor economy in the number of utilized parts (a corollary of parsimony emerging from its emphasis on the smallest number of entities) is important to a system with vast numbers of available parts. Another quite different criterion or guideline that may be much more important for brain studies is *redundancy*—the idea that multiplication of components with the same function may be critical to achieve a robust dependability.

Needless to say, any call for psychology to reject parsimony will fall on unreceptive ears. What is important to observe is that an overly rigid adherence to a vague and what may be an irrelevant criterion such as parsimony for complex sciences such as psychology is another slippery path to the creation of mythical psychological entities.

5.4.2   The Analytic "Méthode"

It is to Rene Descartes (1596–1650) and, to a somewhat controversial degree, his predecessors Roger Bacon (c. 1218–1292) and Francis Bacon
(1561–1626) that one of the most important ideas of experimental science—complex systems should be studied in parts—has long been attributed. The idea of what is literally an analytic[5] guideline for science was summarized in Descartes' famous work *Discours de la méthode* (1649). In this
extremely influential work, he suggested that problems should be analyzed
into their components, each exhaustively studied, and our research based
on clear and distinctive definitions of what it is that is being explored. Descartes may be considered to be an early spokesman for an elementalist and
modular way of thinking that has persisted to this day and is part and parcel
of today's cognitive psychology.

There is little to challenge in Descartes' call for "exhaustive study" or
"distinctive definitions." Persistence and precision go hand in hand in guiding the best of modern science. However, the third component of his rec-
ommendation does deserve a little more attention. As discussed earlier, the
assumption of analyzability is now somewhat more controversial than in
earlier times. This caveat does not extend only to psychology but to all sciences that seek to study complex, interacting systems of components. The
challenge to his modular approach arises because Descartes was not aware
of the contradictory ideas of organizational complexity and nonlinear (due
to interconnecting and interacting components) systems. Such systems are
not amenable to separation into components without being subject to a catastrophic loss of function. Nowadays we appreciate that many physical, biological, and psychological systems are so heavily interconnected that one
cannot separate out a part of a system without disrupting its function.

Thus, as convenient as it may be to assert the utility of a general criterion
of "analysis into components" in our efforts to study the complexly inscrutable, it is unlikely that many interesting psychological systems operate in a
way that would permit that strategy to be followed in the sense proposed by
Descartes or applied by reductionist cognitivists today. The application
(and success in representing complex systems) of powerful analysis techniques such as Fourier analysis adds to this misdirection by suggesting
mythical components that exist only as fictions of the mathematics (see p.
73). Even then, the use of Fourier analysis techniques depends on the systems under study being characterized by superimposition—a property of
linear systems—that may not be a part of the psychological mechanisms in
which we are interested.

---

[5]Analysis, in this case, is defined as "The separation of an intellectual or substantial whole
into its constituent parts for individual study."

The key descriptor here is "nonlinearity." Nonlinear systems have a high nuisance value because they do not have general solutions. Rather, idiosyncratic solutions must be generated for each nonlinear system and often the particular method used in one case does not generalize to other problems that are superficially very similar. It is still the case, as pointed out by Stoker (1950) a half century ago, that:

> The analysis of nonlinear [vibration problems] therefore depends largely on the use of approximation methods, and it is confined for the most part to the discussion of special cases. (p. 11)

The main modification of this 1950s generalization is that *simulation* techniques using computers, both digital and analog, are now available that were not available then.

What is the state of contemporary psychology with regard to the nonlinearity problem? Unfortunately, it is not generally appreciated by experimenters in this field (with the notable exception of the Dynamical Systems types) that most interesting systems, psychobiological and otherwise, consisting of more than few parts are to a major degree nonlinear. In these cases, the application of linear mathematical methods produce what can at best be approximate, rather than precise, solutions. The best method of solving complex nonlinear problems is still to essentially simulate the system and then see what happens when it is stimulated with some kind of a displacement or perturbation. Only in recent years have new mathematical approaches to the study of complex systems based on chaotic and similar methods become available. However, even there, solutions are still heavily constrained to certain basic types of system behavior.

Chaotic mathematics suggests how poorly the *méthode* applies to complex systems. It adds further credence to the argument that problems of this type cannot, in principle, be tracked from their origins to their final states. Chaotic behavior is typical of systems that are subject to many different causal influences, the traces of which are all irretrievably lost as the system proceeds from its original to its end state. For psychology, as already noted, this means it is impossible to either predict global behavior from a knowledge of neural components or to analyze the final behavioral state back to the original neuronal states.

Approximate solutions to nonlinear systems are also sometimes approached by mimicking them with simplified linear systems. The approximation of nonlinear systems by linear ones, however, often leads to the obfuscation of the fact that some essential characteristic phenomena become evident only in the behavior of the original nonlinear system and are just not present in the simplified case. Nonlinear systems, even in simple cases exemplified by vibrating springs, are extremely difficult to solve. Yet, think how much more ambitious are the goals of cognitive neuroscientists! Psychological processes are probably among the most thoroughly nonlinear systems one ever encounters, certainly far more complex than an elastic spring, and yet until recently have only been studied from what must be considered to be an incorrect linear point of view.

Psychologists, in their energetic pursuit of experimental data, have been among the most persistent followers of this most dubious of Descartes' admonitions by assuming a kind of simplistic approximation to linearity that is totally unjustified. This dogmatic persistence has resulted in a fallacious, and unfortunately ubiquitous, commitment to unidimensional experiments. The idea that a single independent variable of a complex aggregate of interacting variables can be isolated to produce a meaningful variation in a single dependent variable is almost certainly an unrealistic interpretation of the nature of cognitive systems. The presentation of unidimensional graphs and charts in standard textbooks leads to a succession of myths about the nature of human nature.

In summary, the idea that psychological phenomena are determined by unidimensional and/or linear relations in such a simple manner that they can be decomposed in accord with Descartes' *méthode* is almost certainly incorrect and misleading. The complexity of psychological systems, in terms of the number of interacting parts and the complexity of their interactions, is so great that the possibility of both obvious and subtle effects should not be overlooked. To do otherwise is to inevitably to add to the corpus of mythical psychological entities. This has been well summarized by Ashby (1960) when he said:

> Science stands today on something of a divide. For two centuries it has been exploring systems that are either intrinsically simple or that are capable of being analyzed into simple components. The fact that such a dogma as "vary the factors one at a time" could be accepted for a century shows that scientists were largely concerned in investigating such systems as *allowed* this method. [However] this method is often fundamentally impossible in complex systems. (p. 5)

Clearly, however well it may have served physical science, Descartes' *méthode* may have offered some very bad advice to psychological science.

5.4.3 Pachella's Analysis of False Cognitive Assumptions

In 1974, Robert Pachella published one of the potentially most important papers in experimental psychology when he analyzed the analytic logic behind a series of reaction time experiments. His goal was not to dissect details of the methodology or statistical analysis, but far more important, to identify the implicit assumptions that underlay this line of empirical research. Unfortunately, the potential of this paper was not realized; its message seems to have been more or less ignored in the quarter century or more since its publication.

Pachella's (1974) specific argument was that both the Sternberg (1969) additive factors and the Donders (1868/1969) subtraction method were terribly flawed by virtue of the network of untenable assumptions required to justify their interpretations. Both these classic studies aspired to develop techniques that would permit them to identify the components and characteristics of reaction time behaviors. Specifically, Pachella identified the following implicit assumptions on which this work was based:

- That a priori information is available that uniquely identifies the sequence of cognitive components that are involved in the process.
- That the cognitive components involved in a more complex process are independent of each other.
- That each cognitive component carries out a specific and isolable operation.
- That it is possible to insert or delete a component process without changing the function of other components.
- That it is possible to insert or delete a component without changing the entire task posed to the subject.
- That so-called "converging operations" actually converged onto the same final cognitive process.
- That cognitive components operate sequentially (i.e., in serial order).
- That the duration of the cognitive components could be added together to determine the total duration of the process.
- That psychological processes could be measured with a precision sufficient to carry out subtractions or meaningfully to determine the effects of adding factors.

(Abstracted and paraphrased from Pachella, 1974)

Pachella argued that none of these assumptions could be proven or was even likely to be valid. Indeed, all seemed frail in the light of other estimates, conjectures, data, and realistic theories concerning the structure and operation of human cognition. As a matter of basic fact, the most fundamental of these assumptions, the ones relating to the immutability, seriality, and additivity of the cognitive components, seemed to be particularly unsupportable when examined in detail. All seemed to emerge from even more fundamental assumptions of cognitive modularity, linearity, and simplicity, of which I have already spoken. None seemed to take into account the actual nonlinearity and complexity of the highly interactive system we now believe to be operating in the brain.

Considering the broad range of experiments in cognitive psychology (above and beyond those reaction time studies targeted by Pachella) that are based on equally flimsy conjectures, the history of modern scientific psychology should have been very different than it has been. One can clearly see the influence of these implicit, but incorrect, assumptions throughout the entire modularity movement as well as on the currently popular efforts to associate particular cognitive processes with specific brain locations.

5.4.4   Equating Analogy With Homology

Biology has a highly developed concept of two terms that have deep relevance to psychological theory. On the one hand, *analogies* can be concisely defined as similarity in form or process. On the other hand, *homologies* can be defined as identity in structural origins with or without similarity in function. Of course, these capsule definitions do not completely capture the flavor of these two terms and, like many of other important concepts in science, their exact meanings have been the subject of discussion for many years by philosophers and scientists alike.

For example, a distinction is often made between formal and material analogies, the first meaning being epitomized by the mathematical model or theory in which the behavior of some system is reproduced in some isomorphic fashion but without necessarily replicating the actual underlying mechanics.[6] For example, electronic analogue computers typically use capacitors, resistors, and driving voltages to describe the behavior of a coiled spring, an ecological interaction, or even another electronic circuit. This kind of formal relationship can provide excellent descriptions and predictions. However, because the same equations may model systems from any of these quite different mechanistic universes, there is nothing in this kind of formal analogy that speaks to the exact inner workings of the system being modeled. As noted elsewhere in this book, such formal systems are, therefore, neutral and are incapable of distinguishing between many different kinds of internal structures that exhibit analogous behavior.[7]

---

[6]I reiterate that this is another way of asserting that mathematical models and behavior are intrinsically neutral with regard to underlying mechanisms. Mathematics is essentially an analogical system capable of representing the common behavior produced by a wide variety of mechanisms. Behavior is also analogical in the same sense that a particular response could be produced by any one of a number of cognitive processes, motivations, or causes.

[7]I must insert, in anticipatory defense, the following comment. Nothing in what I say here about the limitations of the analog approach should be interpreted to suggest that analogy and metaphor have not been powerful intellectual tools throughout scientific history. Nor am I suggesting any change in the course of science. I am suggesting there are some boundaries and constraints to this kind of thinking that must be taken into account. To not do so will inevitably lead to misinterpretations of analogs as homologs and the postulations of totally incorrect theories—psychomyths!

The second kind of analogy, material analogy, is characterized by a real mechanical or physical similarity between the two systems being compared. For example, the wing of a bat and the wing of an insect are material analogies of each other. They share not only a common function or form, but also a similar superficial implementation. However, the two modes of flying are based on very different physical principles; understanding the one does not necessarily provide understanding of the other's mechanical principles. In fact, assuming that it does do so leads to logical absurdities such as assuming that an insect cannot fly since its aerodynamics do not agree with those of the bat.

The idea of a homology, however, goes even further than the concept of a material analogy. The term is taken from biology where structures are assumed to be homologous if they actually share common embryological origins. Thus the leg of a dog and the flipper of a sea lion are homologs of each other, even though evolved over the eons to carry out completely different functions.

The problem faced by those who use similarity of form or function (i.e., those who argue on the basis of analogs, either in its formal or its material sense, as the basis for theoretical explanation), is that neither kind of analogy can provide rigorous insight into the actual mechanical similarities or identities that may or may not exist between analogs. Neither a mathematical model nor a materially analogous solution to a problem such as winged flying is capable of explaining the mechanical principles of some other, albeit analogous, solution to the problem of winged flight. In other words, it is not possible to explain the successful airplane wing by a theory based on the fly's wing. Similarly, vertebrate and invertebrate legs are material analogs of each other, but it requires a much deeper analysis to understand the principles under which each operates. Similarly, the cephalopod eye and the mammalian eye both see and share a kind of material analogy, but are accounted for by a totally different evolutionary and embryological history. However exciting this form of converging evolution may be, an examination of the anatomical or physiological details of the octopus eye does not directly explain why the mammalian eye is organized in the way it is. On the other hand, understanding the structure and action of one member of a pair of homologous structures (e.g., the extremities of a dog and of a sea lion, respectively) does provide deep insight into the way that the other operates.

The operational term in this context is *homology* defined traditionally as "the same organ in different animals under a variety of form and function" by the Victorian anatomist Richard Owen (1804–1892) in 1843 in lectures given at the Royal College of Surgeons. Owen's proposal was actually presented as an alternative to Darwinian Evolution, an idea that he (Owen) fought for most of his life. Owen's concept of homology, that it was an expression of a fundamental "archetype," was used to buttress his strong theological philosophy and as a counterargument to the idea of common ancestry proposed by Darwin.

For the purposes of our present discussion, homologies, unlike analogies, are assumed to have embryologically identical origins and thus, any differences between homologs are supposed to represent modifications that are, in principle, adaptations or modifications of a common ancestral root mechanism. Indeed, homologous structures may end up having very different functions and not even be process analogs. We are long past Owen's Victorian argument that homologs arise out of a long-term plan of God instantiated in the archetype—the basic plan within which all subsequent modifications were supposed to be inherent from the outset. The point being made here, on the contrary, is that many very different mechanisms are capable of producing common behavior.

To reiterate and summarize, the observation of analogous behavior defined either in the formal or the material sense does not permit one to assume that the mechanisms are homologs in the sense of operating on the basis of common mechanical or organizational principles.

Nevertheless, the assumption that one can make the leap from analogous descriptions to common or homologous explanations is implicit in an enormous variety of different kinds of psychological inquiry. This is exhibited most egregiously in erroneous extrapolations made from the analogous behavior of individual neurons and cognition to the idea that those individual neurons encode complex processes.

In sum, the extrapolation from analogous observations to what are essentially homologous theories is fraught with difficulties, is logically invalid, and leads to many different myths in biopsychological theory.

5.4.5 Equating Necessity With Sufficiency

I previously examined (Uttal, 2001 and see p. 154) some of the questionable logic involved in associating particular regions of the brain with specific cognitive processes by means of newly developed and extremely powerful imaging techniques.[8] In that discussion I described one major logical misassumption that seemed to permeate this modern cognitive neuroscience research topic. This misassumption was the equation of necessity with sufficiency. That is, it is often incorrectly assumed that a demonstration of

---

[8]Once again a preemptive defense is in order. My criticism of efforts to localize cognitive processes in particular parts of the brain with modern imaging techniques is in no way intended to suggest that these wonderful machines are not useful in other contexts. The relief of human misery by noninvasive examination of internal anatomy has been a monumental contribution, perhaps of epochal proportions. It is only the psychological–neural bridge theory that seems based on some uncritically examined assumptions that is the source of psychomyths.

correlated activity in a localized brain region with some cognitive function *proves* that the brain region *encodes* the cognitive function. However, here is evidence in one of its most visible forms of a classic logical error. Even if one accepts the empirical data at its face value and ignores many of the technical difficulties in correlating MRI and PET images with behavior, such a *participation* on a part of the brain region in the behavior does not guarantee that the particular brain region is the equivalent or the locale of the psychological function. It should be appreciated that even highly correlated activity may only be a part, and possibly a very indirect one, of the total system of interacting brain regions that collectively represents the cognitive process being studied. In other words, a defined region of the brain may be *necessary* for the behavior but not *sufficient* to implement that psychological process on its own.

On consideration, it is clear that the admonition that necessity should not be misconstrued for sufficiency is of much broader applicability than to just the brain–mind localization problem. In an entirely parallel manner, purely psychophysical problems can also be misconstrued in exactly the same way. A good example is the relationship of wavelength and hue, an exemplar I have turned to several times previously in this book. A unidimensional experiment, typical of those carried out by visual psychophysicists will certainly demonstrate the strong, if not predominant, effect of the incident light's wavelength on the psychological experience of hue. Wavelength differences, therefore, in a sense, are necessary for the discrimination of hues. However, this parameter of the stimulus is insufficient to account for all discriminations; the purity and the intensity of the stimulus are also well known to influence chromaticity as well as are the relative reflectances and other properties of the surrounding regions.

Philosophers and logicians have also dealt with this problem since the time of Aristotle. Clothed in a slightly different language, the distinction between necessity and sufficiency was framed by philosophers as a distinction between necessary and contingent statements. Formal logical systems, such as the one developed by George Boole and further developed into computer design protocols, also take into account the critical conceptual difference between states of implication. On the one hand are statements of logical sufficiency; for example, *a implies b*. On the other, there are statements that imply necessity without implying sufficiency; for example, *a implies b if and only if c is also present*. The first implication represents a tautology of sufficiency whereas the second represents an "and" logical function in which two (or more) states must be present to account for the third. In this latter case, **a** is necessary but not sufficient to produce **b**.

Although clothed in different terminologies, the problems presented to the psychologist or the logician are essentially the same. The psychologist has the more difficult time because the components and their respective contingencies are not simply laid out in a truth table or in a circuit diagram, but must be discovered by rigorous experimentation. All too often, the contingencies that distinguish necessity from sufficiency become lost in the excitement surrounding the discovery of a correlation.

Regardless of the greater subtly of the problems faced by psychologists, caveats and warnings that should have been passed down to psychology from its close past association with philosophy and logic seem to have gone unheeded in the modern science. Sometimes, one wonders just how reckless psychology has been in throwing off the parental methodology of logical analysis and even philosophical speculation in its passion to emulate its distant cousin—physics. The classic misassumption of identifying necessity with sufficiency can influence theoretical understandings and in some cases produces theories or entities that are myths comparable to any of the others discussed in this book. Philosophers, at least, have confronted this problem. Psychologists and other students of cognition have not yet adequately done so.

5.4.6   Some Prevalent Misassumptions Concerning the Physical and Cognitive Worlds

Although not directly influencing theory in psychology, it certainly should be briefly mentioned that there are many cognitive myths about the nature of the real world in which we live. The topic of "folk physics" has been of increasing interest to psychologists. It is characterized in some cases by totally incorrect, but very popular, misconceptions that have been shown on closer examination to contradict known laws of physics. In other instances, these folk physical assumptions about the world make it difficult for humans to move forward on some of the most fundamental questions of the nature of both the microcosm and the macrocosm. If nothing else, these incorrect assumptions are another illustration of how behavior (in the short run) and psychological theory (in the long run) can be affected by preexisting ideas.

David Hestenes, a colleague in the physics department at the Arizona State University and a distinguished scholar of both physical theory and physics education, suggested that one of the most difficult things for the beginning university student of physics to overcome was the conflict between the common sense appreciation of the continuity of physical objects and the now well-known fact that all matter is discontinuous when examined microscopically. The assumption of continuity, Hestenes goes on to argue, also inhibits even some senior physicists from making progress in their scientific endeavors. He argues there are many other "realities" that are counterintuitive from the point of view of ordinary experience, yet which seem to be compelling descriptions of the physical universe. For example, modern string theory postulates a multiplicity of dimensions to explain nature, few of which have any intuitive basis for either the layperson or the basic particle physicist. Similarly, modern quantum mechanical theory raises concepts that are totally foreign to humans. These include the ideas that something may not exist until it is measured, that a particle may be in two different places at the same time, or that a particle may have no exact location but, rather, be localized only as a spatial probability distribution.

Certainly, if deep concepts that run counter to our everyday experience can be present in physics, a science that seems much better disciplined than psychology, they can also occur in psychological thinking with its nebulously defined concepts and constructs. Indeed, such conceptual problems may be even more likely to be found in psychological theory because of the apparent closeness of the language of immediate awareness and that of deep and possibly impenetrable structure.

There is, likewise, a widespread difficulty when laypersons and scholars confront certain questions of cosmology at the other end of the size scale. For example, it is extremely difficult to get across the idea of what may or what may not have been present before the big bang, an event that physicists suggest was when our time began, whatever that can possibly mean. It is difficult for humans to accept such a nonintuitive concept as the "beginning of time." Similarly, what can we make intuitively of what it will be like in many billions of years when the universe runs completely down hill, entropically speaking, and time ends?

The spatial corollary of this conceptual difficulty is the appreciation of what it must mean to be beyond the limits of the known universe. It is equally difficult for people to appreciate an "end of space" as it is an "end of time." Science fiction writers notwithstanding, most people also have a very difficult time grasping the implications of a macroscopic "flat," "positively curved," or "negatively curved" universe. Current cosmology poses many comparable conceptual problems that seem to be inconsistent with our everyday assumptions about and experiences with the world around us. Yet, from one point of view these cosmological and basic particle intuitions may be easier to cope with than those emerging when we consider issues concerning the nature of the human mind. The familiarity of our own self-awareness may make it even more difficult to discern where intuition clashes with psychobiology.

The general difficulty these problems of comprehension pose is that everyday assumptions and intuitions are almost certainly only the grossest approximations to physical reality if not totally incorrect. Even at the scale of ordinary physical experience there is a pervasive misunderstanding of the more familiar laws of Newtonian physics. These misunderstandings have been collected under the rubric of folk physics and include:

- The idea that if something is thrown from a moving platform it will drop straight down (thus ignoring the forward velocity component of the platform). (Kaiser, Proffitt, & McCloskey, 1985)
- The idea that if one cuts the string holding a pail that you are swinging around your head, the pail will continue along the curved path it was previously following (thus ignoring the momentary linear vector that would have it continue in the direction it had been traveling at the moment the constraining string was cut). (Kaiser, McCloskey, & Proffitt, 1986)
- The "Wiley Coyote" physical principle that asserts that you will not fall immediately if you run off a precipice but will enjoy a period of bemusement at your momentary state. (Kaiser, Proffitt, & Anderson, 1985)
- The innumerable "folk psychological" misperceptions about the behavior of liquids discussed in Howard (1978) and in McAfee and Profitt (1991).

Profitt (1999) and Proffitt and Kaiser (in press) presented eloquent general discussions of this general topic of "Intuitive" or "Naïve" Physics in recent encyclopedia articles.

As noted when I began this section, these misconceptions and misassumptions about the nature of the physical world do not always express themselves directly as *psychomyths* (they might better be classified as *physicomyths*). Nevertheless, it is quite clear that the kinds of conceptual difficulties encountered here are for a universe of discourse that is, from many points of view, far simpler than those encountered in psychology. It is not too surprising, then, how many comparable myths have evolved in psychological thinking. Indeed, folk psychology has also become a popular topic for psychological pundits recently (e.g., see Greenwood, 1991.) The problem is that it is not at all clear where the boundary is between folk psychology and scientifically supportable psychology, particularly given some of the other widely accepted but incorrect assumptions that guide this science. Some widespread and very popular assumptions that people have of cognitive processes are:

- Humans are able to decide what their behavior will be. In other words, they exhibit "free will."
- The heart is the seat of emotion.

- Opposites attract.
- Winning a lottery is always a good thing.
- It is always good to receive help.
- It is always good to look deeply into one's past and one's motives to understand the causes of one's current emotional states.
- Financial rewards always improve performance.
- That it is possible for psychics to predict the future or to move objects by mental powers alone.
  (With thanks to Professor John Reich of Arizona State University)

And, at a somewhat more sophisticated scientific or quasiscientific level:

- That observers (previously known as subjects) are stable cognitive entities over time.
- That observers are capable of making precise quantitative evaluations of physical parameters. Ellermeier and Faulhammer (2000) provided an empirical critique of this assumption.
- That memories are both valid and stable indicators of past events. The works of Roediger, Meade, and Bergman (2001); Weldon (2000); and Loftus (1991, 1996; Loftus, Coan, & Pickrell, 1996) are particularly germane in this context.)
- That observers understand the forces, motives, and logic of their decision processes. The study of automatic behavior by Bargh (1997) challenges this assumption, as does the classic study by Nisbett and Wilson (1977), and the work on ironic processes by Wegner (1994).
- That behavior is driven solely by environmental forces. Radical behaviorists preached this extreme theory of human behavior.
- That behavior is driven solely by conscious cognitive decision making. Radical cognitivists and humanists of many other kinds preached this extreme theory of human behavior.
- That it is possible to go from molar behavior (of the organism or of the brain) to a specification of the underlying microscopic mechanisms. See Uttal (1998) for a complete discussion of this flawed assumption.
- That it is possible to go from studies of the microscopic mechanisms to predictions of molar behavior. Here, too, Uttal (1998) may be useful in expunging this psychomyth.
- That a mathematical model that fits psychophysical data (or any other phenomenon, for that matter) is a unique description of the phenomenon.
- That cognitive processes are driven by single parameters rather than being multidimensional.

- That computer simulations of neural nets behave in the same ways as do real brain tissue and thus represent good models of brain action.[9]
- That the behavior of neural nets consisting of more than two simulated neurons can be predicted. Recall that the three-body problem in physics—a much simpler version—cannot be deterministically solved.
- That physiological indicators are valid indicators of cognitive states. Whatever happened to the Galvanic Skin Reflex, The Electroencephalogram, and other classic physiological indicators of cognitive activity? So, too, must be included the widely held myth that the polygraph is a dependable, much less a valid, means of detecting the truth or falsity of verbal statements.
- That attention always improves performance. Although the "Hawthorne Effect" (reported by Elton Mayo around 1930) is one of the most persistent myths in industrial psychology, the fact that virtually any manipulation of the work environment produced increased performance has been long associated with the attention paid to the workers in this experiment. However, even this appears to be largely anecdotal. A very small sample (six) subjects were used and it has been reported that even those six did not remain throughout the study. The experiment was extremely intrusive; the experimenter sat watching the subjects do their work. The implication is that the remaining subjects were terrified of losing their jobs and were, therefore, driven to keep working harder and harder, a strategy that is likely to produce task degradation as well as improvement. Fear, rather the positive effect of attention, was possibly driving the results. Nevertheless, the myth that attention inevitably drives performance continues as it fulfills both a wishful fantasy and an a priori hunch that "people should behave like that."
- That all problems are amenable to solution. Mathematicians are now aware that some problems are impossible to solve for either practical (it would require unrealizable amounts of computer power) or theoretical reasons. An example of the latter constraint is Galois' proof that the general solution of a fifth degree equation is not possible. On a more familiar basis, it is well established that one cannot produce a square with the same area as a circle with a straight edge and a compass, trisect an angle, or represent pi (π) as a terminating fraction of

---

[9]This misassumption can be generalized even further. No matter how well a computer model may simulate or mimic the behavior of a human, there is no way to tell if the methods and processes the computer uses are the same as those used by the human. For example, the newly popular face recognition techniques based on measurements between certain landmarks are not likely to be the same as the human face recognition mechanism—however well the former may work. Again, the bottom line is that analogous behavior is not tantamount to the specification of a unique underlying mechanism.

rational numbers. Many other mathematical problems, that are solvable in principle, cannot be solved in a finite amount of time—they are classified as "NP" problems. Some insoluble NP problems are relatively simple to pose. In a totally different domain, it has long been established that it is not possible to build a perpetual motion machine. How much less likely it would be for contemporary cognitive neuroscience to develop a complete neural net explanation of the emergence of awareness.

However strong may be the scientific "evidence" that affects the credibility of these assumptions, these psychomyths seem to be impossible to eradicate from our popular psychomythology. For example, those interested in the fragility of our memories should refer to Loftus (1996a), Reinitz and Hannigan (2001), and Schacter (2001). For those interested in the lack of a scientific foundation of the polygraph, there is still no better critique than that provided by Lykken (1998). Obviously Folk Psychology, based as it is on very serious misconceptions and misassumptions, can and does have a profound effect on everyday life; its influence propagates to the most esoteric levels of psychological theory.

This brief list does not exhaust the range of psychomyths. Many others permeate psychological science and especially the peripheral and parasitic fields like parapsychology that feed off scientific psychology. Hypnosis, psychotherapeutic procedures, and the direct control of computers by the "mind" are among those still receiving credulity in situations in which a healthy skepticism would be much more appropriate.

5.4.7 Some Questionable Assumptions About Measurement and Statistics

In chapter 3, I discuss some particular frailties of statistical thinking and analysis. Even though it is important to acknowledge the important history of contributions to the psychological and other social sciences made by statistics, it is also important to appreciate that statistics possesses a number of limits and constraints that also arise from erroneous assumptions and conceptual errors. Many of the problems associated with some questionable, if not naïve, applications of measurement or statistical analysis of cognitive processes are discussed in chapter 3. However, it is also useful to tease out the underlying assumptions as a means of illustrating how our a priori axioms can lead us astray. I appreciate that the some of these "questionable" assumption may be held in high regard in some circles, and their inclusion on this list challenged. However, as stressed in chapter 3, there is enough "question" concerning each of them to at least raise the issue of their validity. Here are some of the contentious measurement and statistical assumptions that have been identified:

- The assumption that highly variable cognitive processes can be measured with psychophysical procedures.
- The assumption that the properties of cognitive processes are adequately quantitative and display both regular scales and orderly, if not, linear superimposition.
- The assumption of rational behavior on the part of observers.
- The assumption that the standards and criteria used by observers are stable from time to time and from observer to observer.
- The assumption that the results from individual responses or observers can be pooled in a meaningful way.
- The assumption that slight changes in an experimental protocol are essentially meaningless and without major effect on results.
- The assumption that a sample distribution always accurately reflects the total population distribution.
- The assumption that a "case history" can be validly generalized to the total population.
- The assumption that the outcomes of statistical analyses are immune from logical errors.
- The assumption that correlation is tantamount to causation.
- The assumption that cognitive behavior is determined by single causes.
- The assumption that "statistical significance means theoretical or practical significance."
- The assumption that "the rejection of the null hypothesis establishes the truth of a theory that predicts it to be false."
- The assumption that a .05 significance result is a valid criterion for publication.
- The assumption that the failure to achieve significance means that an experiment has failed.
- The assumption that the best explanatory theory is one that fits the data best.
- The assumption that the rare occurrence of improbable and coincidental random events can be used as proof of equally unlikely theories.
- The assumption that the logical chain from the most primitive assumptions (e.g., Chebyshev's Inequality or the Central Limit Theorem) to final inferences or conclusions is flawless.
- The near universal assumption of normality in a host of different experimental situations.

- The assumption that all data can be uncritically pooled or combined to give improved precision.
- The assumption that data from different populations or sampled according to different rules can be uncritically combined.
- The assumption that small-scale (i.e., toy problems) solutions will scale up into practical large-scale solutions to brain–mind problems.
- The assumption that rounding errors are always insignificant in drawing final conclusions.
- The assumption (or rather the unexpressed practice) evidenced throughout psychology that replication is usually unnecessary to justify theoretical conclusions.
- The assumption that data can be extrapolated and the corollary assumption that discontinuities are unlikely to occur in what had been a continuously trending trajectory.
- And perhaps, most notably, the assumption that behavior and the brain can be dealt with as linear systems.

In summary, there are many conceptual and logical assumptions built into statistical thinking that transcend the simple mechanics of carrying out the actual analysis. It is also important to keep in mind the intrinsic limitations of any procedure that attempts by an inductive process to pass from the particular to the general. Not doing so can lead to incorrect theories and a wide variety of psychomyths.

5.5   SUMMARY AND AN INTERIM CONCLUSION

Much of the wisdom that has accumulated in scientific psychology is based more on a priori assumptions than on obtained experimental results. Although this problem is not specific to the cognitive and behavioral sciences, it is particularly prevalent in these endeavors because of the enormous complexity of the brain–mind system. Some of these incorrect assumptions can lead to "red herring" debates concerning matters that cannot be reconciled or that represent two equivalent statements of what, in the final analysis, must be considered to be the same cognitive entity.

Three fundamental a priori assumptions permeate all of psychology—the acceptance, with inadequate consideration, of analyzability, accessibility, and reducibility of cognitive activity. All three of these assumptions are at the very least questionable and there is compelling evidence that our science should not be based on them. Nevertheless, their uncritical acceptance has led to a host of mythical psychological theories and incorrect conclusions, not the least of which are the various mentalisms that permeate so much of both past and current psychological thinking.

Furthermore, many of the foundational assumptions of science in general may be irrelevant for psychology. This is not to say that the subject matters of psychology are not part of the natural world, but rather that the conditions of psychology often differ in substantial ways from those of, say, physics or chemistry. In particular, the 700-year-old maxim of William of Ockham and its derivatives and corollaries, championing simplicity and a minimum number of axioms or entities, are arguably irrelevant to a system of extreme numerousness in which "fail safe" behavior is more important than economy. In any event, it is clear that William's admonition is honored more in the exception than in the observance throughout psychology. This is clearly evidenced in our science's incessant multiplication of phenomena and explanations. Similarly, Another important example, Descartes' *Méthode* of breaking up a system into its component parts for independent examination may be very useful as a guide for the study of simple linear systems but not for highly interconnected nonlinear systems of which the brain's mechanism and cognitive processes are clear cut examples.

Next, there are some misunderstandings that can contribute to psychological myths. False assumptions required to justify the additive or subtractive approaches to cognitive analysis also lie underneath an enormous amount of empirical research like some kind of intellectual quicksand. Equating an analogy with a homology or necessity with sufficiency provides a fragile foundation for a number of misunderstandings in the theoretical literature of our science. Other "intuitions" (otherwise known as implicit assumptions) lead to erroneous folk physical as well as folk psychological ideas that are deeply held by many people including, unfortunately, many students of the human mind–brain.

The conclusion is that scientific self-deception occurs not only in the development of theories, but also in the often-unacknowledged axioms, assumptions, and premises that are implicitly accepted prior to the initiation of a specific experiment. As previously noted, one can design and carry out an impeccable experiment and follow the logic through in an error-free manner to an totally incorrect conclusion if it was initially based on flawed assumptions. Here, too, is a spawning ground for psychomyths. If nothing else, and regardless of the degree that any of my colleagues may agree with me, it seems unchallengeable that (a) our most primitive and basic assumptions can have effects that propagate throughout our scientific activities and (b) that every effort should be made to identify and justify these assumptions. Indeed, it may be more important to examine them than it is to collect additional data.

Chapter 6

Final Conclusions and Summaries

6.1 INTRODUCTION

This is a book of criticism offered in a positive and constructive sense as a means of reorienting scientific psychology toward a sustainable perspective on the nature of human existence. All-too-much of our current corpus of knowledge is fragile, whimsical, self-serving, and, in not a few cases, so contrary to what is well established in other sciences that we are constantly vulnerable to rejection and even ridicule by scholars from other fields. The only remedy for this vulnerability is for psychologists themselves to filter our scientific contributions by distinguishing the nonsensical, the chimerical, and the unsupportively mythical from the valid aspects of modern psychological thinking. To do so, it is necessary to examine our assumptions, our data, and our conclusions and to reject those that do not do well under the bright light of a detailed scrutiny. Nothing will help more to exorcise some of the psychomyths that bedevil our science.

I could not begin this chapter or end this book without once again expressing my personal belief that scientific psychology is arguably the most important science of all. There is no topic more relevant to understanding humanity's role in the universe than human mentation. However, there is no topic more recalcitrant to robust and rigorous examination than that surrounding the action of the human mind–brain. A reason that this is so has already been alluded to several times in this book; simply put, the structure and function of the brain represent the most complex single entity known to exist in the universe.[1] Given this complexity, psychology can be excused for occasionally wandering off the trail of an objective science. At the very least, any criticism of the field must be tempered by the fact that what we psychologists are attempting to do is profoundly ambitious.

Nevertheless, complexity and difficulty is no excuse for nonsense. It is the responsibility of psychology to be particularly self-critical. For obvious reasons, this is a path not traveled by many of my colleagues except in the defense of detail. It is a dangerous thing to do early in one's career. However, I am at a different career stage and, therefore, there is little damage that can be done by my choosing the role of iconoclast and gadfly. My goal in my recent books has been to filter out of our science the mythical, the untenable, and the unsupportable as well as to identify those conundrums that are not likely, for practical or theoretical reasons, ever to be answered. To do so it is necessary, first of all, to identify possible sources of the psychomyths that permeate contemporary psychology. This is the purpose of this book.

In this final chapter I summarize some of the forces that have affected and influenced thinking in psychology. This summary is presented in the form of summary statements drawn from the more extensive discussions of the previous chapters supplemented by some of the ideas that are now bubbling to the top in the thoughts of others who have chosen to critique the status of modern psychology.

6.2 PREJUDGMENTS AND A PRIORI ASSUMPTIONS

Perhaps the most compelling force pushing scientific psychology toward erroneous conclusions and the creation of psychomyths is the ubiquitous predilection for prejudging the outcome and significance of an experiment. Throughout this book, I have directed my readers attention to the very large number of instances in which prevailing theory or the Zeitgeist has influenced the choice of parameters to be studied, the range over which such parameters will be varied, the analysis of the data and, most seriously, the interpretation of the results obtained. One of the reasons that this prejudgment occurs so frequently in psychology is that so many of the findings of this science are, in principle, indeterminate. In such a situation, expectations, whimsy, a priori judgments, and plain old-fashioned hopefulness replace rigor and robust logic.

The major logical fallacy in an indeterminate science (i.e., one with only the most limited accessibility to its subject matter) such as psychology is the

---

[1]Although some may consider this to be a bit of hyperbole, if one considers that the interconnections between neurons in the brain are far more complex than the forces among physical objects, a case can be made to support this extraordinary statement.

ascription of specific meaning in situations replete with ambiguity or uncertainty. Ambiguous findings free scientists to attach whatever interpretation is preferred to the outcome of an experiment. Furthermore, ambiguous paradigms also permit scientists to select experimental protocols that are pregnant with the kind of findings necessary to support their own particular theoretical positions. In short, it is all too easy in psychology to bias the outcome of experiments and the explanations one infers from that data from the outset. The sensitivity of both empirical findings and theoretical interpretations to one's a priori assumptions is acknowledged to be enormous throughout science; in psychology with all of its indeterminativeness, the neutrality of so many of its methods and tools, and, perhaps most of all, its enormous complexity, the tendency to be dictated to by existing theoretical proclivities is virtually unlimited.

6.3 PHYSICOPHILIA

Another attitude that infects wide areas of psychology is what has been called *physicophilia*, the definition of which was brought to the highest level of exuberant eloquence by Koch (1992) when he said:

> Experimental psychologists have traditionally suffered from a syndrome known as hypermanic physicophilia (with quantificophrenic delusions and methodico-echolalic complications. . . . (p. 264)

Thus, with tongue strongly planted in cheek, Koch was reiterating the criticism that experimental psychologists have been all-too-long enamored by the successes of the physical sciences and have all-too-frequently attempted to emulate them in ways that are not justified. Among the strained efforts at physicophilic mimicry was the adoption of principles and criteria that did quite well for physics but were not suitable for psychology. Among those encountered in this book have been William of Ockham's principle of parsimony and Descartes' *méthode*, both of which were powerful guides during the history of the simpler sciences, but which are questionable benchmarks for a science that should be, on the other hand, guided by criteria of redundancy and indivisibility.

Psychology's passionate embrace of physical science's methodology and criteria as the role model for our science led to injudicious acceptance of premises, criteria, and assumptions that simply do not hold for the much more complex subject matters with which it had to deal. The disappointing thing is that although physicists generally know their limitations, psychologists generally do not. Although, widely accepted in physical circles, many psychologists have not yet received the message that the constraints and limits of physical science also apply to them, perhaps with even greater force. This was so, not because there was any fundamental ontological difference between the two domains, but rather because of practical epistemological constraints emerging from the much greater complexity of mental and neural processes. For these purely quantitative reasons, physics is arguably a poor model for the psychological sciences.

6.4 EXPERIMENTER INTERVENTION AND THE PSYCHOLOGICAL UNCERTAINTY PRINCIPLE

Physics did, however, have some good heuristics to offer psychology—its cousin natural, although much more complicated, science. Usually this came in the form of a general kind of heuristic that provided wise advice even though the details of the two sciences were vastly different. For example, during the development of quantum mechanics, it became appreciated that the momentum and the position of a particle could not simultaneously be measured. This constraint became one of the bedrocks of modern physical science. It was of such great importance that it became an honorific to one of the great physicists who first explicated it. First enunciated in 1927, this profound rule of measurement was designated as the "Heisenberg Uncertainty Principle." This principle stated that there must be a mutual minimum accuracy for joint measurements of momentum and position. Formally this is expressed by

$$\Delta x \Delta p \geq \frac{h}{2} \tag{6.1}$$

where Δx is the most precise estimate of position, Δp is the most precise estimate of momentum, and h is Planck's constant. Since $\frac{h}{2}$ is a constant, to obtain precision in Δx, one must lose it in Δp or vice versa. The philosophical implication that has been drawn is that if you attempt to measure one, you interfere with a measurement of the other. In other words, the possibility of experimenter intervention in the course of making a measurement is raised.

Of course, the dimensions of the numbers and the spatial scale of the domain to which Heisenberg's uncertainty principle was first formulated, and even the origins of it (it was a mathematical deduction based on the particle-wave duality of basic particles) were vastly different than analogous processes at the scale of human thought. Nevertheless, Heisenberg raised two important general issues to which psychologists should have attended—experimenter intervention and the basic indeterminacy of measurements.

With regard to the former, it is well known that one has to be extremely careful to avoid having the experimenter influence the results of an experiment. Thus, double blind experiments are regularly used in medical research, but it is only in the rarest of instances in which psychologists go to such lengths to guarantee the objectivity of their results. Perhaps, they have not made their way into general psychological research protocols because the imminent danger of a flawed behavioral experimental finding is less than that of a medical experiment. However, given the importance given to such techniques to eliminate experimenter influence elsewhere, it is likely that this serious problem is often overlooked in psychological research.

The other general implication for psychology of Heisenberg's uncertainty principle is that it raises to consciousness the fact that, even in the best experiments, there are indeterminacies that cannot be overcome by even the best-designed and controlled experiment. Again the scale of the indeterminacy is not the issue; it is the general concept that no matter how careful we are to control all the variables in an experiment that there may be fundamental limits to what psychological research can tell us about the mind–brain relationship.

6.5   EXPERIMENTS AS EXAMPLES OF ADAPTIVE CONTROL

Just as the experimenter can influence the results of the experiment, so too can the experimental design itself produce misleading results. The problem that psychology faces to a much greater degree than do the physical sciences is that the object of the study is typically a much more dynamic and adaptive entity than found, for example, in the study of materials. Furthermore, in virtually all psychological studies, because of the intrinsic variability of the results that are obtained, trials must be repeated and repeated and then the central tendency calculated to estimate a final result.

The analogy in this case is with an adaptive control system that either self-regulates to maintain a steady state or adapts as a result of previous experience to new conditions. Psychology, therefore, is always in the undesirable scientific position of "shooting at a moving target"—of trying to estimate the state of a constantly changing system. Misjudgments about when one should take a measurement or terminate an experiment can, therefore, lead to erroneous or mythical conclusions.

Similarly, complex nonlinear systems like the brain–mind are very sensitive to even small perturbations in their environment. Thus a very small change can produce drastic behavioral changes, great enough to not only change the quantitative nature of the experiment but also to produce qualitatively different results.

6.6   SOCIAL AND FINANCIAL PRESSURES

Science, of course, is a human creation and, as such, is susceptible to many
of the social and vested interest pressures that infect other aspects of our
existence. I have already mentioned some of the esoteric influences such as
a priori assumptions and prejudgments. However, there are many other
more mundane issues that drive all sciences, physical as well as psychological. Individuals have a strong urge toward fame, an urge that is buttressed
by the generally accepted criterion of "progress." The word "progress"
connotes some of the most basic and honorable defining characteristics of
science—exploration, discovery, novelty, and priority. This powerful moti-
vating force, it cannot be denied, has been enormously influential in expanding human knowledge. There is inherent in it, however, potential
sources of misdirection. The pressure for "progress" (or change of any
kind) sometimes overcomes the caveat of caution, particularly in situations
in which there is doubt about the road being traversed. Progress toward
what may well be a demonstrable dead-end is hardly true progress, no matter how different the next step may seem to be from the preceding one.

Similarly, because fame in science depends so much on novelty, there is
a strong tendency on the part of the individual toward injudicious leaps
from what has demonstrated to much more fragile ideas that are hardly justified. It can be argued that such inspired leaps sometimes produce intellectual magic and this, too, cannot be denied. There are, however, contrary examples (e.g., cold fusion) that seem to be based on a frailer foundation that
were at least partially motivated by the siren "progress."

Coming from the opposite direction (from the community rather than
from the individual) is the influence of social pressure that may act on the
way scientists behave as much as it does on their subjects in experiments. It
is very difficult to not "go with the flow" of contemporary ideas. It is dangerous professionally and often personally. Iconoclasm is not held in high regard in what is (and properly should be) a conservative science. Anyone
challenging the Zeitgeist is confronted with enormous resistance and must
demonstrate not only overwhelming empirical evidence but also a persistence that is rare.

Much more insidious, particularly in the last half century when science
became a national rather than an individual pastime and huge amounts of
public funding became available, was the financial motivation. Few things
in science are sadder or more offensive than hearing scientists suggest that
they are working on a topic because "that is where the money is."

Finally, among the strongest social pressures of all on psychology are
those from other fields of intellectual endeavor that seek to deal with the
same kinds of problems with which psychologists struggle. Theology, for
example, is as concerned with the mind (although they often prefer to use

the S word) as are psychologists. The supernatural premises that theologians invoke to explain behavior are usually in direct and immediate conflict with the natural ones on which scientific psychology depends. Many a scientist has had to cope with the conflict between a personal theology and scientific objectivity. It is difficult to estimate just how much influence has been exerted on modern psychology when the conflict with theological doctrine and scientific objectivity becomes extreme. There is a strong suggestion that the conflict between behaviorism and cognitivism is influenced by such factors.[2]

6.7 THE VAGUENESS OF OUR LANGUAGE

Another barrier to the development of scientific psychology is our language. The definitions that we use to characterize the entities of concern are often so circular and imprecise it is not always clear exactly what is the topic of an argument. Over the years that I have tried to define perception, mind, consciousness, emotion, and related terms I have never succeeded. Yet, some of us are so dogmatically attached to our personal connotations for these critical words that any hope of achieving a consensual appreciation of a specific denotation seems completely elusive. Then, too, many psychological entities are more manifestations of the operations involved in an experimental protocol than valid psychoneural realties. Certainly, far too many of the mental "things" that we deal with so glibly are actually hypothetical constructs conjured up to provide some sense of tangible substance to the behavioral observations we make in the laboratory. Disagreement over definitions has often led to unending arguments or to those that terminated abruptly when it suddenly became clear that the two combatants were (or were not) talking about the same thing.

6.8 OVERESTIMATING AND UNDERESTIMATING THE POWER OF MATHEMATICS

Mathematics, the "queen of the sciences," is indisputably the keystone of psychology as well. However its role in our science is profoundly misunderstood by many of its most ardent practitioners. The reason is that mathematics is at once too powerful and too weak to carry out the roles sometimes

---

[2]For a fuller discussion of the conflict between theology and science as it was instantiated in the conflict between behaviorism and mentalist cognitivism, see Uttal (2000, p. 39). I am now at work on a manuscript that deals with the influence of dualism on psychological theory in a more general way.

asked of it. Mathematics is too powerful in the sense that it can inject its own properties into an analysis of a system. For example, Fourier analysis, which has proven to be so useful in manipulating images and evaluating responses, creates analytical fictions in the form of sets of basis functions *that can be used to recreate a function in spite of the fact that those components may have no physical reality in the actual system.* The ability of mathematics to disseminate its own properties by creating these analytic, but physically nonexistent, functions is the basis for the gross misunderstanding of its power that permeates thinking in scientific psychology.

Furthermore, it is still not universally appreciated that mathematics is a descriptive method that is neutral with regard to the actual underlying mechanisms of the system under study. That is, there is nothing in even the best fitting mathematical model that can distinguish between the multitudes of possible mechanisms that could produce identical behavioral functions. Reductive psychology strangles on this "many to one" difficulty; many quite different internal structures and processes can produce the same external behavior. In this sense, mathematics (as well as all computational models, however powerful they are in providing a means of description and even prediction) is incapable of reductive explanation. This is a fundamental limitation and the basis of much overestimation of the power of mathematics.

I must reiterate that these criticisms of mathematics by no means diminish its role as the great interpreter in science. Many different kinds of mathematics are capable of serving important roles in cognitive research. Nevertheless, we have to be aware of its limitations and constraints and not ask that impossible magic be added to its fundamental utility.

6.9   SMALL SCIENCE—LOW STANDARDS OF PROOF

The span of psychological science is enormous. Problems ranging from the most elevated philosophical to the merest of pragmatic applications of its methodological tools attract the attention of psychologists. Journals dedicated to the philosophy of psychology sit side by side on library shelves next to journals explaining how computers can be used to manipulate stimuli, control experiments, and reduce the obtained data. Arguably, there are few other sciences in which such an enormous variety and range of topics is considered. On the other hand, unlike physics, there are relatively few "hot" topics on which the community of researchers are collectively working.

The outcome of such a situation is that psychology in the main has become a science of small problems each of which is of interest to only a relative few. Small science suffers structurally from a lack of replication; the few who are interested in a particular problem are typically unwilling or unable to recheck their findings and often there are no other laboratories working on the same topic to confirm or deny. What is published by one laboratory is often unrefuted or unconfirmed.

The sheer economics of the situation mean that only modest amounts of data germane to a particular topic can be collected either by the individual investigator or *by the community at large* and, therefore, relatively low levels of proof have to be accepted. The traditional .05 criterion for statistical significance that characterizes psychological research acceptability means that at least 1 of every 20 published findings is probably a statistical accident leading to spurious conclusions. Given the sampling errors and biases of one kind or another that are discussed in chapters 4 and 5, even that is probably an optimistic estimate. Given the unarguable importance of what psychologists are trying to do, this compares poorly with the extremely high criteria used in other science.

6.10   EXTREME DICHOTOMIES VERSUS ECLECTIC COMPROMISE

Psychological controversies have an inexplicable tendency toward extremes. Although this writer is not innocent of ascribing a warlike status to some debates (see e.g., Uttal, 2000) I have also pointed out that most of the resolutions of differences of opinion in psychology that are eventually resolved, are done so on the basis of reasonable and eclectic compromises. Nevertheless, many of our empirical studies and theoretical controversies are still posed in the form of exclusive dichotomous positions. Most of the historical debates that have torn psychology apart over the centuries have typically been posed in that vein—exclusive and extreme positions being championed in situations in which reasonable compromise would have been far more desirable. Debates about serial versus parallel processing, the critical spatial frequency components of a stimulus form, and nature versus nurture, being among the most familiar examples of such contentious dichotomies.

Closely related to this extremism is the use of a particular experimental paradigm to champion one or the other side of a contentious issue. There are two flaws in this approach. First, many "empirical" arguments offered up to support one position or another in theoretical debates are so constrained from the original inception of the experimental design that they are predetermined to provide support for a particular point of view. A narrow selection of stimulus classes or the task itself can do as much to determine the outcome of an experiment as the psychobiological process that is supposedly being assayed.

Second, and more seriously, most experiments, even the most constrained, are actually neutral, and can intrinsically offer no support for either side of a controversy. When scrutinized carefully there are only a very few that can support any conclusion about the very positions that they are purported to defend. Given that this is the case, it appears far more reasonable to describe situations in which a stimulus exerts some influence on behavior without assuming an extreme and universal answer to some of the most fundamental of psychobiological questions.

6.11   INACCESSIBILITY, IRREDUCIBILITY, NONANALYZABILITY, NEUTRALITY, AND THE NEED FOR A BEHAVIORAL SCIENTIFIC PSYCHOLOGY

Throughout this book and in my earlier studies of scientific psychology, I have made several arguments about the fundamental nature of our study of cognitive process. I reiterate and summarize them here to emphasize that an unknown portion of our beliefs in psychology has little more credibility than those of some nonscientific enterprises.

1. For many empirical and logical reasons, there is ample evidence that intrapersonal human cognitive processes are not accessible to the techniques available to us now or to those that might conceivably be developed in the future (see Uttal, 2000, wherein this argument is made).

2. Because of the enormous complexity of the network of huge numbers of individual neurons—*the level at which cognitive processes are instantiated*—any aspirations that cognition might eventually be reduced to the terms of the underlying neurophysiology is a hopeless goal, incapable of ever being achieved (see Uttal, 1998, wherein this argument is made).

3. Because of the chain of unsupportable assumptions required to justify the division of cognitive processes into modules or components, aspirations that cognitive processes might be analyzed into parts susceptible to independent assay are equally forlorn (see Uttal, 1998, and Pachella, 1974, wherein this argument is made).

4. An important corollary of these three arguments is, as noted earlier, that mathematics, computational, modeling, as well as behavioral data are all neutral with regard to internal processes and mechanisms. At best, they describe and predict, sometimes with enormous precision; however, they can provide nothing in the way of reductive explanation in the sense that chemical reactions can be reduced to physical principles.

If my arguments are convincing, they must suggest that the current mentalistic tone of contemporary psychology should be replaced with a more descriptive, molar behaviorism. This should not be the behaviorism of past times but one that is characterized by the following attributes:

- Psychophysical—Stimuli and responses must be anchored to physical dimensions and parameters and response modes are kept as simple as possible
- Mathematically and behaviorally descriptive
- Neuronally nonreductive
- Experimental
- Molar
- Eclectic with regard to the influence of learning and heredity on behavior
- Eclectic with regard to the influence of direct and mediated influences on behavior
- Objectively scientific instead of pragmatic

Finally, I must repeat my deep conviction that scientific psychology is confronted with what are arguably the most important scientific challenges of all time. It is up to those of us who labor in the laboratories, libraries, and studies to understand humanity to do our utmost to make it the best possible science. The iconoclastic role I have undertaken here is presented as a small part of what should be a continuing effort by all psychologists to understand the fundamental assumptions on which our science is based.

References

Abe, S., & Rajagopal, A. K. (2000). Justification of power law canonical distributions based on the generalized central-limit theorem. *Europhysics Letters, 52*, 610–614.

Abraham, F. D., Abraham, R. H., & Shaw, C. (1990). *A visual introduction to dynamical systems theory for psychology*. Santa Cruz, CA: Dakota Books.

Abraham, F. D., & Gilgen, A. R. (Eds.). (1995). *Chaos theory in psychology*. Westport, CT: Greenwood Press.

Ackoff, R. L. (1971). Toward a system of system concepts. *Management Science, 17*, 661–671.

Adamic, L. A. (2001). *Zipf, power-laws, and pareto—A ranking tutorial*. Available: http://www.parc.xerox.com/istl/groups/iea/papers/ranking/ranking.html.

Alieva, T., & Barbé, A. (2000). Macroscopic 1/f behavior of fractal signals generated by additive substitution. *IEEE Transactions on Information Theory, 46*, 2261–2268.

Amari, S.-I. (1977). Neural theory of association and concept-formation. *Biological Cybernetics, 26*, 175–185.

Amazeen, E. L., & Turvey, M. T. (1996). Weight perception and the haptic "size-weight illusion" are functions of the inertia tensor. *Journal of Experimental Psychology: Human Perception and Performance, 22*, 213–232.

Amazeen, P. G., Amazeen, E. L., & Turvey, M. T. (1998). Dynamics of human intersegmental coordination. In D. A. Rosenbaum & C. E. Collyer (Eds.), *Timing of behavior: Neural, psychological, and computational perspectives* (pp. 237–259). Cambridge, MA: MIT Press.

Ashby, W. R. (1960). *Design for a brain* (2nd ed.). New York: Wiley.

Axtell, R. L. (2001). Zipf distribution of U.S. firm sizes. *Science, 293*, 1818–1820.

Bargh, J. A. (1997). The automaticity of everyday life. In R. S. Wyer Jr. (Ed.), *Advances in social cognition*. Mahwah, NJ: Lawrence Erlbaum Associates.

Bartoshuk, L., Fast, K., Duffy, V. B., Prutkin, J. M., Snyder, D. J., & Green, B. G. (2000). Magnitude matching and a modified LMS produce valid sensory comparisons for PROP studies. *Appetite, 35*, 277 (abstract).

Bateson, G. (1972). *Steps to an ecology of mind*. New York: Ballantine Books.

Beier, E. G., Starkweather, J. A., & Miller, D. E. (1967). Analysis of word frequencies in spoken language of children. *Language and Speech, 10*, 217–227.

Benford, F. (1938). The law of anomalous numbers. *Proceedings of the American Philosophical Society, 78*, 551–572.

Best, J. (2001). *Damned lies and statistics: Untangling numbers from the media, politicians, and activists.* Berkeley: University of California Press.

Biernat, M., & Kobrynowicz, D. (1997). Gender- and race-based standards of competence: Lower minimum standards but higher ability standards for devalued groups. *Journal of Personality and Social Psychology, 72,* 544–557.

Biernat, M., Manis, M., & Kobrynowicz, D. (1997). Simultaneous assimilation and contrast effects in judgments of self and others. *Journal of Personality and Social Psychology, 73,* 254–269.

Biernat, M., Vescio, T. K., & Manis, M. (1998). Judging and behaving toward members of stereotyped groups: A shifting standards perspective. In C. Sedikides, J. Schopler, & C. A. Insko (Eds.), *Intergroup cognition and intergroup behavior* (pp. 151–175). Mahwah, NJ: Lawrence Erlbaum Associates.

Blalock, H. M. J. (Ed.). (1971). *Causal models in the social sciences.* Chicago: Aldine-Atherton.

Boring, E. G. (1950). *A history of experimental psychology.* Englewood Cliffs, NJ: Prentice-Hall.

Borret, D., Kelly, S. D., & Kwan, H. (2000). Phenomenology, neural networks, and brain function. *Philosophical Psychology, 13,* 213–266.

Bradford, S. C. (1948). *Documentation.* London: Lockwood.

Brady, N., Bex, P. J., & Fredericksen, R. E. (1997). Independent coding across spatial scales in moving fractal images. *Vision Research, 37,* 1873–1883.

Breslau, L., Cao, P., Fan, L., Phillips, G., & Shenker, S. (1998, June). *On the implications of Zipf's law for web caching.* Paper presented at the third International WWW Caching Workshop, San Diego, CA.

Bridgeman, B. (1998). Simple conscious percepts require complex unconscious processing: Review of Indirect Perception by Irvin Rock. *Psyche, 4.*

Brindley, G. S. (1960). *Physiology of the retina and the visual pathway.* London: Edward Arnold.

Brooks, R. A. (1991, August). *Intelligence without reason.* Paper presented at the 12th International Joint Conference on Artificial Intelligence, Sydney, Australia.

Bruner, J. S., & Postman, L. (1947). Emotional selectivity in perception and reaction. *Journal of Personality, 16,* 69–77.

Bruner, J. S., & Postman, L. (1948). An approach to social perception. In W. Dennis (Ed.), *Current trends in social psychology* (pp. 71–118). Pittsburgh: University of Pittsburgh Press.

Campbell, S. K. (1974). *Flaws and fallacies in statistical thinking.* Englewood Cliffs, NJ: Prentice-Hall.

Cannon, W. B. (1932). *The wisdom of the body.* New York: W. W. Norton.

Carello, C., Turvey, M. T., Kugler, P. N., & Shaw, R. E. (1984). Inadequacies of the computer metaphor. In M. Gazzaniga (Ed.), *Handbook of cognitive neuroscience* (pp. 229–248). New York: Plenum.

Carpenter, S. (2000). A taste experts sniffs out a long-standing measurement oversight. *Monitor on Psychology, 31.*

Carroll, J. B. (1995). Reflections in Stephen Jay Gould's The Mismeasure of Man. *Intelligence, 21,* 121–134.

Casti, J. L. (1996). Confronting science's logical limits. *Scientific American* (October), 102–105.

Clayton, K., & Frey, B. (1995, August). *Studies of mental noise.* Paper presented at the fifth annual conference of the Society for Chaos Theory in Psychology and the Life Sciences, Garden City, New York.

Costall, A. (1989). A closer look at "direct perception," *Cognition and social worlds* (pp. 10–21). New York: Clarendon Press.

Cox, D. R., & Smith, W. L. (1954). On the superposition of renewal processes. *Biometrika, 41,* 91–99.

Cutting, J. E. (1986). *Perception with an eye for motion.* Cambridge, MA: MIT Press.

Day, R. H. (2001). Laurel and Hardy and me. In T. E. Parks (Ed.), *Looking at looking: An introduction to the intelligence of vision* (pp. 83–94). Thousand Oaks, CA: Sage.

Dennett, D. C. (1997). *Brainstorms: Philosophical essays on mind and psychology.* London: Penguin.

Descartes, R. (1649). *A discourse of a method for the well guiding of reason, and the discovery of truth in the sciences (English edition).* London: Thomas Newcombe.

Donders, F. C. (1969). On the speed of mental processes (W. G. Koster, Trans.). *Acta Psychologica, 30,* 412–431. Originally published in 1869.

Dooley, K. J., & Van de Ven, A. H. (1999). Explaining complex organizational dynamics. *Organization Science, 10,* 358–372.

Downes, S. (2000). *Stephen Downes guide to the logical fallacies.* Available: http://www.intrepidsoftware.com/fallacy/.

Dunlap, R. A. (1998). *The golden ratio and fibonacci numbers.* Singapore: World Scientific.

Eliasmith, C. (1998, April). *Attractive and in-discrete: A critique of two putative virtues of the dynamicist theory of mind.* Paper presented at the Southern Society for Philosophy and Psychology Annual Meeting, New Orleans.

Ellermeier, W., & Faulhammer, G. (2000). Empirical evaluation of axioms fundamental to Steven's ratio-scaling approach: I. Loudness production. *Perception and Psychophysics, 62,* 1505–1511.

Elman, J. L. (1995). Language as a dynamical system. In R. F. Port & T. van Gelder (Eds.), *Mind as motion: Explorations in the dynamics of cognition* (pp. 195–226). Cambridge, MA: MIT Press.

Epstein, W. (1973). The process of "taking-into-account" in visual perception. *Perception, 2,* 267–285.

Ernst, B. (1976). *The magic mirror of M. C. Ernst.* New York: Ballantine Books.

Estoup, J. B. (1916). *Gammes stenographiques.* Paris: Institut Stenographique de France.

Evans, B. (1946). *The natural history of nonsense.* New York: Knopf.

Farley, B. G., & Clark, W. A. (1954). Simulation of a self-organizing system by a digital computer. *Institute of Radio Engineers Transactions of Information Theory, 4,* 76–84.

Fast, K., Green, B. G., Snyder, D. J., & Bartoshuk, L. (2001). Remembered intensities of taste and oral burn correlate with PROP bitterness. *Chemical Senses, 26,* 1069.

Fechner, G. (1860/1966). *Elements of psychophysics* (H. E. Adler, Trans.). New York: Holt, Rinehart, & Winston.

Fisher, R. A. (1960). *The design of experiments* (7th ed.). New York: Hafner.

Fourier, J. B. J. (1822/1878). *Theorie analytique de la chaleur.* Paris: F. Didot.

Fujii, H., Aya, K., & Shima, K. (1991). 1/f-like power spectra of interspike interval fluctuations in model and real neurons. *Medical and Biological Engineer and Computing, Supplement 29,* 1103.

Gardner, M. (1978). White and brown music, fractal curves, and one-over-f fluctuations. *Scientific American, 238*(4), 16–32.

Garner, W. R., & Hake, H. W. (1951). The amount of information in absolute judgments. *Psychological Review, 58,* 446–459.

Gewolb, J. (2000). Exorcizing extrapolation. *Science, 294,* 45.

Gibson, J. J. (1950). *The perception of the visual world.* Boston: Houghton Mifflin.

Gibson, J. J. (1966). *The senses considered as perceptual systems.* Boston: Houghton Mifflin.

Gibson, J. J. (1973). Direct visual perception: A reply to Gyr. *Psychological Bulletin, 79,* 396–397.

Gibson, J. J. (1977). The theory of affordances. In R. Shaw & J. Bransford (Eds.), *Perceiving, acting, and knowing: Toward an ecological psychology.* Hillsdale, NJ: Lawrence Erlbaum Associates.

Gibson, J. J. (1979). *The ecological approach to visual perception.* Boston: Houghton Mifflin.

Gilden, D. L. (1997). Fluctuations in time required for elementary decisions. *Psychological Science, 8,* 296–301.

Gilden, D. L. (2000). Cognitive emissions of 1/f noise. *Psychological Review, 108,* 33–56.

Gilden, D. L., Thornton, T., & Mallon, M. W. (1995). 1/f noise in human cognition. *Science, 267*, 1837–1839.

Gnedenko, B. V., & Kolmogorov, A. N. (1968). *Limit distributions for sums of independent random variables.* New York: Addison-Wesley.

Goldberger, A. L., & West, B. J. (1987). Applications of nonlinear dynamics to clinical cardiology. *Annals of the New York Academy of Sciences, 504*, 195–213.

Gonzalez, R. (1994). The statistical ritual in psychological research. *Psychological Science, 5*, 321–328.

Goode, E. (2001). *Researcher challenges a host of psychological studies.* Available: http://www.adhdfraud.org/commentary/1-4-00-2.htm.

Gould, S. J. (1981). *The mismeasure of man.* New York: Norton.

Granger, C. W. J., & Newbold, P. (1974). Spurious regressions in econometrics. *Journal of Econometrics, 2*, 111–120.

Greenwood, J. D. (Ed.). (1991). *The future of folk psychology: Intentionality and cognitive science.* New York: Cambridge University Press.

Gregory, R. L. (1970). *The intelligent eye.* New York: McGraw-Hill.

Gregson, R. A. M. (1997). Signs of obsolescence in psychological statistics: Significance versus contemporary theory. *Australian Journal of Psychology, 49*, 59–63.

Guerin, B. (1990). Gibson, Skinner and perceptual responses. *Behavior and Philosophy, 18*, 43–54.

Gyr, J. (1972). Is a theory of direct visual perception adequate? *Psychological Bulletin, 77*, 246–261.

Halford, D. (1968). A general mechanical model for f^2 spectra with special reference to 1/f flicker noise. *Proceedings of the IEEE, 56*, 251–258.

Hausdorff, F. (1919). Dimension und ausseres mass. *Mathematische Annalen, 79*, 157–179.

Hausdorff, J. M., & Peng, C.-K. (1996). Multi-scaled randomness: A source of 1/f noise in biology. *Physical Review E, 54*, 2154–2157.

Hayes, A., Beevers, C., Kumar, S., & Winett, C. (2000, June). *What dynamical systems theory can tell us about the study of change in psychotherapies for depression.* Paper presented at the 31st annual meeting of the Society for Psychotherapy Research, Chicago.

Hayes-Roth, F. (1977). Critique of Turvey's Contrasting orientations to the theory of visual information processing. *Psychological Review, 84*, 531–535.

Hebb, D. O. (1949). *The organization of behavior.* New York: Wiley.

Helmholtz, H. v. (1856). *Handbuch der Physiologishen Optik.* Leipzig: Voss.

Helson, H. (1948). Adaptation-level as a basis for a quantitative theory of frames of reference. *Psychological Review, 55*, 297–313.

Helson, H. (1964). *Adaptation-level Theory: An experimental and systematic approach to behavior.* New York: Harper & Row.

Hendry, D. F. (1993). *Econometrics: Alchemy of science.* Oxford: Blackwell.

Heylighen, F. (in press). The science of self-organization and adaptivity, *Encyclopedia of life support systems.* Oxford, England: EOLSS Publishers Co. Ltd.

Hill, B. M. (1970). Zipf's law and prior distribution for the composition of a population. *Journal of American Statistical Association, 65*, 1220–1232.

Hochberg, J. (1970). Attention, organization, and consciousness. In D. I. Mostofsky (Ed.), *Attention: Contemporary theory and analysis* (pp. 99–124). New York: Appleton-Century-Crofts.

Howard, I. (1978). Recognition and knowledge of the water level problem. *Perception, 7*, 151–160.

Howson, C., & Urbach, P. (1994). Probability, uncertainty, and the practice of statistics. In G. Wright & P. Ayton (Eds.), *Subjective probability* (pp. 39–52). West Sussex, England: Wiley.

Hölder, O. (1901). Die Axiome der Quantitat un die Lehre vom Mass. *Berichte uber die Verhadlungen der Koniglich Sachsischen Gesett der Wissenschaften zu Leipzig, Mathematisch-Physische Klass, 53*, 1–46.

Huberman, B. A., Pirolli, P. L. T., Pitkow, J. E., & Lukose, R. M. (1998). Strong regularities in world wide web surfing. *Science, 2830*, 95–97.

Huff, D. (1954). *How to lie with statistics.* New York: Norton.

Hurst, H. E. (1951). Long-term storage capacity of reservoirs. *Transactions of the American Society of Civil Engineers, 116*, 770–808.

Ingvaldsen, R. P., & Whiting, H. T. A. (1997). Modern views on motor skill learning are not representative. *Human Movement Science, 16*, 705–732.

Johnson, J. B. (1925). The Schottky effect in low frequency circuits. *Physical Review, 26*, 71–85.

Kaiser, M. K., Proffitt, D. R., & Anderson, K. (1985). Judgments of natural and anomalous trajectories in the presence and absence of motion. *Journal of Experimental Psychology, 11*, 795–803.

Kaiser, M. K., Proffitt, D. R., & McCloskey, M. (1985). The development of beliefs about falling objects. *Perception and Psychophysics, 38*, 533–539.

Kaiser, M. K., McCloskey, M., & Proffitt, D. R. (1986). Development of intuitive theories of motion: Curvilinear motion in the absence of external forces. *Developmental Psychology, 22*, 67–71.

Kantor, J. R. (1924). *Principles of psychology, Vol. 1.* New York: Knopf.

Kantor, J. R. (1926). *Principles of psychology, Vol. 2.* New York: Knopf.

Kantor, J. R. (1947). *Problems of physiological psychology.* Bloomington, IN: Principia Press.

Kantor, J. R. (1958). *Interbehavioral psychology.* Bloomington, IN: Principia Press.

Kantor, J. R. (1971). Preface to interbehavioral psychology, *The aim and progress of psychology and other sciences: A selection of papers by J. R. Kantor.* Chicago: Principia Press.

Karsenti, E., & Vernos, I. (2001). The mitotic spindle: A self-made machine. *Science, 294*, 543–547.

Kaulakys, B., & Meskauskas, T. (1998). Modeling 1/f noise. *Physical Review E, 58*, 7013–7019.

Kelso, J. A. S. (1995). *Dynamic patterns: The self-organization of brain and behavior.* Cambridge, MA: MIT Press.

Khinchin, A. I. (1949). *Mathematical foundations of statistical mechanics.* New York: Dover.

Killeen, P. R. (2001). The four causes of behavior. *Current Directions in Psychological Science, 10*, 136–140.

Kinston, W. (1985). Measurement and the structure of scientific analysis. *Systems Research, 2*, 95–104.

Koch, S. (1992). Psychology's Bridgman vs. Bridgman's Bridgman. *Theory and Psychology, 2*, 261–290.

Kohonen, T. (1982). Self-organized formation of topologically correct feature maps. *Biological Cybernetics, 43*, 59–69.

Kolmogorov, A. N. (1941). Dissipation of energy in a locally isotropic turbulence. *Doklady Akad. Nauk USSR, 32*, 141.

Kuhn, T. S. (1962). *The structure of scientific revolutions.* Chicago: University of Chicago Press.

Kuznetsov, I. A. (1998). *Elements of applied bifurcation theory (Vol. 112, 2nd ed.).* New York: Springer-Verlag.

Land, E. H. (1977). The retinex theory of color vision. *Scientific American, 237*, 108–128.

Landau, L. D. (1944). Turbulence. *Doklady Akad. Nauk. SSSR 44, 8*, 39–342.

Leeper, R. (1935). A study of a neglected portion of the field of learning—The development of sensory organization. *Journal of Genetic Psychology, 46*, 41–75.

Li, W. (1999). *Zipf's law.* Available: http://linkage.rockefeller.edu/wli/zipf/.

Li, W. (2000). *A bibliography on 1/f noise.* Available: http://linkage.rockefeller.edu/wli/1fnoise/.

Lloyd, A. C. (1967). Simplicity. In P. Edwards (Ed.), *The encyclopedia of philosophy, Vol. 7.* New York: Macmillan.

Loftus, E. F. (1991). Made in memory: Distortions in memory after misleading communications. In G. Bower (Ed.), *The psychology of learning and motivation: Advances in research and theory* (pp. 187–215). New York: Academic Press.

Loftus, E. F. (1996). *Eyewitness testimony: With a new preface by the author.* Cambridge, MA: Harvard University Press.

Loftus, E. F., Coan, J. A., & Pickrell, J. E. (1996). Manufacturing false memories using bits of reality. In L. M. Reder (Ed.), *Implicit memory and metacognition* (pp. 195–220). Mahwah, NJ: Lawrence Erlbaum Associates.

Lorenz, E. (1963). Deterministic nonlinear flow. *Journal of Atmospheric Sciences, 20,* 130–141.

Lotka, A. J. (1926). The frequency distribution of scientific productivity. *Journal of The Washington Academy of Science, 16,* 317–323.

Luce, R. D., & Tukey. (1964). Simultaneous conjoint measurement: A new type of fundamental measurement. *Journal of Mathematical Psychology, 1,* 1–27.

Lundstrom, I., & McQueen, D. (1974). A proposed 1/f noise mechanisms in nerve cell membranes. *Journal of Theoretical Biology, 45,* 405–409.

Lykken, D. T. (1998). *A tremor in the blood: Uses and abuses of the lie detector (Second ed.).* New York: Plenum.

Mace, W. M. (1986). J. J. Gibson's ecological theory of information pickup: Cognition from the ground up. *Approaches to cognition: Contrasts and controversies.* Hillsdale, NJ: Lawrence Erlbaum Associates.

MacLeod, R. B., & Pick, H. L., Jr. (Eds.). (1974). *Perception: Essays in honor of James J. Gibson.* Ithaca, NY: Cornell University Press.

Malcolm, N. (1971). *The problems of mind.* London: George Allen and Unwin.

Mandelbrot, B. B. (1960). The Pareto-Levy law and the distribution of income. *International Economic Review, 1,* 79–106.

Mandelbrot, B. B. (1961). On the theory of word frequencies and on related Markovian models of discourse. In R. Jakobson (Ed.), *Structures of language and its mathematical aspects* (pp. 190–219). New York: American Mathematical Society.

Mandelbrot, B. B. (1967). Some noises with 1/f spectrum, a bridge between direct current and white noise. *IEEE Transactions on Information Theory, 13,* 289–298.

Mandelbrot, B. B. (1983). *The fractal geometry of nature.* New York: Freeman.

Mandelbrot, B. B. (1999). *Multifractals and 1/f noise: Wild self-affinity in physics (1963–1976).* New York: Springer-Verlag.

Mantegna, R. N., Buldyrev, S. V., Goldberger, A. L., Havlin, S., Peng, C. K., Simons, M., & Stanley, H. E. (1994). Linguistic features of non-coding DNA sequences. *Physical Review Letters, 73,* 3169–3172.

Matsumoto, T., & Aizawa, Y. (1999). Punctuated equilibrium behavior and Zipf's law in the stochastic branching process model of phylogeny. *Progress of Theoretical Physics, 102,* 909–915.

May, R. M. (1974). Biological populations with nonoverlapping generations: Stable points, stable cycles, and chaos. *Science, 186,* 645–647.

May, R. M. (1988). How many species are there on earth? *Science, 214,* 1441–1449.

McAfee, E. A., & Profitt, D. R. (1991). Understanding the surface orientation of liquids. *Cognitive Psychology, 23,* 669–690.

Michell, J. (1999). *Measurement in psychology: Critical history of a methodological concept.* Cambridge, England: Cambridge University Press.

Miller, G. S. (1965). Introduction. In G. K. Zipf, *Psycho-biology of languages* (pp. v–x). Cambridge, MA: MIT Press.

Miller, J. G. (1978). *Living systems.* New York: McGraw-Hill.

Milotti, E. (1995). Linear processes that produce 1/f or flicker noise. *Physical Review E, 51,* 3087–3103.

Moore, E. F. (1956). Gedanken-experimental studies on experimental machines. In C. E. Shannon & J. McCarthy (Eds.), *Automata studies* (pp. 129–153). Princeton, NJ: Princeton University Press.

Mueller, S. (1998). *New poll shows correlation is causation.* Available: http://www-personal.umich.edu/~smueller/HappHour/correlation.html.

Narens, L. (1996). A theory of ratio magnitude estimation. *Journal of Mathematical Psychology, 40,* 109–129.

Narens, L. (1997). On subjective intensity and its measurement. In A. A. J. Marley (Ed.), *Choice, decision, and measurement: Essays in honor of R. Duncan Luce* (pp. 189–205). Mahwah, NJ: Lawrence Erlbaum Associates.

Neal, A., & Hesketh, B. (1997). Episodic knowledge and implicit learning. *Psychonomic Bulletin and Review, 4,* 24–37.

Neisser, U. (1967). *Cognitive psychology.* New York: Appleton-Century-Crofts.

Neisser, U. (1976). *Cognition and reality.* San Francisco: W. H. Freeman.

Newcomb, S. (1881). Note on the frequency of use of the different digits in natural numbers. *The American Journal of Mathematics, 4,* 39–40.

Nickerson, R. S. (2000). Null hypothesis significance testing: A review of an old and continuing controversy. *Psychological Methods, 5,* 241–301.

Nimh, S. D. (1976). Polynomial law of sensation. *American Psychologist, 31,* 808–809.

Nisbett, R. E., & Wilson, T. D. (1977). Telling more than we can know: Verbal reports on mental processes. *Psychological Review, 84,* 231–259.

Ogawa, Y. (1998). Firing properties of olfactory bulb neurons during sniffing in rats. *Physiology and Behavior, 64,* 755–764.

Pachella, R. G. (1974). The interpretation of reaction time in information processing research. In B. H. Kantowitz (Ed.), *Human information processing: Tutorials in performance and cognition* (pp. 41–82). Hillsdale, NJ: Lawrence Erlbaum Associates.

Parks, T. E. (2001). *Looking at looking: An introduction to the intelligence of vision.* Thousand Oaks, CA: Sage.

Peale, N. V. (1952). *The power of positive thinking.* New York: Prentice-Hall.

Penrose, L. S., & Penrose, R. (1958). Impossible objects: A special type of illusion. *British Journal of Psychology, 49,* 31–33.

Poincaré, H. (1890). Sur le probleme des trois corps et les equations de la dynamique. *Acta Mathematica, 13,* 1–270.

Poincaré, H. (1903). *Science and method* (English Ed., Trans. by F. Maitland in 1952). Mineola, NY: Dover.

Pressing, J. (1999). *Sources of 1/f noise effects in human cognition and performance.* Available: http://www.paideusis.matco.ro/n1ciss.html#jp.

Pressing, J. (2001). *Sources for 1/f noise effects in human cognition and performance.* Available: http://www.paideusis.matco.ro/e ln2jp.html.

Pressing, J., & Jolley-Rogers, G. (1997). Spectral properties of human cognition and skill. *Biological Cybernetics, 76,* 339–347.

Proffitt, D. R. (1999). Naive physics. In R. Wilson & F. Keil (Eds.), *The MIT encyclopedia of the cognitive sciences* (pp. 577–579). Cambridge, MA: MIT Press.

Proffitt, D. R., & Kaiser, M. K. (in press). Intuitive Physics.

Rashevsky, N. (1948). *Mathematical biophysics.* Chicago: University of Chicago Press.

Raup, D. M., & Sepkoski, J. J., Jr. (1984). Periodicity of extinctions in the geological past. *Proceedings of the National Academy of Science USA, 81,* 801–805.

Reinitz, M. T., & Hannigan, S. L. (2001). Effects of simultaneous stimulus presentation and attention switching on memory conjunction errors. *Journal of Memory and Language, 44,* 206–219.

Roberts, S., & Pashler, L. (2000). How persuasive is a good fit? A comment on theory testing. *Psychological Review, 107,* 358–367.

Robertson, R., & Combs, A. (Eds.). (1995). *Chaos theory in psychology and the life sciences.* Mahwah, NJ: Lawrence Erlbaum Associates.

Rock, I. (1983). *The logic of perception.* Cambridge, MA: MIT Press.

Rock, I. (1997). *Indirect perception.* Cambridge, MA: MIT Press.

Roediger, III, H. L., Meade, M. L., & Bergman, E. T. (2001). Social contagion of memory. *Psychonomic Bulletin and Review, 8,* 365–371.

Rosenbaum, D. A. (1998). Is dynamical systems modeling just curve fitting? *Motor Control, 2,* 101–104.

Rosnow, R. L., & Rosenthal, R. (1989). Statistical procedures and the justification of knowledge in psychological science. *American Psychologist, 44,* 1276–1284.

Russell, B. (1937). *The principles of mathematics.* New York: Norton.

Ryle, G. (1976). *The concept of the mind.* Baltimore: Penguin.

Sagan, C. (1995). *The demon-haunted world: Science as a candle in the dark.* New York: Random House.

Schacter, D. L. (2001). *The seven sins of memory: How the mind forgets and remembers.* Boston: Houghton-Mifflin.

Schmitt, B. H. (1987). The ecological approach to social perception. A conceptual critique. *Journal for the Theory of Social Behavior, 17,* 265–278.

Schroeder, M. (1991). *Fractals, chaos, power laws: Minutes from an infinite paradise.* New York: Freeman.

Schulz, T. (1989). Direct perception or unconscious inference? Some remarks on the valence of affordances within the debate between "direct" realism and rationalism, *Gestalt theory* (Vol. 11, pp. 52–67). Wiesbaden, Germany: Westdeutscher Verlag GmbH.

Seife, C. (2000). Cern's gamble shows perils, rewards of playing the odds. *Science, 289,* 2260–2262.

Shannon, C. E. (1948). A mathematical theory of communication. *Bell System Technical Journal, 27,* 379–423; 623–656.

Shaw, R., & Turvey, M. T. (1981). Coalitions as models for ecosystems: A realist perspective on perceptual organization. In M. Kubovy & J. Pomerantz (Eds.), *Perceptual organization* (pp. 343–416). Hillsdale, NJ: Lawrence Erlbaum Associates.

Shaw, R. E., & Turvey, M. T. (1999). Ecological foundations of cognition: II. Degrees of freedom and conserved quantities in animal-environment systems. *Journal of Consciousness Studies, 6,* 111–123.

Shepard, R. N. (1987). Evolution of a mesh between principles of the mind and regularities of the world. In J. Dupré (Ed.), *The latest on the best: Essays on evolution and optimality* (pp. 251–276). Cambridge, MA: MIT Press.

Skinner, B. F. (1953). *Science and human behavior.* New York: Macmillian.

Skinner, B. F. (1974). *About behaviorism.* New York: Knopf.

Sornette, D., Knopoff, L., Kagan, Y. Y., & Vanneste, C. (1996). Rank-ordering statistics of extreme events: Application to the distribution of large earthquakes. *Journal of Geophysical Research, 101(B6),* 13883–13894.

Sternberg, S. (1969). The discovery of processing stages: Extension of Donders' method. *Acta Psychologia, 30,* 276–315.

Stevens, S. S. (1939). On the problem of scales for the measurement of psychological magnitudes. *Journal for the Unification of Science, 9,* 94–99.

Stevens, S. S. (Ed.). (1951a). *Handbook of experimental psychology.* New York: Wiley.

Stevens, S. S. (1951b). Mathematics, measurement, and psychophysics. In S. S. Stevens (Ed.), *Handbook of experimental psychology* (pp. 1–49). New York: Wiley.

Stevens, S. S. (1956). The direct estimation of sensory magnitude—loudness. *American Journal of Psychology, 69,* 1–15.

Stevens, S. S. (1971). Sensory power functions and neural events. In W. R. Lowenstein (Ed.), *Principles of receptor physiology* (pp. 226–242). New York: Springer-Verlag.

Stewart, A. L., & Pinkham, R. S. (1991). A space-variant operator for visual sensitivity. *Biological Cybernetics, 64,* 373–379.

Stewart, A. L., & Pinkham, R. S. (1994). Space-variant models of visual acuity using self-adjoint integral operators. *Biological Cybernetics, 71,* 161–167.

Stoker, J. J. (1950). *Nonlinear vibrations in mechanical and electrical systems.* New York: Interscience.

Stroop, M., Turvey, M. T., Fitzpatrick, P., & Carello, C. (2000). Inertia tensor and weight-percept models of length perception by static holding. *Journal of Experimental Psychology: Human Perception and Performance, 26,* 1183–1147.

Thelen, E., & Smith, L. (1994). *A dynamic systems approach to the development of cognition and action.* Cambridge, MA: MIT Press.

Thorndike, E. L. (1913). *Educational psychology, Vol. 2: The psychology of learning.* New York: Teachers College.

Thurstone, L. L., & Chave, E. J. (1929). *The measurement of attitude.* Chicago: University of Chicago Press.

Titchener, E. B. (1896). *An outline of psychology.* New York: Macmillan.

Townsend, J. T. (1994). Methodology and statistics in the behavioral sciences. *Psychological Science, 5,* 321–325.

Tufte, E. R. (1983). *The visual display of quantitative information.* Cheshire, CN: Graphics Press.

Tufte, E. R. (1990). *Envisioning information.* Cheshire, CN: Graphics Press.

Turvey, M. T. (1977). Contrasting orientations to the theory of visual information processing. *Psychological Review, 84,* 67–88.

Turvey, M. T. (1992). Ecological foundations of cognition: Invariants of perception and action. In H. L. Pick Jr., V. D. Broek, & D. C. Knill (Eds.), *Cognition: Conceptual and methodological issues* (pp. 85–117). Washington DC: American Psychological Association.

Turvey, M. T. (1998). Dynamics of effortful touch and interlimb coordination. *Journal of Biomechanics, 31,* 873–882.

Turvey, M. T., & Carello, C. (1995). Dynamic touch. In W. Epstein & S. Rogers (Eds.), *Perception of space and motion* (pp. 401–490). San Diego: Academic Press.

Turvey, M. T., & Shaw, R. (1979). The primacy of perceiving: An ecological reformulation for understanding memory. In L. G. Nilsson (Ed.), *Perspectives on memory research: Essays in honor of Uppsala University's 500th Anniversary* (pp. 167–222). Hillsdale, NJ: Lawrence Erlbaum Associates.

Turvey, M. T., & Shaw, R. E. (1995). Towards an ecological physics and a physical psychology. In R. L. Solso & D. W. Massaro (Eds.), *The science of the mind: 2001 and beyond* (pp. 144–169). New York: Oxford University Press.

Turvey, M. T., & Shaw, R. E. (1999). Ecological foundations of cognition: I. Symmetry and specificity of animal-environmental systems. *Journal of Consciousness Studies, 6,* 95–110.

Ullman, S. (1980). Against direct perception. *Behavioral and Brain Sciences, 3,* 373–415.

Uttal, W. R. (1973). *The psychobiology of sensory coding.* New York: Harper & Row.

Uttal, W. R. (1981). *A taxonomy of visual processes.* Hillsdale, NJ: Lawrence Erlbaum Associates.

Uttal, W. R. (1988). *On seeing forms.* Hillsdale, NJ: Lawrence Erlbaum Associates.

Uttal, W. R. (1998). *Toward a new behaviorism: The case against perceptual reductionism.* Mahwah, NJ: Lawrence Erlbaum Associates.

Uttal, W. R. (2000). *The war between mentalism and behaviorism: On the accessibility of mental processes.* Mahwah, NJ: Lawrence Erlbaum Associates.

Uttal, W. R. (2001). *The new phrenology: The limits of localizing cognitive process in the brain.* Cambridge, MA: MIT Press.

Uttal, W. R. (2002). *A behaviorist looks at form recognition.* Mahwah, NJ: Lawrence Erlbaum Associates.

van der Pol, B., & Van der Mark, J. (1927). Frequency demultiplication. *Nature, 120,* 363–364.

van Gelder, T., & Port, R. (1995). It's about time: An overview of the dynamical approach to cognition. In R. Port & T. van Gelder (Eds.), *Mind as motion: Explorations in the dynamics of cognition* (pp. 1–43). Cambridge, MA: MIT Press.

Vandewalle, N., & Ausloos, M. (1999). The n-Zipf analysis of financial data series and biased data series. *Physica A, 268,* 240–249.

Von Bertalanffy, L. (1968a). *General systems theory: Foundations, development, applications.* New York: G. Braziller.

Von Bertalanffy, L. (1968b). *Organismic psychology and systems theory.* Worcester, MA: Clark University Press.

Von Foerster, H. (1960). On self organizing systems and their environments. In M. C. Yovits & S. Cameron (Eds.), *Self-organizing systems* (pp. 30–50). London: Pergamon Press.

Voss, R. F., & Clarke, J. (1975). 1/f noise in music and speech. *Nature, 258,* 317–318.

Voss, R. F. (1978a). 1/f noise in music; music from 1/f noise. *Journal of the Acoustical Society of America, 63,* 258–263.

Voss, R. F. b. (1978b). Linearity of 1/f noise. *Physical Review Letters, 40,* 913–916.

Ward, L. M. (1994, July). *Hypothesis testing, nonlinear forecasting, and the search for chaos in psychophysics.* Paper presented at the fourth annual international conference of the Society for Chaos Theory in Psychology and The Life Sciences, Baltimore MD.

Watanabe, T., Nåñez, J. E., & Sasaki, Y. (2001). Perceptual learning without perception. *Nature, 413,* 844–848.

Wegner, D. M. (1994). Ironic processes of mental control. *Psychological Review, 101,* 34–52.

Weiner, N. (1948). *Cybernetics.* New York: Wiley.

Weldon, M. S. (2000). Remembering as a social process. In D. L. Medin (Ed.), *The psychology of learning and motivation* (pp. 67–121). San Diego: Academic Press.

Wenger, M. J., & Townsend, J. T. (2000). Spatial frequencies in short-term memory for faces: A test of three frequency-dependent hypotheses. *Memory & Cognition, 28,* 125–142.

Wertheimer, M. (1923). Unterchungen zur Lehre von der Gestalt, II. *Psychologische Forschung, 4,* 301–350.

Wilkinson, L., & the Task Force on Statistical Inference. (1999). Statistical methods in psychology journals. *American Psychologist, 54,* 594–604.

Wright, B. D. (1999). Fundamental measurement for psychology. In S. E. Embretson & S. L. Hershberger (Eds.), *The new rules of measurement: What every educator and psychologist should know* (pp. 65–104). Hillsdale, NJ: Lawrence Erlbaum Associates.

Wright, C. E. (1979). Duration differences between rare and common words and their implications for the interpretation of word frequency effects. *Memory & Cognition, 7,* 411–419.

Wright, S. (1921). Correlation and causation. *Journal of Agricultural Research, 20,* 557–585.

Wundt, W. (1874/1910). *Principles of physiological psychology.* Millwood, NY: Krau Reprint.

Wundt, W. (1894/1907). *Lectures on human and animal psychology.* London: Swan Sonnenschein.

Yule, G. U. (1926). Why do we sometimes get nonsense-correlations between time series? A study in sampling and the nature of time series. *Journal of the Royal Statistical Society, 89,* 1–64.

Zanone, P. G., & Kelso, J. A. S. (1992). The evolution of behavioral attractors with learning nonequilibrium phase transitions. *Journal of Experimental Psychology: Human Perception and Performance, 18,* 403–421.

Zipf, G. K. (1935/1965). *Psycho-biology of languages.* Cambridge, MA: MIT Press.

Zipf, G. K. (1941). *National unity and disunity: The nation as a bio-social organism.* Bloomington, IN: Principia Press.

Zipf, G. K. (1949). *Human behavior and the principle of least effort.* Cambridge, MA: Addison-Wesley.

Author Index

Subject Index